Tweeted Heresies

TWEETED HERESIES

Saudi Islam in Transformation

Abdullah Hamidaddin

OXFORD
UNIVERSITY PRESS

OXFORD
UNIVERSITY PRESS

Oxford University Press is a department of the University of Oxford. It furthers
the University's objective of excellence in research, scholarship, and education
by publishing worldwide. Oxford is a registered trade mark of Oxford University
Press in the UK and certain other countries.

Published in the United States of America by Oxford University Press
198 Madison Avenue, New York, NY 10016, United States of America.

© Oxford University Press 2020

CIP data is on file at the Library of Congress
ISBN 978–0–19–006258–3

Contents

Acknowledgments

THERE ARE MORE people to thank than I can remember or mention; as so many have been instrumental in the accomplishment of this book, directly or indirectly.

This book started as a PhD project, and I first extend my utmost gratitude to my supervisor Dr. Carool Kersten, whose patient guidance, advice, and understanding through my time as a student was fundamental to my completion of this project. I want to also thank my interlocutors, who trusted me and shared with me sensitive details from their personal lives. I learned so much from them, and this book benefited so much from their generosity in sharing their time and their stories with me.

My family's support had been the reason I was able to start and complete this book. I want to thank my mother, my children - Mariam, Muhammad, al-Muhsin, and al-Qasim - who continuously encouraged me and carried the burden of my absence as I worked on this book. Wijdan, my wife, was always there making it easier with her unconditional care and emotional support.

Finally, I thank those who prefer not to be mentioned. They know who they are, and I am wholly indebted to them.

My father has long passed on. I hope he is looking down on me pleased and proud, and I dedicate this to him.

Note on Translation and Transliteration

TRANSLATION OF THE Quran is taken from Sahih International. Other translation is mine. For the transliteration I used a simplified version of the *International Journal of Middle Eastern Studies*'s (*IJMES*) transliteration guidelines. Exceptions were made for some names (such as Abdulaziz instead of Abd al-Azis) and for names already covered in English media.

Introduction

UNTIL THE TURN of the 21st century, what later became known as the "the modernity battle" (*ma'rakat al-hadatha*) was the only cultural war outside the lines of religious orthodoxy.[1] The impact of modernity[2] on Islamic beliefs and practices had preoccupied Saudi intellectuals and ulama during the 1980s, leading to a fierce debate, especially between proponents of modernism in literature and religious orthodoxy. The Saudi debate over *hadatha* (modernity) was not merely a question of political, economic, or technological modernization—themselves faits accomplis—but of still-unsettled questions of authenticity (*al-asala*) and religious identity (*al-hawiyya al-diniyya*). Though this debate was framed around the battle between ostensibly foreign Westernization and indigenous Salafism, it centered on basic questions of daily life in which this dichotomy is far less clear. Taken to its logical end, this debate over *hadatha* could interrogate creed and cosmology and assess the role of religion in personal

---

1. By contrast, the cultural tumult of the 1990s and 2000s would be fought within the bounds of religious orthodoxy (al-Khidr, 2011)

2. Modernity is an elusive concept (Elvin, 1986; Saler, 2006). It has raised contention and disagreement, due to its ambiguity and sometimes due to its use as a "Western" normative standard for other societies and cultures (Bendix, 1967; Eisenstadt, 2000). For the purposes of this book—and following Eisenstadt's (2000) discussion on modernities and Faubion's (1993, pp. 114–116) discussion on the common ground between modalities of modernity— I take "modernity" to be a value-free term that refers, first, to institutions, technologies, and ideas that originated from the West and, second, to the various outcomes arising from the interaction of Western and non-Western societies and cultures with those institutions, technologies, and ideas. In this sense the whole world is living in a state of ongoing and changing modernity, and each society or culture is creating its own contemporary version of it. Also see Stoeckl and Rosati (2012), Kozlarek (2014). For a critique of "modernities" see Schmidt (2006), and for an in-depth critique of the concept of modernity see Jameson (2002), especially his "Four Maxims of Modernity" (pp. 17–95).

and public life and the authority of religion and the religious establishment. Yet such a course had been stifled by Saudi religious institutions, and, following a brief period of openness, the Ministry of Culture and Information launched in the late 1980s a fierce campaign against literary modernity and also banned the mere use of the word "modernity" by any public media outlet (Kraidy, 2012).

The 1990s witnessed a revolution in the consumption, production, and communication of culture. Satellite television and the Internet entered Saudi Arabia during that decade, the former in the early 1990s and the latter in 1998, bringing about important changes in the issues discussed and debated by Saudis. Cultural wars started again, this time through a new medium, with a new generation, and with fundamentally different outcomes. Whereas in the 1980s the public cultural wars were restricted to modernity in the literary domain, between 2012 and 2014 the Saudi public was hearing and reading about a religious war waged against the spread of atheism throughout the country. On August 13, 2012, the Saudi-owned Islamic channel, ʾIqraʾ, aired a program that tackled the pathological roots of atheism (al-Habib, 2012). On August 19, 2012, a prominent daily paper, *Gulf News*, published an article that asked "Are Gulf Youth Increasingly Drawn to Atheism?" (National, 2012). And in 2014 *Global Post* published an article on the rise of atheism in Saudi Arabia (Murphy, 2014). The period between 2012 and 2014 had seen the blossoming of an internal Saudi debate over the fundamental tenets of religion. Most of those debates were on Twitter under hashtags that questioned the legitimacy of Saudi religion or raised questions on the foundations of Islam, or even rejected Islam and religion all together. Whether concerns over the absence of divine intervention in the Syrian civil war, the Muslim monopoly of heaven, or a politically subversive comparison of "Saudi religion" to Islam, the challenge within Saudi Arabia to religious orthodoxy has never been greater.

When did this challenge emerge? Until the late 1990s, critics of religion were mainly reformist, seeking to maintain the basic religious paradigm and the fundamental tenets of Islam while reforming scriptural interpretations. Competing religious visions in Saudi Arabia operated within a paradigm structured by a number of basic and fundamental tenets including the quest for an authentic and pure Islam, adherence to a religious authority, belief in the ahistorical legislative applicability of scriptural injunctions, moral commitment to Muslim brethren, and firm belief in the monopoly of religious truth and the afterlife. Groups as diverse as Shiʿa, Salafis, and Sufis all shared these basic tenets (al-Khidr,

2011; al-Mushawwah, 2012). Indeed, it is considered heretical in any of these groups to question these premises.

Saudis who criticize[3] the basic foundations of Islam within and beyond Saudi Arabia have recently emerged, challenging the existing paradigm and criticizing some of its fundamental tenets. These critics sometimes criticize religion, sometimes reject it, sometimes question it, and often demonstrate a passive nonadherence to its dictates. I explore the emergence of this trend at the intersection of individual experiences of religion and structural factors brought about by modernity. I believe this trend can reveal much about religious development in Saudi Arabia, and cast light on the broader transformation of religion in other Muslim communities.

My first experience with this new critical trend was in 2008, when I found myself interacting with individuals who were what I later characterized as proponents of the voice of religious criticism. The interaction intensified when I initiated and moderated a discussion circle, titled Harmonious Being, in Jeddah around April 2008, whose explicit objective was to discuss religiosity (Hamidaddin, 2016). The first few meetings took place weekly. At that point the purpose was to discuss religion openly and critically with just six people, three of each gender. Initially the objective was to develop analytical skills and concepts relevant to a rational spirituality, defined as spirituality not based on altered states of consciousness—such as some of the Sufi sessions—but rather on an understanding of one's existential situation. I was keen to make the sessions and discussions fit in with the busy lives of those attending, all of whom were employed. More importantly, there was no expectation that the moderator—myself in this case—knew more about or was an expert on the subject matter. From the beginning, the sessions were premised on the fact that this was a discussion of a very personal matter, where each opinion counted and all had equal weight.

Soon a new type of audience started to attend: younger, more diverse in their opinions, ranging from the ultraconservative to the ardently atheist. This created a challenge, as the basic rule of the meeting was unrestricted expression, and some of the attendees could not tolerate ideas or arguments that were, in their view, blasphemous. But there was no

---

3. "Religious criticism" is a broad term. The type of criticism I will be exploring here is that which sought to demonstrate internal inconsistencies in Islam or criticism to the fundamentals of Islam, both in a way that could lead to its undoing in the view of religious orthodoxy.

compromise on the principle of unrestricted expression, so those who could not tolerate it realized that they would not be accommodated. Some stopped attending, while others started to listen and were listened to in return. The goal of the sessions changed. Acquiring skills and developing a rational spirituality did not appeal to the new attendees, who were keener on open discussions of religiosity and theology. However, the democratic structure of the sessions remained the same, in contradistinction to the authoritarian structure of existing religious institutions and practices.

To accommodate the new audience, the meetings were held biweekly rather than weekly. The average number of attendees was 12, going up to 40 at some meetings and down to 4 at others depending on the topic being discussed and on college vacations. A Facebook page was set up where each meeting was announced and invitations were sent to members of the group. Usually attendees invited others who were interested in intellectual sessions. Within a few months, people in the social networks of the attendees, who by then were mostly students, began to hear about the meetings. While some found them agreeable, others were very critical of both the broad lines of discussion and the joint participation of men and women therein. Still others objected to the absence of traditional scholars of religion, or *ulama*[4] (sing. *alim*), as young attendees unlearned in religion had an open floor on religion no matter how little they knew. For them this was part of what gave the sessions value, but others considered it a threat to the sanctity of religion. They believed that legitimate religious discussions depend on the presence—explicit or implicit—of a teacher–disciple relationship in which even discussions *among* disciples always assume that there is a teacher to whom they can turn to for answers. Holding meetings where no such teacher is present and where questions on religion need not be answered by an authority challenged existing structures and expectations of religious authority, and was thus considered improper and even deviant.

The topics discussed lay within the broad meaning and experience of religion. One of the more provoking meetings tackled the question of why we pray;—"pray" in the sense here of performing *salat*, the obligatory ritual performed five times a day. This was not a discussion or a debate

---

4. Here I use *ʿalim* / *ʿulama*ʾ for scholars of religion who are socially considered authorities to give a religiously binding opinion, more commonly known as *fatwa* (pl. *fatwas*). And I use "scholars of religion" to refer to those who have academically studied it, but do not have the authority—formal or informal—in most Muslim communities to give a fatwa.

over particular doctrinal or legal questions. Instead, each attendee was given a couple of minutes to give a personal answer to the question: "Why do I pray?" The attendees were instructed to answer in an experiential manner without invoking normative expectations. The answers varied greatly between those who said they did not pray at all, those who said they gained nothing particularly useful from praying, those who thought that praying gave them peace, those who felt it was adherence to the command of Allah, and those who said they prayed to avoid going to hell. That meeting resulted in giving voice not only to the motivations and benefits derived from prayer but also, as it turned out, to benefits derived from ritual abstention.

As such discussions went deeper I had a sense that it was not just the personal experience of the individual that influenced these critical approaches to religion; this sense was more evident to me in those who had a critical approach to religion without being intellectually oriented. It was not surprising to me to find someone who had read books critical of tradition to be critical of religion; but to see the same approach among the less-read was a clue that there could be something structural behind the criticism. Moreover, the way the less intellectually oriented expressed their views was experiential. They made statements such as, "It doesn't feel relevant"; "There are gaps"; "My morality can't accept it." These individuals also spoke about structural causes such as increased exposure to different opinions and religions, growing resentment of authority imposed on personal life, and especially the religious establishment's influence and the growing belief that the traditional voices are incapable of providing answers.

The Harmonious Being meetings continued until December 18, 2011, when its last session was held at Jusur café in Jeddah to discuss personal experience of religious transformation. This purpose was shared in the open invitation sent through Facebook, as usual. The session was intended as a personal discussion, with each attendee given 3 to 5 minutes to express, in his or her own words and style, the religious changes they had personally undergone and the reasons behind them. Then the listeners would be given a chance to ask questions. They were instructed to avoid the immediate impulse to challenge or assess the correctness of the change experienced by the speaker; rather, they were to work toward understanding the subjective or objective reasons behind that change. When some of the participants in this meeting struggled at first to speak publicly about their inner beliefs, I intervened to share my own experiences of change. Soon enough, many in the group were ready to share their experiences. One shared his shift from judging people morally for their religious behavior to not doing so; another, a shift from believing in Allah to questioning His existence; a third had moved from homophobia to accepting homosexuality as a natural and amoral issue. My particular challenge in moderating this session was in foregrounding both the importance of experience and the necessity of setting aside normative judgments.

Group dynamics, however, would not be my only challenge. During this session, members of *Ha'yat al-'Amr Bi-l-Ma'ruf wa al-Nahy 'An al-Munkar* (the Committee for Ordering Virtue and Forbidding Vice), commonly known in Saudi Arabia as "The Committee" and in the foreign media as "the religious police," came in. The session was abruptly halted and they escorted me to their offices. I was released within an hour with a verbal warning that I should desist from holding Harmonious Being sessions. I learned later from a friend, whose friend worked with the Committee, that this premier enforcer of religious orthodoxy had visited in response to complaints from the parents of some of the young men and women who had attended meetings and then returned home to share the ideas they had heard. Some had also started challenging the ideas they had been brought up to believe.

The intervention of the Committee was thus not entirely unexpected. The meetings had already crossed many red lines, whether by rejecting gender segregation, providing an open space for challenging religious orthodoxy and negotiating their understanding of religion including the ideas of Allah and Prophecy, or disregarding the authority of the ulama. Equally troubling, I suspect, was that these sessions had created a public space outside the institutional structures of the state and the religious establishment.

Despite the intervention of the Committee, the Harmonious Being sessions had introduced me to a group of young people actively involved in an alternative religious project, who then gave me access to their intellectual peers over e-mail, Facebook, and Twitter. Far from solely reflecting an expression of individual disillusionment or an intellectual criticism of religion, however, the emergence of this trend reveals a structural shift within Saudi Arabia's religious landscape instigated by modernity and enabled by the rise of social media. Criticizing religion in Saudi Arabia is not merely a personal or individual response to religion, although it is partially that; it is also an expression of the individual experience of structural change in the country.

I.1. Public Space in Saudi Arabia

I planned to observe the beliefs that have been expressed in Saudi public space, and not those in private spaces. This raised a challenge, as the term "public space" cannot be applied accurately to Saudi Arabia since there are no such physical spaces available for discussions on religion due to the state monopolization of public space. Public space has always been something the state closely controls in alliance with religious institutions. Indeed, until the second decade of the 21st century, universities, mosques, and literary clubs were the only available physical spaces in which ideas could be publicly voiced and debated. Outside these spaces, gatherings and assemblies were, and still are, restricted, and freedom of expression in public is extremely limited (State, 2015). While newspapers hosted many heated debates, there was no physical space outside newspaper columns to allow free and general discussion of issues. The limitations on face-to-face interaction limited the impact of newspaper debates on the general population. Soon newspaper debates would become a manifestation of the turf wars among the intellectual elites of the country rather than a reflection of vibrant and interactive discussion between the populace on matters of mutual concern.

The alternative to the limitation of public space is private salons. They have been around since the 1940s, but in the last 30 years or so have multiplied to meet the growing demand for expression. Generally hosted by wealthy or prominent social figures, these salons are frequently named after the day of the week on which they convene. For example, in Jeddah there is the *Thaluthiyya* or "Tuesday Salon" of Muhammad Said Tayyib (b. 1939), one of the most prominent Saudi political dissidents and reformers (Matthiesen, 2009). Tayyib's salon does not proceed according to a set structure, and the participants usually engage in a critical review of the important events of the past week. Another important salon was the *'Ahadiyya* or "Sunday Salon" hosted by Rashid al-Mubarak (1935–2015) in Riyadh, which had provided a platform for dissident voices such as those of Mansour al-Nogaidan and Hasan al-Maliki (b. 1970). Salons for women have emerged, too, most notably that of Hatun al-Fasi (b. 1964) in Riyadh (al-Muhammad, 2004). While such meetings brought Saudis together to speak and share ideas of common concern, they could not accommodate significant numbers of participants and incorporated a narrow segment of the population.

I.2. Nonphysical Public Space: From Satellite TV to Twitter

The introduction of satellite television in the early 1990s provided a new venue for exploring and introducing new ideas and perspectives that could expand the public conversation in Saudi Arabia. Notwithstanding an initial legal ban on satellite television and a ruling by a leading religious figure that defined it as sinful (bin ʿUthaymin, 1996), such injunctions were largely toothless, as this medium quickly grew in popularity. Like their print predecessor, the newspaper, satellite television channels provided Saudis with a space in which they could interact with a broader audience. This medium, however, had its limits insofar as this conversation was mediated by the program host. Instead, broad conversation *among* participants would have to wait for the introduction of the Internet in 1998.

Yet even with the advent of Internet access, the Saudi state kept tight control by centralizing Internet traffic through the King Abdulaziz City for Science and Technology, giving the state some capacity for controlling what comes into the country (Bunt, 2009; OpenNet Initiative, n.d.). These roadblocks, however, did not stop young Saudis from unleashing the full potential of the Internet. Paltalk, Yahoo, and MSN chat rooms were soon sources for many interactions with the outside world and among Saudis themselves. Saudis set up Internet forums to facilitate in-depth written discussions with people of all backgrounds and from all countries. Saudis were now meeting each other in ways never experienced before. Limitations of geography, culture, gender, and social restrictions would dissolve in this virtual world, allowing for diverse and intense meetings. Saudis now had the opportunity to voice their doubts and concerns regarding highly sensitive issues such as class relations, religion, and gender norms. While these initiatives led to shock and disdain among conservative social leaders, the Internet provided a forum through which Saudi youth could explore religious and cultural differences.

Religion has been on the Internet since the early 1980s, starting with the use of bulletin board systems (BBSs) and then moving on to the creation of online forums. Through the 1980s and 1990s religious and nonreligious people expressed their views, critiques, and aspirations as well as marketing their religious views or proselytizing online, learning, informing, exploring, and experimenting with religious ideas, even performing acts of worship online through forums, mailing lists, and online periodicals (Campbell, 2006; Cowan, 2007; Hackett, 2006).

Research on the Internet has developed in many ways, facing methodological challenges due to the "fluid, almost volatile, nature of the Internet," raising questions about the usefulness of "distinctions between public and private, orthodox and heterodox, and religious and secular" (Hacket, 2006, pp. 67, 73). One of the main questions raised is whether or not we can distinguish what has been termed as "online religion" (Bunt, 2009), "cyber religion" (Cowan, 2007), or "digital religion" (Campbell, 2013) as objects of research distinct from the offline religious experience. The premise behind such questions is that religion's presence online is not merely a mirror reflection of its offline presence; rather, religion and religious actors accommodate themselves in a way that allows them to fit into the medium, generating a transformational dynamic for religion and religious authority online; and its effect can possibly be offline (Hjarvard, 2016). Religion and religious experience develop differently in the virtual space, and there are religious communities or experiences that exist only online; this demands studying it as an object of study independent from the studying religion in other spaces (Bunt, 2009; Campbell, 2013; Cowan, 2007). A more fundamental question being raised is about the uniqueness of the online religious experience and the degree to which we can or cannot consider that the Internet generates a fundamentally new religious experience (Bunt, 2009; Dawson, 2005; Helland, 2013), even creating a totally different "digital interface" (Bunt, 2009, p. 81) in the relationship with the Divine.

Another issue pertaining to this research is the issue of authority. Has the Internet affected religious authority, and if so, how (Barker, 2005; Hackett, 2006; van Dun, Versteeg, & Roeland, 2015)? Notwithstanding the many existing layers of religious authority, and the different concepts of authority among different religious individuals (Campbell, 2007), the discussion on the influence of the Internet on religious authority is predicated on the space it creates for religious experience away from the control of any given religious authority (El-Sayed, Greenhill, & Westrup, 2015). The discussion took various directions, such as the influence of the Internet on the erosion of religious authorities by challenging their monopoly and allowing new leaders to come in (Hjarvard, 2016), or altering the credentials for giving and receiving guidance (Bunt, 2009), or strengthening authority through strategies of gatekeeping (Knowles, 2013), or through being "there" for religious individuals who previously found it difficult to get access to their traditional scholars (Halim, 2015).

With the advent of social media in general, new questions were raised regarding its role in empowering the citizenry through increasing public participation in public life, giving voice to those without platforms and breaking through the limitations of access to a wider public. There is research that suggests that social media is an enabling force (Khannous, 2011; al-Saggaf, 2012) while other research suggests the opposite (Bakshy, Hofman, Mason, & Watts, 2011; Larsson & Moe, 2012). I do not think one can take a single position regarding this matter, as social media has different outcomes and impacts in different societies. While the research may not support it being a leveling field for all players in the community, it does support it being—as an Internet medium—a means of circumventing censorship and creating a new public sphere for interaction and the production and diffusion of knowledge (Bunt, 2000, 2009; Eickelman & Anderson, 2003).

In Saudi Arabia the Internet had been from its onset *the* public space and not just an addition to available public spaces. The history of this type of interaction in Saudi society is yet to be written, in particular that of online forums documenting the nature of these interactions. The research and writing about these forums says much about their importance in the early phases of Internet penetration of Saudi Arabia (Bunt, 2009; al-Harithi, 2010; al-Quwayfili, 2002a, 2002b, 2002c, 2002d). Many forums and sites were shut down either due to state pressure or by their owners, but what remains still constitutes a rich source of information.

Following the expansion of Internet access and the suppression of particular forums, Twitter has become very popular in Saudi Arabia; people tweet while they work or eat, in the mosque as they listen to sermons, and sometimes even as they drive. Individuals have used fame on Twitter to increase their profile locally and internationally. During the peak of the Saudi Twitter debates, Saudis had ranked on Twitter as the first among Arab users, representing 38% of Arab users of this social media tool (al-Saggaf, 2012).[5] In the absence of public physical spaces in Saudi society, Twitter was at one point the premier space for discussing everything from politics to religion to sex (Kinninmont, 2013; MacFarquhar, 2011). In turn, leading figures within the Saudi religious establishment have criticized Twitter specifically and the Internet more generally for its perceived role in facilitating the transmission of "corrupt and deviant" ideas into the minds of Saudi youth (al-Arabiyya,

---

5. By 2016 this had dropped to about 29%, but the absolute number of Saudis on Twitter continues to rise (Salem, 2017).

2012; Al Omran, 2013; al-Qanat al-Rasmiyya Li-l-shaykh Nasir al-Qitami, 2014). Indeed, this criticism of Twitter by the religious establishment is merely the latest instance of ulama opposition to new communications technology, whether mobile phones equipped with cameras or Bluetooth (Bunt, 2009). The Saudi state had at one point struggled to respond in the face of Twitter's popularity; one Saudi minister of culture and information, Abdulmaqsud Khuja, even stated that the state censor is unable to control its content (@Saudi_Gazette, 2013). Social media was a means of circumventing censorship and creating a new public sphere for the interaction, production, and diffusion of knowledge, and Twitter for Saudis has become the preferred form of social media[6] (Bunt, 2000, 2009; Eickelman & Anderson, 2003).

Due to restrictions on the public criticism of religion outside the bounds of the Internet, it was not possible to carry out any form of observation in a physical public field. Instead, I observed the criticism of religion as it unfolded online. Given the popularity of Twitter, broad acknowledgment of its reach and the intensity of religious criticism that it hosts, it is an ideal site through which to study contemporary Saudi negotiations of faith.

I consider physical and virtual spaces, the offline and online worlds, not as separate but as continuous arenas or different theaters of self-presentation. Social interaction today takes place in different types of space; some are digital, others physical, and the nonembodied space of the Internet is one of them. Whatever my subjects did in a virtual space said something about them and about their lives in nonvirtual space. If they were being genuine in their self-presentation, this presented real facts about their lives outside the virtual world. At the same time, though, even if they were not being genuine this too revealed something about them. There are many ways of being disingenuous, and choosing criticizing religion for example as a tactic is in itself a statement about how perceptions about religion are developing. Ultimately, deceit should be looked at according to the objective of the study, and truth does not always matter if "'fabrications' can tell us something about the manner in which specific social and cultural ideas such as morality are constructed" (Hookway, 2012, p. 159). Whatever I observed, I would be observing a version of who they were, which in itself cannot be anything but what it is.

---

6. This has of course changed, and the Saudi Twitter sphere has ceased to be a public space, instead a tightly censored space.

In that sense, Twitter would be my *field* of study, not as an independently existing social space, but as an extension of the spaces available to social actors as they interact, communicate, self-present, and share information. Gruzd, Wellman, and Takhteyev (2011) even suggest that Twitter users can be considered an "imagined community" and that, in particular instances, followers of a particular user can be considered an "online community" and not merely an imagined one, due to the degree of interaction and influence they exhibit with one another. This approach reinforces the idea of using Twitter as a distinct, but not disconnected, field wherein one is actually embedded, much as one would use a hospital or a school.

To complement my observations of Saudis interacting with one another on Twitter as they question and criticize fundamental Islamic tenets, I interviewed 26 Saudis, but used for my research the interview results of only 20; 13 males and 7 females aged 18–35, living in different countries and cities. I chose them based on my access to them, their willingness to share their thoughts and experiences, and their opinions posted on various platforms. While Twitter provides us with a good sense of the range of issues being discussed, the interviews provide insights into the personal experiences that have led some Saudis to venture into criticizing religion.

But it is not enough to merely explore the narratives of criticism of religion. I place this study in the context of studies on disengagement from religion and studies on contemporary Islam. Following that I explore the Saudi religious landscape in a way that places the criticisms of religion in the context of Saudi Islam. Then, after exploring the criticisms of religion, I explore the reaction of Saudis to the public emergence of such criticism. I do this by dividing this book into the following chapters:

Chapter 1: Criticizing Religion: This chapter explores the impact of modernity on religion in general, and the main Muslim response to modernity. I highlight here the difference between two ways of understanding the impact of modernity on Muslim religiosity: the first being the disengagement from religion in the same way modernity impacted religion in other societies, the second being the Muslim response to modernity and the evolution of religion into an identity. My purpose is to place my book within the context of the first way, that is, within the context of disengagement from religion due to modernity using social theories that highlighted some of the key reasons individuals disengage from religion and revert to indifference, heresy, nonbelief, or other varying forms of disengagement.

Chapter 2: Ambivalent Religiosity: This chapter examines the Saudi religious landscape, interrogating the widespread assumption that Saudi society and state are religious, and highlights the internal contradictions and ambivalence of religiosity in Saudi society and the ways in which these contradictions create spaces for criticism.

Chapter 3: Criticizing Religion on Twitter: This chapter demonstrates the types of critical discussion on religion, showing that Saudis on Twitter have been critical of Islam in all its aspects.

Chapter 4: Religious Disengagements: Here I explore in detail some of the stories of Saudis who underwent changes in their belief system, specifically changes away from the basic fundamental precepts of Islam.

Chapter 5: Backlash: *Takfir* Campaigns: This chapter explores the response of Saudi religious orthodoxy to the challenge of criticism and the ways in which it has sought to mobilize society against such a phenomenon and called on the security forces to repress leading actors. It further analyzes the methods of control employed by state institutions, their underlying sociopolitical motivations, the state's response, and the consequences for the phenomenon.

Chapter 6: Evolution of Saudi Religion: The final and concluding chapter summarizes the main points raised in the previous chapters, highlighting the challenges of translating virtual criticism into dialogue in physical spaces. It also states the main learnings gained about the emerging phenomena of criticizing religion in Saudi Arabia. Moreover, it points to some of the learnings gained about disengagement from religion in terms of causes and outcomes. Finally, I point to some of the questions left unanswered that need further research.

Writing this was a personal journey as much as it was a study of religious transformations among many Saudis. I was once an intellectual activist, keen on promoting certain ways of thinking about religion, which I did through the Harmonious Being sessions. At the time of writing this I have stopped my activism, but that does not mean that I have become a detached and neutral observer of religion and its criticism. I myself have a personal engagement with the process of criticizing religion. I had and still have a strong affinity with many of those involved in this process, as many of them are friends in either the virtual world or the physical one. I have also recounted an unpleasant encounter with the religious establishment, in which a meeting I was moderating was interrupted and I was escorted away. What I am essentially saying is that I do not claim to be neutral toward the topic of criticizing religion. Nor do I claim to be an objective observer; I am a participant and collaborator in writing the story of other Saudis. I am not neutral with regard to the topic I observed; rather, I am fascinated by the experiences that lead to change even more than by the change itself. I have already developed my own assumptions about what matters in ideas and what does not matter, and also about the reasons that may lead someone to change his/her beliefs. Even my experiences during my observation of Twitter and during the interviews was a source of many intellectual surprises, and it is quite possible that these led to my overlooking some important and relevant data or shaped my interpretation of them.

While I went through thousands of tweets, I ultimately depended on a small sample of them. Also, Twitter is limited in its capacity to offer a representative sample of a given population, and I cannot extrapolate from Twitter to Saudi social life. As I present Saudis' opinions and discussions on Twitter later, it would be difficult to say to what extent they were a reflection of discussions happening in Saudi Arabia between people in physical spaces. I cannot claim that these discussions are happening outside Twitter. It is unavoidable that my account is anecdotal and sometimes even impressionistic; I am not claiming to present prevailing or dominant trends. However, the limited sample used does give an insight into how religious discourses are developing in a society like Saudi Arabia's along different lines than those discussed in the literature that has appeared so far. Thus this book does not seek to represent the criticism of religion in Saudi Arabia broadly speaking, nor does it seek to examine the social life of Saudi Arabian citizens. Instead, it seeks to show that a phenomenon of religious criticism is emerging and increasingly becoming public, and to highlight key issues that Saudis discuss when criticizing religion. One can see this as a "black swan" case study (Flyvbjerg, 2006, pp. 224–225), where the main purpose is to prove that the black swan exists more than to discuss its numbers or all of its characteristics.

1

Criticizing Religion

HOW SHOULD WE understand religion in Saudi Arabia? To what extent does religion control the various aspects of Saudi life? Why are more and more Saudis and generally Muslims leaning toward heresy, and many others exhibiting an indifference toward religion? And how does our understanding of the state of religion in Saudi Arabia inform us about the state of religion in other Islamic communities? Those interrelated questions are the subject of this book where I explore the emergence of nonbelief and the response to it from the Salafi-Wahhabi[1] country's religious institutions. While previous studies have focused on particular institutions and

---

1. "Salafi" (pl. "Salafis"; n. "Salafism") (literally means a follower of predecessors) is highly problematic. On the one hand it has had more than one academic definition; on the other, Muslims who define themselves as Salafis have contested its use by other Muslims different from them who also define themselves as Salafis. Moreover "Salafi/s" has been used to refer to the "modernist" Muslim "reformers" of the 19th and early 20th century who, among other things, promoted a metaphoric interpretation of the Quran, and those Salafis are considered heretical or misguided by contemporary Salafis. The term has also been used to refer to "religious reformers" who promoted a literal view of the Quran as Wahhabis (Griffel, 2015; Lauziere, 2010, 2016). Among today's adherents of Salafism there are many competing groups, most significantly disagreeing in issues relating to the relationship between religion and the state, and to *jihad* (Abdel-Latif, 2009; Meijer 2009). "Salafis" in this work denotes the Salafism of Saudi Arabia, or what is known as Wahhabi Salafism.

"Wahhabi"/ "Wahhabis"/"Wahhabism" was first used as a derogatory term to demean the status of the movement of Muhammad Ibn Abdulwahhab, but was later used in positive ways in the late 19th and early 20th century. King Abdulaziz al-Saud, the founder of the kingdom, eventually banned its use, preferring the term "Salafism" or "*Salafiyya,*" although this did not stop the positive usage of "Wahhabism." Today there are mixed feelings about the term "Wahhabism." Those who argue against the authority of the established Saudi religious institutions prefer to use it to imply that Wahhabis are followers of Muhammad Ibn Abdulwahhab (d. 1792); that is, they are not authentic followers of the first three generation of Muslims as other Salafis claim. Those who support that authority prefer to be called "Salafis" (Lacroix, 2011a; Mulin, 2011; al-Rasheed, 2007). I refer to them here using the term

their role in religious change, here I focus on individuals who have criticized religion by taking advantage of the virtual space of social media. In doing so, they have raised questions on the most fundamental aspects of Saudi society: politics, religion, social justice, gender, sexuality and the future of the country. Just as importantly, these individuals, who emerged first on the Internet, have mounted a frontal challenge to religious orthodoxy, whether through calls for religious reform or, even more provocatively, through debates over concepts of deity, duty to Allah, and morality.

This subject of this book—the criticism of religion in Saudi Arabia—falls within the scope of three theoretical frameworks: first, theories on secularization and disengagement from religion that study both issues and identify their causes; second, theories on Muslim's diverse responses to modernity; and third, theories on religion in Saudi Arabia. As I engaged with the literature on those three areas I sensed that I was moving among parallel conversations that hardly engaged with one another. The literature on the factors that bring about secularization focuses on modernity as an organic reality, with various effects on personal and social life, one of which is its effect on religion. In parallel, the literature on the way Muslims responded to modernity examines this shift as a product of the interaction between two monolithic entities: Islam and modernity. Finally, studies of Islam in Saudi Arabia disproportionately center on questions of political violence and security as they relate to religious activism. Yet although those three areas hardly intersect, together they provide key insights and a theoretical background for understanding the subject of this book.

1.1. Religion, Modernity, and the Secular Horizon

"Religion" is heavily contested, both as a discipline of study and as a human phenomenon. One of the primary reasons for this is that it does not have an "autonomous essence" (Asad, 1993, p. 28; Stringer, 2011). Rather, it is a social construct that defies universal definitions or theorizing about it "as if it were a generic object" (Beckford, 2003, p. 16), leading some scholars even to deny the validity of studying religion as an academic discipline, and undermining its analytic value (Fitzgerald, 2000; Flood, 2006). The most important source of tension, however, is that religion in modernity has always been studied in the context of the secular, and

---

they prefer—"Salafis"—unless I am quoting or using a source or referring to a context that uses the term "Wahhabism."

especially the secular experience of the West (Beckford, 2003; Casanova, 1994). The secular resides in the background of most scholarship on religion in modernity (Asad, 1999; Berger, 1999; Casanova, 1994; Karpov, 2010; Lambert, 1999; Tschannen, 1991). Even literature on religion and the media proceeds from the premise that the public sphere is by definition a "radically secular" sphere "that is constituted by nothing outside of the common action we carry out in it" (Taylor, 2004, pp. 93–94), and that the presence of religion in the public sphere of the media is an anomaly—"a sign of the society's backwardness, or at least the backward orientation of the religious movement in question" (Meyer & Moors, 2006, pp. 4–5)—because religious discourse only operates from assumptions "that transcend contemporary common action"(Taylor, 2004, p. 93), rendering the term "religious public sphere" an oxymoron—at least in the view of some. At the same time, though, recent scholarship has highlighted the Western-centric nature of the secular paradigm, the normative restrictions placed on religion in public life, the transformation of religiosity in the West and the neglect of transnational global dimensions in which religion has always been strong (Casanova, 2008; Habermas, 2003; Karner & Aldridge, 2004; Speck, 2012; van Harskamp, 2008).

While acknowledging the Western background of most theories on the disengagement of religion, there is still much to be gained by taking them as a starting point for thinking about religion in Saudi Arabia. Specifically, theories of global structural manifestations of modernity such as differentiation, institutionalization, and the spread of the media enable us to examine the Saudi case in broader perspective while also challenging Western-centric theory to account for Muslim contexts. In this chapter I divide these theories into three categories: the first argues that religion has failed in the modern period due to its inability to serve social or individual needs; the second examines the poor fit between religion and daily life; and the third considers the breakdown of the social foundations that facilitate the continuity of religion.

The first set of theories includes the theories on religion of Emile Durkheim (1857–1917) and Thomas Luckmann (1927–2016). Both ascribe to religion a set of functions, and both assume that when religion does not serve these functions then religion either becomes functionally redundant or transforms itself in order to be able to serve these functions once more. Durkheim attributes to religion a function of solidarity, and Luckmann, a function of meaning. In the former case, Durkheim believes that social institutions exist to perform a function that serves the continuity of society, and that religion is a social institution that functions as a source of social solidarity for societies organized around kinship (Durkheim, 1984). In such societies, according to Durkheim, there is little differentiation between individuals at a functional level; instead, there is an overarching collective consciousness that cements society and is projected and objectified as religion (Turner, 1991).

With the advent of societies that embrace a high degree of functional differentiation due to the division of labor, collective consciousness is weakened and society turns to other means of solidarity. In this situation solidarity becomes based on reciprocity and exchange (Durkheim, 1984; Giddens, 1986; Turner, 1991). Accordingly, since the role of religion is contingent on the existing social structure, and as this social structure changes, the role of religion also changes (Turner, 1991). Thus as traditional societies modernize their division of labor, their need for religion decreases. However, Durkheim does not say that religion will disappear; rather he suggests that the needs of the social order will transform religion (Collins, 1988; Durkheim, 1984, 1995; Turner, 1991).

Luckmann (1967) takes a similar view. Durkheim considers religion an expression of the soul of society, while Luckmann states that religion provides societies with "systems of meaning" (1967, p. 43). Yet while Durkheim relates this expression of society's core to social solidarity, Luckmann argues that these systems of meaning are crucial to the development of human consciousness. His view is technical and can be summarized as follows: a society objectivizes meaning; an instance of this objectivation is formalized; then the particular instance of those systems of meaning that have become formalized is what we consider to be "religion," which is then consolidated and transmitted through authority and education. However, society continues to objectivize meaning and while doing so also continues to assess the gap between the previously formalized meaning—that is, religion—and the current objectivized meaning. Yet, society connects to that previously formalized version as long as it is close to the informal socially objectivized meanings that it continuously creates in order to express the actual collective experiences of its adherents.

If there is a fit between formal meaning—that is, religion—and informal experience, society once more internalizes and transmits religion; if on the other hand, the gap between the two meanings is too wide, society will not internalize it and people leave religion, moving toward either another system or toward a state of abyss. For example, the cosmological view provided by religion has been challenged by the ongoing development of science over the past four centuries. The church could not adapt to the new meaning, and soon it was in the position of offering a cosmological worldview that was detached from the beliefs of its adherents. In this scenario, institutionalized meanings become disconnected and people seek new systems of meaning. This does not mean that the transmission of religion totally ceases, as that is contingent on the authority and power of the religious establishment. For Luckmann, religion can still play a role if it fits into the systems of meaning needed by particular societies. Luckmann, however, has been criticized for "excessive conceptual confusion" and for the broadness of his definition, in which either everything or nothing is religious. This breadth also implies that "all normal functioning societies and socialised individuals are essentially religious" and that the only questions to be put forward are those such as "How is man religious?" (Weigert, 1974, pp. 181–184). But his theory nevertheless captures an important aspect of explaining the relationship between religion and individual life experience, which is that when individuals' sensibilities become contradictory to religion this leads some individuals to disengage from religion. As Charles Taylor (b. 1931) notes:

> The religious life or practice that I become part of not only must be my choice, but it must speak to me; it must make sense in terms of my spiritual development, as I understand this. (Taylor, 2011, p. 241)

The second approach to religion and modernity is represented by the work of Max Weber (1864–1920), Peter Berger (b. 1929), and Charles Taylor. Weber's thesis of disenchantment presents the paradigmatic theory of the uneasy coexistence of religion and modernity. Weber ties the dissolution of religion to the structural changes of the modern era, which make religion incongruent with the logic and demands of the modern (Weber, 2009). Modernity, according to Weber, voids the world of the "overarching meanings, animistic connections, magical expectations, and spiritual explanations that had characterised the traditional world" (Saler, 2006, p. 695); it is a disenchanted world.[2] In Weber's modernity, religious motivation loses its relevance (Seidman, 2013) and "ultimate values rationalise and devalue themselves, and are replaced increasingly by the pursuit of

---

2. Many researchers have recently challenged the notion of disenchantment. Saler (2006) provides a detailed historical overview to the positions toward disenchantment. Yet the concept is still valid in explaining at least part of the role and impact of modernity on religion.

materialistic, mundane ends" (Gane, 2002, p. 15). While Weber said that "the routines of everyday life challenge religion," and that old gods who insisted on returning would be "disenchanted and hence take the form of impersonal forces" (Weber, 2009, p. 149), he was not explicit in saying that disenchantment would lead to religion's demise; religion, rather, is "detached" in some form.

Berger (1967) and Taylor (2007) also attribute the disengagement from religion from modern life to disenchantment. People once believed in "a worldview in which sacred forces were continuously permeating human experience": a world full of magic, miracles, and mystery (Berger, 1967, p. 34). The person in that world was a "porous self," vulnerable and anxious due to being surrounded by unpredictable, uncontrollable, unknowable, and unseen forces in a world in which "going against God is not an option." Disenchantment transformed the person into a "buffered self": a person invulnerable and confident due to the science that has made forces predictable, controllable, and knowable, either actually or potentially (Taylor, 2007, pp. 38–44). Moreover the enchanted world was one of not just unseen forces but also meaningful natural events. In the face of the erosion of traditional religious cosmology based on a meaningful order for mankind, an alternative idea of a universe in which order has no human meaning arose (Taylor, 2007). We thus now live in a universe emptied of mythology and miracle (Berger, 1967). Here Berger and Taylor also focus on the factors that lead to changes in sensibilities which in turn lead to a tension between the old and the new sensibilities.

The third set of theories is based on religion not as a tool that performs a function, nor as a cultural entity implanted in an unconducive environment. Instead, it considers religion as a body that needs society for its existence and persistence: as a unit in a network without which it loses meaning and significance. One can conceive of two types of religious network, the first synchronic and the second diachronic. Berger's theory of plausibility structures explains how the synchronic religious network is being eroded, while Danièle Hervieu-Léger's (b. 1947) theory of religion as memory explains the diachronic erosion of the religious network. Both explanations highlight the challenge faced by religions when they are in an environment that is unconducive to their validation and transmission.

A plausibility structure, according to Berger, is a social base: a society large and cohesive enough to enforce in its members a sense of confidence in the worldview that it offers (Berger, 1967, pp. 45–46). It is a society in which most individuals' experiences are similar, and whose internalization techniques can transmit faith from one generation to the next and protect its members from the polluting effects of alternative and deviant worldviews. These processes, in turn, enable the individuals within it to take its world view for granted. Its theodicy (and theology) can be intellectually reproduced and then "refracted on different levels of sophistication throughout the society." When this "plausibility structure" is massive and durable the religious world will then be simply taken for granted. However, as the plausibility structure is weakened, so is the subjective reality of the religious world in question, and uncertainty appears (Berger, 1967, p. 54).

Hervieu-Léger's thesis is that religion is a particular belief that implies reference to the authority of tradition, and that the crisis of religion in modern societies lies in those societies no longer being "collective depositories—custodians—of memory" (2000, p. 4). Societies where memory still plays a role are more religious, and the religion is more persistent. Changes in religion are a natural response to being away from, or lacking, a memory network. The reason memory plays such a vital part in religious transmission and continuous commitment is that believing is a mode of conviction that is not susceptible to verification or experimentation. It "must be attested by others" (Hervieu-Léger, 2000, p. 94) and thus given social confirmation. It validates meaning, and the older the tradition, the stronger the validation. Tradition is thus retained and sustained through memory. Yet modernity has broken down previous techniques of meaning validation by breaking down chains of memory, and when collective memory crumbles, so does religion (Hervieu-Léger, 2000, p. 127).

One of the ways modernity breaks down the integrity of the memory chain is through the "overabundance of information available at any moment [which] tends to obliterate a meaningful continuity" (Hervieu-Léger, 2000, p. 128). This factor exists in all societies—even in memory societies such as Saudi Arabia—and thus, according to Hervieu-Léger's thesis, the advance of modernity will make it increasingly hard for individuals to sustain an ongoing commitment to religion. It also means that the more networks one belongs to, the more fragmented memory becomes, making it more difficult for a group, especially a large one, to create and transmit a collective memory. Instead, individuals are left with fragmented memories "composed of bits and pieces." Accordingly, the main culprit in the weakening of religious belief is not Weber's rationalization but collective amnesia (Hervieu-Léger, 2000, p. 129).

There are elements of Berger throughout Hervieu-Léger's work, although instead of locating the central factor of continuity of religion in the synchronic she goes to the diachronic. Hervieu-Léger, however, also discusses how religion can successfully transform itself through those same factors that represent a seemingly existential threat to its reproduction. While collective amnesia has caused traditional religions to lose ground, it also has facilitated the survival of religions. A consequence of collective amnesia is "the passion commonly felt for everything concerned with the celebration of roots," which "may be seen as the converse of the intensely felt sense of the loss of collective memory" (Hervieu-Léger, 2000, p. 92). Thus, paradoxically, it is modernity that prompts a need for religion, and religion only survives today because modernity demands it. Modernity created the reasons to let go of religion, but those reasons themselves create a situation where religion becomes more relevant.

However, there is more to religion's survival than mere nostalgia: there is also meaning. Science cannot replace religion's role in defining the place of humans in the universe, facing our mortality, and the need for ritual. What will happen, as Durkheim predicts, is a new religion of humanism, without a church, not organized and yet providing grounds for sacrifice and devotion and transcending instinct (Durkheim, 1984, 1995). Hervieu-Léger essentially says the same: amnesia leads toward the dissolution of religion; nostalgia leads toward retaining religion in a reconstructed form; and the quest for meaning leads toward creating a new religion. Hervieu-Léger has been criticized for being too reliant on the Western Christian framework and overemphasizing the authority of tradition, linear time, and doctrine—there are religious experiences independent of the chain of memory such as mystical experiences, and the development of Indian traditions is best understood as cyclic (Geaves, 2009)—yet her theory remains an important tool for understanding some aspects of the individual relationship to religion in the modern world.

Ultimately each of these approaches has its critics, but it is not the accuracy of the theories in their own contexts that matters at this point but rather their usefulness. The functional redundancy of religion, the compatibility or incompatibility of religion and modern life, and the breakdown of the religious networks provide three approaches to understanding disengagement from religion in modern life due to changed sensibilities rather than intellectual argumentation against religion. Although these authors approach this question from the vantage point of secularization, they nonetheless provide a useful starting point for understanding religion in Saudi Arabia.

1.2. The "Authenticity/Identity" Prism

The literature on Muslims in modernity reveals a different focus of attention than that on religion in modernity in Western societies. The literature on Western societies focuses on explaining secularization and then desecularization and, more importantly, treats modernity as an inexorable process of change that has emerged in Western societies. By contrast, literature on Muslims in modernity refracted Muslim responses to modernity through the "Authenticity/Identity" prism or "within a modern politics of cultural authenticity" (Hirschkind, 2006, p. 19). Muslims have responded to the foreign project of modernity that came with colonial control by either responding to it through religion *or* embracing it in spite of religion. Most studies of religion and modernity in the Muslim world are in effect about the different forms of Muslim response.

The framing of the literature on Muslims in modernity within a paradigm of authenticity is partially due to the way Muslims themselves have responded to modernity in the past 150 years. At the center of this response was the question of how to relate to modernity: Embrace it? Or reject it? The initial response of some leading Muslims in the 19th century and part of the 20th century was to embrace Western modernity by "harmonising Islamic teaching with European philosophy and science" (Haddad, 1991, p. 4), creating what could be called a " 'modernised' Islam, or even what was in effect an alternative to Islam" (Voll, 1991, p. 23). Some of the leading characters in this endeavor were Sir Seyyid Ahmad Khan of India, Khayr al-Din Basha of Tunisia, Muhammad Abdu of Egypt, and Jamal al-Din al-Afhgani of Iran (Haddad, 1991, p. 4). They believed that the essence of Islam and Western modernity are compatible, and that through reviving and transforming the practice of *ijtihad*[3] Islam could be represented in a way that allows for a Muslim renaissance. (Ahmad, 1960, Abu-Rabi', 1996; Hassan, 2015; Parray, 2011). Perhaps the main and most consequential ideas that came out of that era—both of which were advocated with

---

3. Traditionally *ijtihad* denotes a process by which a religious scholar (*alim*) develops a jurisprudential opinion. Some Muslim reformers wanted to expand its scope beyond jurisprudence so as to cover all aspects of religious interpretation and to permit nonreligious scholars to practice *ijtihad* as well.

intense passion by al-Afghani—were that of pan-Islamism and the conceptualization of Islam and the West as two clashing civilizations (Keddie,
1983; Lee, 1942).[4]

In the early 20th century a new response was being developed that
shifted the focus from "'modernising' Islam to the Islamisation of the
modern experience" (Voll, 1991, p. 24). This had many manifestations, the
most important of which was what could be called selective modernity.
This essentially meant that a Muslim should not totally reject modernity,
nor totally embrace it, but rather should select from modernity what is
compatible with and reject what is antithetical to Islam. This was summed
up in a statement by the key Muslim ideologue of the 20th century Abu
al-A'la al-Mawdudi (1903–1979): "'yes' to modernisation but 'no' to blind
Westernisation" (quoted in Nasr, 1996, p. 52). There were also were calls
for the total rejection of modernity or its absolute assimilation, but these
were peripheral (Tibi, 2002, 2009).[5]

Amid this array of responses, many Muslims started asking themselves
whether they could be modern while still holding onto their Muslim identity (Lee, 1997; Tibi, 2009); or "can the Muslim world accede to modernity without denying some of the fundamentals of the Islamic religion?"
(Ramadan, 2009). This question has shaped competing articulations of
Islam and generated an urge for authenticity as a means of self-preservation
and the construction of identity (Gole, 2003). This urge prompted an effort to be differentiated from both Western and traditional forms of religiosity: a dual criticism of modernity and traditionalism in which being
Islamic becomes a quest for authentication that expertly melds tradition
and modernity (Deeb, 2006; Gole, 2003; Tibi, 2002, 2009). Subsequently
authenticity became the primary context of much theoretical analysis of
Muslims. There was more focus on the consequences of religion emerging as a source of identity and a fountain of authenticity than on the transformation of religion per se.

The quest for a pure authentic Islam, however, is not limited to the
modern period. It also served as a basic motif of the religious reform movements of the 17th and 18th centuries. The purpose there was to search for a
purified Islam and is fundamentally different from the modern quest for

---

4. For a historical analysis of the ideas related to a pan-Muslim nation, see Aydin (2017).

5. For a detailed presentation and analysis of the Muslim response to modernity and its different variations across times and places see Moaddel and Kamran (2000); Cooper, Nettler,
and Mahmoud (1998); Haj (2009); and Masud, Salvatore, and van Bruinessen (2009).

an authentic Islam, which is coupled with a sense of a unique identity vis-à-vis a stronger and dominant "other." This modern quest for *authenticity* arose out of the predicament faced by Muslims in dealing with the West and modernization in the 19th century (Tibi, 2009). While the previous quest for an authentic Islam was about being true to Allah, the new quest for authenticity was about responding to the overwhelming presence of the "other."

This modern quest only developed with the rise of nationalism and Islamists' adoption of nationalist motifs (al-Azmeh, 1993). To the Muslims and nationalists of the 19th century, the only response to weakness and destruction was revivalism through "the retrieval and restoration of the original qualities that made for strength and historical relevance" (al-Azmeh, 1993, p. 46). This was premised on the belief that only an authentic self can resist decay from within or defeat from without (Hoebink, 1999). As an outcome of the quest for authenticity Islam was presented as self-sufficient: "a complete divine system with a superior political model, cultural code, legal structure, and economic arrangement—in short, a system that responded to all human problems" (Bayat, 2007, p. 7). Islam, according to this view, held within it all the solutions to the "ills" of modern civilization. Islam here does not need to borrow any idea or social system, especially from the West. In this view the Muslim predicament was regarded as a product of either lapses in practice among Muslims or impurities within its existing form. Muslims must therefore reform their practice and seek a genuine Islam cleansed of all impurities (Esposito & Voll, 2001; Watt, 1988). The need to preserve identity has thus become a central Islamist concern (al-Azmeh, 1993; Watt, 1988). From this vantage point, political and developmental failures are due to a failure to live up to Islamic ideals that had previously enabled Muslims to lead the world. Seeking authenticity implies the renouncing of universal foundations and a quest to:

> refound the human experience on a deeper, inner, non-rational source, which the individual sees as authentic. They search for what "we" are as opposed to what "they" would want us to be. (R. D. Lee, 1997, p. 14)

The modern quest for authenticity was of course not restricted to religious thinkers, although such figures ultimately dominated it. Just as important were nationalist and liberal voices: the Moroccan philosopher Muhammad 'Abid al-Jabiri (1936–2010) says that Arabs were preoccupied during the 20th century with the question of authenticity (Safi, 1994). Exposure to modernity initiated an approach that sought to "meld Western ideas and institutions with Muslim [and Arab] values and society" (Norton, 2002, p. 378). When Taha Husayn (1889–1973), a leading Arab intellectual, called for the absolute adoption of Western values, he situated this call within a framework of identity and authenticity. Part of his argument was that Egypt should be Westernized because it is an authentic part of the West and not the East (Safi, 1994). Conservatism and fundamentalism developed as a reaction to those calling for the absolute adoption of Western values (Norton, 2002), and a "discourse of authenticity" emerged, supposing "a self defining historical subject with a fundamental continuity over time" (al-Azmeh, 1993, pp. 82–83).

In turn, the issue of modernization in the Arab world quickly became connected to the politics of identity. Leftists, Islamists, and liberals adopted the "authenticity" paradigm. For example, Michel 'Aflaq (1910–1989)—the Syrian Arab nationalist and founder of Ba'athism—rejected Marxism as a Western product that does not respond to society's internal problems (Safi, 1994). Authenticity would inform Islamist discourse in the Muslim and Arab worlds (Matthee, 1989; Zubaida, 2000), becoming a commodity without which many ideas find themselves alienated. For example, Arab Marxist and Liberal writers found themselves under pressure "to locate their ideas within the historical framework of Arab thought." Prominent Arab intellectuals came to realize that lack of authenticity was a serious charge and resorted to validating themselves by connecting the roots of their thought to Arab and Islamic historical practice (Safi, 1994, p. 175).

Of the studies that reflect the role of authenticity in the process of reappropriating religion in modern times, those on the veil—*hijab*—stand out strongly. According to Nilufer Gole, the debate in Turkey about the veil is not "against the grandmother's headscarf" but rather against the political symbolism that it embodies (Gole, 2003, p. 29). This sartorial choice has been transformed from a mere personal expression of piety or modesty to "a political cultural symbol" of Muslim women who are critical of both religious tradition and assimilative modernity (Gole, 2003). This approach is echoed by Leila Ahmed (2011), who traces the existing narrative of the veil to the colonially endorsed narrative of unveiling, explaining how the wearing of the veil has changed from a personal behavior to a form of identity and a political statement. This analysis of the veil can be extended to the change in how religion is viewed in general: from a means of piety to a means of resistance through identity. Women who wore the hijab changed their interpretation of it due to their changed consciousness. The crucial point for this study, however, is not the changing political meaning of the veil but rather its specific location within a paradigm of authenticity.

There are studies on issues more general than the veil. "Globalized Muslims" (Roy, 2006), "Enchanted Modern Muslims" (Deeb, 2006), and "Post-Islam Muslims" (Bayat, 2007), although different in many aspects, exhibit a constant thread: the quest to achieve compatibility between Islam and modernity by reshaping Islam to accommodate modern values and reappropriate modern values in Muslim terms; that is, by being authentic and at the same time modern. Olivier Roy's globalized Muslims are seeking to create or construct a deculturalized Islam to practice as a means of experiencing a religious identity that is not linked to a given culture; thus every culture can be suited to a privatized religion that is primarily concerned with identity (Roy, 2006). Lara Deeb (2006) points to the narratives of the Shiʿa in contemporary Lebanon, which are charged with references to being authentic. Their form of understanding and expression of modernity is mediated through the quest for authenticity. Deeb's informants are keen to demonstrate that Islam and modernity are not merely compatible but actually go hand in hand, and that being a pious Muslim does not mean being antimodern. Throughout her book, Deeb presents narratives of Shiʿa women that express the quest for authenticity and present a dual criticism of modernity and traditionalism. Finally, Asef Bayat's (b. 1954) post-Muslims seek to make Islam and democracy compatible, not intellectually, as had been the case, but politically. For Bayat's interlocutors, "the compatibility or incompatibility of Islam and democracy is not a matter of philosophical speculation but of political struggle" (Bayat, 2007, p. 6).

1.3. Islam in Saudi Arabia

While most studies on Islam in modernity focus on the politics of cultural authenticity, most research on Islam in Saudi Arabia centers on security and oil, emphasizing the religious dimensions that influence security and mostly neglecting aspects that have little to do with security. When the question of modernity is tackled, it is limited to exploring how the various religious groups in the country have exploited modern means of communication and organization, particularly the relationship between radical religiosity and the media, to further their political agendas (Fandy, 1999a, 1999b).

Even when religious minorities in Saudi Arabia are studied as a distinct topic, this is done in the context of their relevance to security issues. When one looks at the very limited studies on Shiʿa, for example, the security focus is clear. The literature looks at the complex and nonsystemic yet strategic discrimination against them (al-Rasheed, 2011); their violent contestation with the Saudi state (Jones, 2006; Matthiesen, 2010, 2012); their efforts to nurture a Shiʿa identity by means of resisting the prevalent discourse and developing their own narrative about their identity and place in Saudi Arabia (Matthiesen, 2015; al-Rasheed, 1998); their reintegration into local politics by civil activists post 9/11 (Jones, 2006; Raphaeli, 2005); how sectarianism is used by the state, such as in its latest utilization of it in the Arab Spring (al-Rasheed, 2011); and the identity challenges that arise from their status as a demographic minority (al-Sayf, 2013b). In all cases, however, questions of security and political rule stand at the forefront. By contrast, there has been little research on Shiʿa outside the oil-rich region of the Eastern Province of Saudi Arabia, notwithstanding the existence of small communities of Shiʿa living in al-Madinah, in the Western Province of Saudi Arabia, also known as *nakhawila* (Ende, 1997; al-Khoei, 2001). There is also an Ismaili Shiʿa community in Najran in the south of the country, but other than a Human Rights Watch report by Christoph Wilcke (2008), scholars have not studied them. Even more notably, studies of contemporary Sufism in Saudi Arabia are very few, such as Mark Sedgwick's (1997) article on Saudi Sufis in the mid-20th century and al-Zekri's (2004) work on the Sufi-Wahhabi encounter in Eastern Saudi Arabia. Ultimately, the majority of the academic literature on religion in Saudi Arabia centers on Salafism or Wahhabism as both a state religion and a contested ideology.

Salafism is the officially sanctioned version of Islam in Saudi Arabia. It seeks a pristine and pure past, claims a vision of an "authentic, unmediated Islam," and aims to create a "Wahhabised social sphere" which itself is not monolithic and includes "multiple interpretations" (al-Rasheed, 2007, p. 25). In this it is no different from other Muslim groups within and outside of Saudi Arabia. It is, however, distinct in that the Salafi establishment was given authority over the social sphere by the Saudi state and sought to shape it through ritualistic Islam (al-Rasheed, 2007). Meanwhile, the state did not adjust to becoming Islamic, but rather Islam was adjusted to support the state (Fandy, 1999b). Social strains brought about by a rich

rentier state and the massive demographic shift that disrupted the traditional tribal social structure led to the emergence of an Islamism that is
socially and religiously conservative but politically radical and militant in
practice (Fandy, 1999b, p. 77). Until the 1990s Saudi Islamism focused on
affecting change abroad:

> due to the relative lack of socio-economic grievance and to the
> development of a peculiar political culture in which support for
> Muslims abroad became a major source of political legitimacy and
> social status. (Hegghammer, 2010, p. 1)

In the 1990s, Saudi Islamists gradually shifted to the creation of inner political contestation (al-Rasheed, 2007). After being largely restricted to the
social sphere, groups emerged seeking to influence the political sphere by
expanding the religious realm from mere ritual and the personal. Their
appearance in the 1990s was due to the breakdown of the state's efforts
to create distinct spaces, leading to "desectorisation" (Lacroix, 2011a). This
desectorization led to the emergence of the specific discourse of al-Sahwa.
With globalization, the capacity of traditionally oriented active scholars
was enhanced. Specifically, they used modern forms of communication—
first the tape-recorder and then the Internet—to spread their message,
yet also accommodated their message to those forms (Fandy, 1999b;
Teitelbaum, 2002). Although this movement failed, a new movement
emerged in 2003 to contest the Saudi state through violence and jihadism
(Lacroix, 2011a).

Although the majority of research on religion, society, and the state in
Saudi Arabia has focused on radicalism and fundamentalism, this literature also provides much insight into three important themes that pertain
to my research. The first is the changes affecting the capacity of the religious scholars, or *ulama,* to shape the social arena; the second is the role
of education in transmitting Islam, and the types of outcome this generates; the third concerns the growing activism of non-Islamists or liberal
Islamists, which reveals the growth of nonreligious forms of sociopolitical
expression (al-Rasheed, 2014). These three themes relate to my research in
that they represent the main units within the structure of cultural change
in Saudi Arabia, and although the literature in these three areas is still developing, that which is available is of great benefit.

How should we understand the role of ulama in Saudi Arabia? Part
of the challenge is that it has changed rapidly, particularly since 1990.

Generally, efforts to conceptualize the role of the ulama start with the 1744 alliance between Muhammad bin[6] Abdulwahhab (1703–1791) and Muhammad bin Saud (1710–1765) (Mulin, 2011), but since this original union the Saudi state has diminished the centrality of this alliance. The ulama are not a monolith, nor are they a static category. Rather they have shifted in terms of political allegiance as well in their religious ideas (al-Khidr, 2011).

Analysts are split over the influence of ulama in Saudi Arabia. According to one school of thought, the influence of Saudi ulama has declined in the face of the expanded bureaucratization of state activities and the incorporation of the ulama into the institutions of the modern Saudi state,[7] leading to the loss of many of their traditional functions (al-Atawneh, 2009; al-Rasheed, 1996). Alternatively, a second approach argues that this incorporation constituted a restructuring of their power and authority through the same process of bureaucratization, thus formalizing their powers and securing their monopoly over particular sites of religious thought and practice (Mulin, 2011). Whatever can be said about their diminished or growing power, ulama have played important roles at times of major crisis, whether in supporting King Abdulaziz al-Saud, the founder of modern Saudi Arabia (1876–1953), against the Ikhwan in 1929 (Mulin, 2011); in their support for King Faisal bin Abdulaziz al-Saud (1906–1975) in the deposition of King Saud bin Abdulaziz al-Saud (1902–1969) in 1964 (Kechichian, 2001; Mulin, 2011); in their role in supporting the state after the 1979 occupation of the Mecca Grand Mosque (Kechichian, 1986; Mulin, 2011); in their legitimation in 1990 of the invitation of American forces into the country (Mulin, 2011; al-Rasheed, 1996); in their stand against those calling for public protest in 2011 (al-Rasheed, 2011); and most recently in supporting the Saudi state's decision to allow women to drive and to develop the Saudi entertainment industry including opening of cinemas in 2017.

Notwithstanding those roles, the ulama prefer the dialectical binary of ulama/umara (scholars/princes) whereby the legitimating authority is retained for the ulama and the material power is for the umara. The

---

6. *bin* and *ibn* mean: son of. *bin* is used when it is between two proper names. *ibn* is used when it is mentioned before a proper name.

7. The modern and third Saudi state was established in 1902. It was preceded by the first Saudi state, established in 1744 and ended in 1818; and the second Saudi state, established in 1824 and lasted till 1891.

umara, according to this binary, should be obeyed on the condition that their decrees are in accordance with Islam, which is defined by the ulama (al-Atawneh, 2009; Mulin, 2011). There is almost no explicit articulation from the Saudi state to contradict this, though in fact ulama have almost no influence on the major political and administrative aspects of Saudi Arabia, and are absent when it comes to formulating Saudi Arabia's economic and political policies (al-Atawneh, 2009). One rare instance of a response to the ulama/umara binary was made by Turki al-Faisal (b. 1945), a prominent Saudi prince and intellectual who wrote an article responding to such a claim that both the umara and ulama have a right to obedience and allegiance. This claim was presented by a prominent Saudi alim and politician Abdullah al-Turki (b. 1940) in the presence of King Abdullah bin Abdulaziz al-Saud in 2002 (Crown Prince at the time). Al-Faisal's article presents a jurisprudential argument to assert that that only the umara are entitled full obedience and allegiance, while the ulama are counsellors (al-Faisal, 2002).

Even the authority of the ulama that has primarily been exhibited in social matters is now receding. Their vision of a pious Saudi society has failed; instead they see Saudis heading toward moral degeneration and there is growing division among them on matters that were once held in consensus (Otterbeck, 2012). One of the important indicators of the shrinking role of the ulama is their influence on issues pertaining to women, for instance regarding gender mixing in the workplace, women's education, and women in the workforce. In all of these areas the ulama are losing their grip. While gender mixing in the workplace was previously totally prohibited, it is now largely accepted in Saudi Arabia. Moreover such mixing is now being presented as an issue for debate, whereas its prohibition was once considered a given. Most importantly, the ulama have lost their long-held influence over the education of girls. Girls' education had been institutionally separate from that of boys, with separate state institutions each with its own jurisdiction: the General Presidency of Girls' Education and the Ministry of Education. The former, heavily influenced by the ulama, controlled girls' education until 2002, when it was abolished, while the latter controlled boys' education (Hamdan, 2005; al-Rawaf & Simmons, 1991; El-Sanabary, 1994).

Much of the literature that seeks to understand education and its role in Saudi Arabia is framed by the legitimating role of religion in Saudi Arabia and the subsequent weight of religion in its curriculums (Nevo, 1998). Religious matters used to make up more than 30% of school texts

(Nevo, 1998; Prokop, 2003; Rugh, 2002). Since 9/11 the Islamic tone of the curriculum has been the focus of analysis and criticism of those trying to understand why 15 of the 19 hijackers on 9/11 were Saudis (Rugh, 2002). There are two main views in this regard: on one side there are those who consider that Saudi education has largely led to the creation of a generation prone to radicalism due to an emphasis on religious education, including educational texts that portray the "other" in negative terms, the development of apocalyptic thinking whereby the student is placed in a world of an ongoing struggle against the enemies of Allah and Islam, and teaching methods that inhibit critical and independent thinking (al-Nafjan, 2012; Prokop, 2003; Rugh, 2002). On the other hand there are those who argue that extensive religious education does not necessarily produce religious radicals. Saudi youth's knowledge of Islam is very limited, despite 12 years of schooling, and according to this view, the purpose is to build loyalty to Islam, not understanding (Doumato, 2003, pp. 232–243). The practice of listening to music may support Doumato's argument. While the official decree of the religious institution is that listening to music is a grave sin, most Saudis carry on listening to it, albeit with occasional feelings of guilt (Otterbeck, 2012). Between these two opinions there are those who argue that religious education leads indirectly to radicalism; that is, it does not create radicals but rather produces unemployable students "susceptible to recruitment for religious terrorism" (Walsh, 2009, p. 44). This third opinion reflects, in my view, the reality of youth in Saudi Arabia much more precisely.

Western criticism of Saudi school books has stirred many internal reactions. The religious establishment saw it as a Western attempt to break into the local culture, and some liberals as an infringement of national sovereignty. Saud al-Shuraym (b. 1964), once an imam[8] at the Mecca Grand Mosque, declared that changing the content of religious education was tantamount to high treason (Prokop, 2003, p. 89), despite many Saudis welcoming such a change and participating actively in advocating it. The best-known Saudi criticism is written by two Salafis, Ibrahim al-Sakran and Abdulaziz al-Qasim (al-Sakran & al-Qasim, 2002). Yet despite pressure from both within and outside of Saudi Arabia to reform religious

---

8. The title of whoever leads the Muslim prayer. Important to note that a prayer imam is not always a trained alem. However, the imams of the Grand Mosques of Mecca and Medina have usually been learned men—if not from the ulama—and are always officially appointed. Imam is also a title for the political leader of a Muslim community.

curricula, there have been very few changes to a curriculum that promotes intolerance (al-Nafjan, 2012; Center for Religious Freedom, 2006).

Speaking about literature on religion in Saudi Arabia would not be complete without reference to some of the scholarship on Saudi liberals who are in a way considered the "other" of the religious. The word "liberal" is frequently used in Saudi Arabia as an umbrella term for anyone critical of tradition or Salafism, but the two main factors that distinguish those who belong to this trend are a commitment to challenging the religious establishment and a focus on the emancipation of women (Dekmejian, 2003; Meijer, 2010). This alone complicates the conceptualization of liberals in Saudi Arabia. What further complicates the analysis is that "liberal" is often used as a pejorative term, sometimes combined with or replacing the term "secular" and often attached to the spread of corruption and the decay of society (Meijer, 2010). The Saudi liberal reformist spirit is "derived from the *practice* of Western liberalism," although not the liberal philosophy, which makes understanding liberals difficult as it is dependent on their demands and not their ideas (Dekmejian, 2003, p. 401, my italics). Moreover there are wide divisions on religious issues between liberals and the various positions they take regarding the authority of the religious establishment. Many of those classified by the religious elite as liberal or secular believe in the legitimacy of the fatwa and the authority of the ulama in Saudi Arabia (bin Sunaytan, 2004).

One cannot yet speak of a Saudi liberal movement, for although there is a liberal impulse, "liberals have been unable to acquire official sanction to convert their following into a cohesive movement" (Dekmejian, 2003, p. 408). Ondrej Beranek (2009), who speaks of such a movement, states that it is fragmented, lacks an independent financial base, and is wholly dependent on the state for protection and financing. Much of the research on liberals has focused on their political activism and ideology. Since 1990, they have been ever-present on the political stage, where they pressure the state to change and reform through petitions and demands for reform that they have presented to it in 1990, 2003, and 2011 (Lacroix, 2011b; Raphaeli, 2005).

More attention, though, had been paid to a special form of liberals, or what Lacroix (2004) calls the "Islamo-Liberal." These are Salafi liberals, whose roots can be traced to the fierce Salafi-Salafi debates in Saudi Arabia after foreign forces were invited to defend Saudi Arabia from Iraq in 1990. The debates were between those who supported the state's decision and those who rejected it (Fandy 1999; al-Khidr, 2011; Lacroix, 2011;

al-Rasheed, 2007; Alshamsi, 2011). After 9/11 the self-critique among Saudi
Salafis intensified, and since 2003 there have been many discussions and
publications seeking to recreate a Salafism that incorporates civil, plural-
istic, and even democratic values. Their opponents call these new Salafis
"enlightened Salafis." While this sounds like a commendation, the actual purpose is to discredit them with such a label as it associates their
new form of thinking to Western cultural origins, thus accusing them of
inauthenticity (Madawi, 2015). After the events of the Arab Spring, this
trend intensified, and although the goal of its leading figures was to re-
establish Salafism and Islam in a way that makes them more compatible
with human rights, what they also did was delegitimize the authority of
many Saudi Salafi ulama (Madawi, 2015), opening up space for more fundamental criticism of Islam.

1.4. Religion and Society

The previous discussion thus far has pointed to two different approaches
to the study of religion in Western and in Muslim societies. The research
on religion in Western societies has focused on secularization. The literature I have reviewed explains secularization by reference to factors
ranging from the functional disconnect between religion and modern
life, the conflict between religious cosmology and a scientific outlook on
the universe and nature, and the breakdown of the social ties that main-
tained religious communities and facilitated a continuous transmission
of faith. These explanations are structural; that is, they are not about individual traits such as lack of spiritual disposition or even individual choices
but refer to systemic social and cultural phenomena. The consequence
of these factors has been exaggerated at times, most notably when many
scholars assumed that modernization would bring about total secularization. What came to be known as the secularization thesis argues "that
society is on the road to irreversible or reversible secularization and that,
because of this, religion is in decline at the level of social process, or individual consciousness or both" (Hanson, 1997, p. 157). The resilience of religious institutions and the return of religion to public spaces—especially
the media—cast doubt on the validity of the thesis. Some have argued that
it has totally failed, while others contend that it has been successful in
explaining the trend of secularization in the world (Bruce, 2013; Norris &
Inglehart, 2004).

Moreover, notwithstanding the limitations of the secularization thesis, scholars have also probed the impact of these structural factors on the ways in which religion is experienced, mediated, and transmitted. There is much research about the various manifestations of secularization and desecularization, such as the deinstitutionalization of religion, the development of spiritualties without religion, individual religions, new forms of rituals, and "believing without belonging," among other forms of new religiosities (Bruce, 1996; Davie, 1994; Heelas & Woodhead, 2005). I have not included these as they are beyond the scope of this research, which is concerned with the detachment, disengagement, and criticism of religion and not the development of alternative forms as a consequence of such processes.

In contrast, the research on Muslim societies has had a very different focus, that of authenticity, while studies of Islam in Saudi Arabia have focused on religion through the security prism. The studies I have reviewed focus on one important part of the reality of religion in Muslim societies, namely the will to resist modernity and to remain authentic to a "past self" as a means of that resistance. The irony is that the discourse of authenticity is based on modern concepts of nationalism. Fundamentalism, the politicization of Islam, the articulation of religious duties and modernity in Islamic idioms, the development of an enchanted modernity and the redefinition of religious decrees through an authentic language are all presented in the literature as manifestations of the quest for the pure and pristine Islam as a basis of religious legitimation or for social and political identity. As mentioned previously, this is partly due to the fact that Muslims themselves highlight this aspect of authenticity. Other manifestations of religion are largely overlooked or underresearched, in particular aspects of atheism, areligiosity, and criticism of the fundamentals of Islamic faith, all of which are important undercurrents. The existing studies focus on the intellectual efforts and thoughts involved in such manifestations (Barlas, 2002; Esack, 1997; Fluehr-Lobban, 1998; Kersten, 2011; McGinty, 2007; Safi, 2003), but little is done to understand the nonintellectual and popular manifestations. There are several studies that use statistics to examine the popular presence of these issues, but these remain in the minority (Moaddel & Azadarmaki, 2002; Tezcur & Azadarmaki, 2008; Zuckerman, 2007).

One tentative conclusion that I reached from the literature review on Islam in modernity is that studies of religion in Muslim societies do not take into account the factors associated in Western societies with disengagement from religion or the transformation of religious life, even as Western and Muslim societies share these factors. Instead, modernity is looked at as "an object" imported into Muslim societies, and the analysis of religion in Muslim societies is effectively an analysis of the response of Muslims to this "object"—that is, modernity and the quest for authenticity, and the competing projects that emerge from it. Modernity is also reduced to some of its basic values, such as freedom and rationality, and most studies focus on how Muslims have responded to such values being imposed on their societies. Most problematically, these studies do not consider modernity from the perspective of considering it a structural (and ubiquitous) change that has already occurred but rather from the perspective of considering it as a challenge that can be warded off.

Along related lines, little attention is paid to the subtle and underlying changes occurring in everyday Muslim religious practice due to these structural changes. For example, when Grace Davie (1994) speaks of "belief without belonging," she does not mention it as a fact exclusive to religion but as a general state of social existence that also influences how people relate to religion. The factors mentioned above—the functional mismatch between religion and modern life, between religious cosmology and the scientific outlook on the universe and nature, and the breakdown of the social ties that kept religion intact and facilitated a smooth transmission of faith—are outcomes of changes in political, economic, and scientific life and thought, rather than a value of modernity that can be accepted or rejected. Modernity has brought a new state of social existence in Muslim societies, and this aspect of the relationship between modernity and religion in Saudi Arabia is understudied.

In this book I make the assumption that modernity has transformed Saudi Arabia, and in the process the relationship between Saudis and Islam. My central hypothesis is that the same factors that have led to disengagement from religion in Western countries are also at play in Saudi society, albeit with different manifestations and outcomes. In my study, I focus on the contemporary process of criticizing religion and how it is related to these structural factors as they play out in Saudi Arabia. Although there have not been studies that focused on Saudis who have stepped outside the bounds of Islam or challenged its fundamental tenets, there have been strong indicators of fundamental changes in the religiosity of Saudis. According to a survey published in 2006, 17% of Saudis define themselves as Saudis first and Muslims second (Moaddel, 2006): almost a fifth of the Saudi population believe in a concept antithetical to a common modern

Muslim understanding that the Islamic identity comes first or, to be more precise, that "the Muslim's nationality is his faith" (Zubaida, 2011, p. 175); and in Saudi Arabia acknowledging a national identity is problematic, and the celebration and commemoration of National Day is considered heretic by many Saudi scholars (A. al-Fawzan, n.d.). In a Saudi context the results of Moaddel's survey is quite telling.

This book first describes the visible process of the criticism of the grand religious beliefs by a small but growing population of urban youth in Saudi Arabia. I focus on observing a small number of Saudis involved in this process at different levels of depth and sophistication. Second, I explore the relationship between modernity and the criticism of religious beliefs, placing the critical process within two contexts: the individual biographies of the people that I observed and with whom I interacted, and the structural factors within which an individual finds him/herself. Third, I consider the legal consequences of engaging in such a debate in public physical spaces, exploring on the one hand how communications technology has facilitated the growth of the debate, and on the other how it has constricted the discussion that followed. Fourth, I examine the social and legal backlash to the public phenomenon of criticizing the grand religious beliefs, describing in detail some of the actions of various religious agents in response to the criticism of religion. I place these actions within the larger context of Saudi Arabia, highlighting the decreasing role and influence of the religious establishment and the political manipulation of that establishment for nonreligious ends.

1.5. Conclusion

This chapter has explored the literature on modernity and religion in Western contexts, the literature on Islam in modernity, and studies of Islam in Saudi Arabia. In particular, it has shown how the "Islam and modernity" literature centers on a prism of authenticity and identity. This approach may construct our view of Islam as much as it explains it. There is a need to complement these efforts with theories that explore the actions of Muslims outside the bounds of circular claims to authenticity. Moreover, it is important to study the Muslim voices within Islam that are breaking away from the authenticity/identity paradigm: an Islam that is continuously being shaped by modernity. To go beyond that prism one needs a new theoretical starting point. In the following chapters I explore disengagement from religion outside the context of authenticity in the hope of a different understanding of religion in Muslim countries and in Saudi Arabia.

The three approaches to religious disengagement and transformation discussed earlier, when combined, could be a very important starting point. The reason I use all three approaches is that they raise issues from different perspectives, which could help in understanding a multifaceted reality. They also resonate with the discourse on religion and the rejection of religion among Saudis in ways that will become apparent as the research moves on. For example, in the Harmonious Being sessions I heard ideas about religion as a function in the social and even the cosmological order. I also heard opinions on the incapacity of religion to provide a collective identity. Other voices at the sessions complained that religious authority is unable to transform experience into meaning. I heard statements reflecting the erosion of the plausibility structure, emphasizing the dearth of people who believed as they did. I felt that individuals have been leaving their memory networks, and as a consequence find themselves breaking away from their old form of religiosity, with some exposed to other forms. All of this prompted me to study this phenomenon in an attempt to present an initial understanding and some useful parameters for future research.

2

Ambivalent Religiosity

THE PURPOSE OF this chapter is to place the emergence of the criticism of religion in a Saudi context. For that purpose, I seek to answer one key question: What is the state of religion in Saudi Arabia? Answering that question will allow me to approximate whether or not criticizing religion is a totally alien phenomenon or one with local precursors. More importantly, answering it will tell us more about the nuanced and ambivalent nature of religiosity in Saudi society, which in turn creates space for various forms of religious criticism to arise.

As I have noted, existing studies on religion in Saudi Arabia focus mainly on manifestations of religiosity in both state and society. The constant theme of most of those studies is that Allah, and religion more broadly, is omnipresent in Saudi Arabia. By virtue of this approach, previous studies uphold a narrative in which Saudi Arabia, born out of a pact between religion and politics, an alem and a prince, upholds Islam; through the full implementation of the Shari'a, state institutions are assumed to create an "Islamised social sphere" (al-Rasheed, 2007, p. 25). This narrative is supported by Article 23 in the Saudi Constitution, called *The Basic Law of Government*, which was announced by royal decree on March 1992:

> The State shall protect the Islamic Creed, apply the Sharia, encourage good and discourage evil, and undertake its duty regarding the Propagation of Islam (*Da'wa*). (Council, 1992)

Thus, the state defines itself as a religious country and positions its mission as a religious one. With the state's past and present enmeshed in religion, it is easy to assume that Saudi Arabia's society is enchanted and "predominantly preoccupied with ritualistic Islam" (al-Rasheed, 2007, p. 59). Al-Atawneh takes this somewhat further to say that Saudi Arabia is "a 'theo-monarchy' shaped by religion" in which ulama shape the politics and the social form of society (al-Atawneh, 2009, p. 733). And Frank Vogel even claims that Saudi Arabia is "a state that aspires to adhere literally to classical Islamic law among and despite the drastically changed circumstances of today" (Vogel, 2003, pp 749). To prove these claims, scholars point to the number and the authority of religious formal institutions that exist in Saudi Arabia and to the state's religious discourse, which asserts time and again that its mission is to uphold Islam. Such findings are supported by the fact that religious institutions are in full control of the judiciary, and women must adhere to strict limitations to their personal freedoms—such as the need for a male guardian's approval to travel out of the country or the previously held ban on Saudi women driving—because of the dictates of the religious institution. Moreover, religion is a central part of the institutional structure of the state, as an estimated 25% of state employees work in religious institutions (al-Sayf, 2013b).

Thus, to speak of the emergence of the criticism of religion in Saudi Arabia may sound as if it were an anomaly totally disconnected from the lives of most Saudis. In this chapter, however, I seek to show that religion—at least in its Salafi version—is not as central to the Saudi state or to Saudi social life as it is assumed to be; that Allah is not everywhere; that people are critical of religion and religious institutional authority; that while there are many religious people there is also frustration surrounding the prevailing interpretations of sacred scripture; and that religion is more intense as an identity for both the state and individuals than it is as a guide to belief and behavior. In doing so, I show that there exists another side to Saudi Arabia, one that is as prevalent as the religious aspect yet underexplored. In other words, I want to show that Saudi Arabia cannot be considered a religious country on either a state or an individual level. This does not mean that we can say it is an areligious country, nor can we say it is a country where religion does not matter to the state or to the majority of the population. Rather, the country maintains what I call ambivalent religiosity, a place where religion matters and religiosity is valued, but religion does not fully or largely guide the state nor the individual; that is, religion is important but not central, and a better view of Saudi Arabia can be attained if we decentralize religion in our analysis of the country and its society.

2.1. Ambivalent Religiosity?

I mentioned in the first chapter that religion has no conclusive or agreed-on definition—the word "religion" has no clear meaning and it seems that there will not be one (Bergunder, 2014). Abandoning the word "religion" altogether has been suggested, and some even recommend dropping the discipline of studying religion (Fitzgerald, 2000; Hubert, 2015). This can also apply to the derivative of "religion," "religious." Thus, any sentence that includes the words "religion" and/or "religious" can almost be said to be without a meaning that is common to all users and listeners.

Subsequently statements such as "a religious society," "a religious state," or "religion and the state" can theoretically mean so many things to different listeners. Nevertheless, this multiplicity of the meaning of religion is to some degree restricted to those who have been exposed to the theoretical literature on religion as a social phenomenon. By contrast, my concern is how the average person in Saudi Arabia understands and uses the word. And for that person, a state's or society's religious nature depends on its role in applying the Shari'a and abiding by the guidance of its ulama. In turn, a person is religious if he/she performs duties prescribed by religion and avoids sin. This approach to defining religiosity is very similar to Kecskes and Wolf's definition of religiosity as agreement with the prescriptions of one's religion (cited in Hubert, 2015, p. 43). This definition is also compatible with the various attempts to measure Muslim religiosity by identifying its dimensions, all of which are based on determining the specific prescription for a Muslim (Khraim, 2010; el-Menouar, 2014). Indeed, the approach of using the lay Saudi's understanding of religiosity has also been used to develop a concept of religiosity (Berghammer & Fliegenschnee, 2014). Here, I use a simple definition of "religious" as generally understood in Saudi Arabia, and my sources are fatwas and sermons by popular ulama.

Being religious in Saudi Arabia implies first and foremost avoiding sin and performing good deeds, with the former serving as the most notable indicator of religiosity. Indeed, even if a Muslim performs all the good deeds prescribed in the Quran and in the *Hadiths*[1] of the Prophet Muhammad yet consistently and publicly commits grave sins, he/she would not be considered religious (Asbar, n.d.). Having said that, I consider *ambivalent religiosity* as a situation whereby according to the standards of orthodox

---

1. "Hadiths" generally means the teachings and deeds of the Prophet Muhammad. Sometimes referred to as the *Sunna*.

religious authority a person is not religious but the person him/herself considers him/herself religious. Or a situation in which an individual accepts an alim's authority in theory, fails to adhere to it in practice, yet still insists that he or she is following the alim's guidance. One finds such a situation in Saudi Arabia: sin prevails and is sometimes protected by the state—such as the sin of listening to music—and in other cases is institutionalized by it—such as the sin of gender mixing. Based on this, one can question the assumption made about the religiosity of Saudi Arabia. I do not say this to make a judgment on whether a person or a community or an institution is religious. That is not my purpose, nor is it my place. I am merely questioning some of the assumptions raised in the literature on Saudi Arabia.

2.2. Is Saudi Arabian Society "Religious"?

The opinion that Saudi society is religious is not unfounded. Before I present my argument for its ambivalent religiosity, I want to present some further support for the claims made in the literature that Saudi Arabia is a religious country, and that religion is central to both the state and society. My purpose is not to support their case but rather to emphasize the ambivalence of religiosity in Saudi Arabia. It is only by examining the factors that we associate with religiosity and nonreligiosity that we can understand a middle space of ambivalence within religiosity. I mentioned in the first chapter that there are two striking features in the religiosity of Saudi Arabia, namely the presence of the ulama and the intense religious education at Saudi schools. In what follows I present two common arguments for the claim that Saudi Arabian society is religious, the first based on the presence of the Committee for Ordering Virtue and Forbidding Vice (more commonly referred to in Saudi Arabia as "the Committee"), and the second based on the position of women.

A first supporting case for those claiming that Saudi Arabia is religious is that the ulama in Saudi Arabia hold formal and informal authority. Formal authority is derived from state institutions controlled by the ulama, and informal authority is derived from the traditional social status given to the ulama by Muslim communities. In this context, formal authority is particularly consequential as it shows the role of the state in endorsing and cultivating religiosity. The formal ulama of the country are divided across a number of state institutions such as *al-Lajnah al-Da'imah Li-l-Buhuth al-Ilmiyyah wa al-'Ifta'* (Permanent Committee for Scholarly

Research and Fatwa [PCSRF]), which is a body that provides the state with fatwas. This institution comprises ulama who are members of another powerful institution, *Hay'at Kibar al-ulama* (Council of Senior Ulama), a body comprising ulama appointed by the king who are formally the country's top ulama. The Permanent Committee is the only officially approved entity permitted to issue fatwas in Saudi Arabia. The Saudi state has been keen to control the issuing of fatwas that define what is permissible or prohibited and, according "to the August 2010 royal edict, only ulama associated with the Council of Senior Ulama are now authorised to issue fatwas" (Boucek, 2010). There is also the *Majlis al-Qada' al-'A'la* (High Judiciary Council), a judicial body similar to the Supreme Court in other countries, and its members are also ulama appointed by the king. *Al-Ri'sah al-'Ammah Li-l-Haramayn* (Presidency of the Two Holy Mosques) supervises the management of the two Grand Mosques in Mecca and Medina, is led by ulama, and employs a significant number of religious preachers. Furthermore, the Committee is also led by ulama, and this institution employs preachers and pious individuals who want to reform society—sometimes forcefully—in accordance with the injunctions of Shari'a. There are also publicly funded and ulama-controlled religious universities in Saudi Arabia, such as Imam Muhammad bin Saud Islamic University in Riyadh, Umm al-Qura University in Mecca, and the Islamic University in Medina. A country that has such a vast number of institutions whose mandate is religious, which are led by ulama, and which are state funded can only be perceived as religious.

The number of institutions is but one factor that contributes to the perception that the Saudi state is religious. Another important factor on this front is the influence that these institutions exercise on the daily life of Saudis. Here one institution stands out for its influence on Saudi society, and subsequently for emphasizing perceptions of a religious Saudi Arabia. It is the Committee; a state entity whose raison d'être is to uphold virtue and forbid sin. Its existence is premised that ordering virtue and forbidding vice is a Quranic commandment to which Muslims must adhere, and the Committee is considered the institutional embodiment of this commandment (Cook, 2000, 2015). To be more accurate, one can say that the original idea of the Committee was as an embodiment of that commandment in the sense of observing moral and legal transgressions practiced in public, but in Saudi Arabia it has outgrown this to acquire "all-encompassing and flexible powers to suppress crime" (Vogel, 2003, p. 763). The reason it stands out is its visibility and daily encroachment on

Saudi social life. The Committee had—until very recently—the power to disrupt people's personal lives, leading to Saudis' impression that religion has a tight hold on the country.

Indeed, this encroachment on social life had sometimes had tragic consequences, which are then picked up by the media (@HaiaWatch, 2013). This media focus, whether supportive or critical, has amplified the Committee's sense of presence and subsequently the perception of the ubiquity of religion. Attitudes toward the Committee vary and are difficult to assess accurately. It has its supporters and its detractors, but the point is not what people think about the Committee but rather that people think of the Committee all the time when they step out into a public space such as a market, a park, or a public play area.

The Committee first arose in 1927, when King Abdulaziz ordered its creation. The motive was not purely religious; instead, it served as a pressure valve by which he could control to his advantage the zeal of some of his followers, who were shocked by the supposedly decadent lifestyles of the people of their contemporaries (al-Nogaidan, 2012, p. 16). Known as the *Ikhwan*, these zealot followers of King Abdulaziz al-Saud had previously sought to forcefully impose their understanding of right and wrong on various populations in the newly founded kingdom (Kostiner, 1985). Incorporated into the Committee, they and others enforced public morality through various practices, most notably by reminding people to close their shops during prayer times. While the Committee initially reported to the local judge or police, it shifted in 1953 to report directly to the Council of Ministers, which is the highest legislative and executive body in the country and is presided over by the king (al-Nogaidan, 2012, p. 19).

The Committee has enjoyed continuous support from all the Saudi monarchs, beginning with the kingdom's founder, Abdulaziz Al-Saud, but especially after the Mecca incident in 1979, in which Juhayman al-Utaybi (1936–1980) led a group mostly consisting of tribal and economically marginalized individuals and took over the Grand Mosque in Mecca. Since the 1960s, Juhayman had been lamenting the corruption of Islam and actively "promoting a purified Wahhabism" (Hegghammer & Lacroix, 2007, p. 106). He was first a member of a group called *al-Jamaʻa al-Salafiyya al-Muhtasiba* (the Salafi Group that Commands Right and Forbids Wrong) but underwent a process of radicalization and became the leader of a new group called the *ikhwan* (brothers). To this day his motivation for taking over the Grand Mosque is not clear, but the most likely explanation is his messianic and apocalyptic views, which demanded allegiance to the Mahdi[2] at the Ka'aba in Mecca. The Saudi state regained control of the Grand Mosque, and Juhayman, along with 60 of his companions, was executed (Dekmejian, 1994; Hegghammer & Lacroix, 2007; Kechichian, 1990; Trofimov, 2007).

Following this incident, the state took serious steps to support the Committee specifically and the religious establishment more generally "by imposing stricter enforcement of the religious laws, censorship of television programmes, and prohibition of female singers on television" (Dekmejian, 1994) and reinforcing "the powers of the religious establishment and its control on Saudi society" (Hegghammer & Lacroix, 2007, p. 113). Prior to the Juhayman incident the state had supported the Committee but had limited its authority; from 1980 the Committee acquired more leeway. It gained further support after 1990, when Saudi Arabia faced an existential crisis after the Iraqi invasion of Kuwait, as well as a crisis of legitimacy due to the presence of foreign troops in Saudi Arabia, to which the state responded by giving more support to the religious establishment (al-Nogaidan, 2012, pp. 117–118).

The Saudi state not only consistently supported the Committee but also adamantly rejected any demands to dismantle it, even after many complaints from the public about the behavior of its members. As important as those rejections were, what mostly matters is the way the Committee was framed. For example, on May 18, 2003, roughly a week after the Riyadh bombing of May 12, 2003, Prince Nayif bin Abdulaziz al-Saud (1934–2012), the Minister of Interior, met with the editors-in-chief of Saudi newspapers and other journalists. The editor-in-chief of the Saudi newspaper *The Gazette*, Ahmad al-Yusuf (b. 1968), asked if it was time to shut down the Committee, considering it an institution that breeds radicals and terrorists. The prince's response was to lament that a Saudi would want the Committee to be closed down; instead, he reaffirmed the commitment of the Saudi state to the Committee. He said that the Committee is a state body, that it is part of the State, and that since Saudi Arabia is the Islamic state the Committee will continue to exist because ordering virtue and forbidding vice are vital pillars of Islam (krt455, 2008). His answer reflected not only the State's commitment to the Committee but also the

---

2. The Mahdi is a Muslim eschatological figure. Many Muslims believe he will come at the end of times to bring justice to all humanity before the return of Jesus, after which the Day of Judgment will arrive.

way that the State presents itself to its public, as well as what it expects from its citizens. Nayif "associated attacks on the Committee with other attacks on the state and its sovereignty" (Vogel, 2003, p. 759), and this was not totally new, as it only emphasized the rhetoric of the Saudi state since its establishment.

Even liberal ruling members of the royal family have shown support for the Committee. Prince Khalid al-Faisal (b. 1940), a very liberal prince and governor of the Mecca region, and widely criticized by the conservatives of the country, has affirmed that the state will continue to order virtue and forbid vice (al-Nogaidan, 2012, p. 120). Such statements when taken in isolation from the larger reality of Saudi Arabia could lead to an assumption that Saudi Arabia is indeed a religious country and that the state follows the precepts of religion to the last detail. But as I show later, this is not the case. These statements have to be understood as a legitimizing tool more than as a reflection of religiosity. Political statements serve in creating legitimacy (al-Rasheed, 1996, p. 360), and the State was stating its support for the Committee—and Islam in general—as a means of establishing its legitimacy and to clarify the foundations of its politics. This continuous and consistent verbal and actual support for the Committee gives the impression that Saudi Arabia is a religious state, or even a theocratic one.

I need to mention here that support for the Committee was not purely instrumental. The State believed that by preserving the Committee, it they would ensure Allah's support. It believed strongly in the verse of *tamkin* (enablement):

[And they are] those who, if We give them authority in the land, establish prayer and give zakah and enjoin what is right and forbid what is wrong. And to Allah belongs the outcome of [all] matters. (Quran: Hajj 41)

The State wants to be of those who "enjoin what is right and forbid what is wrong" in the hope that Allah will support them (al-Nogaidan, 2012, p. 123). This also made the Committee a crucial component of authority in Saudi Arabia, and the Saudi state would continuously reiterate its central importance.

Having said that, it is important to add that while successive kings affirmed the role of the Committee they did not support it in executing most of its mandate; to be more accurate, the Saudi state did not allow the Committee to execute its mandate. A glance at the list of things that the Committee considered sins which it had to forbid implies that while the state wants the Committee to exist, it does not want it to execute its mandate. For example the Committee was supposed to prevent barbers shaving the beards of men; to stop people selling and consuming tobacco; to stop people taking photographs of live creatures; to destroy musical instruments, and to whip whoever is found with them (al-Nogaidan, 2012, pp. 49–51). All of these acts are considered sinful, according to Wahhabi interpretations of Islam, but the Committee is not allowed to act against them, and all of these actions that the Committee is supposed to forbid are part of Saudi daily life. Moreover, the Committee's authority in controlling public space had been weakened to the point where they were stripped of any authority to forcefully intervene against a public sin (Said-Moorhouse, 2016). Already we see the ambivalence of religiosity. An institution such as the Committee is given full support by the Saudi state to forbid sin, and at the same time prevented from executing its mandate. The Committee thus serves as the quintessential symbol of the religiosity, albeit ambivalent religiosity, of the Saudi state.

Another symbol of the religiosity of the Saudi state in the view of outside observers is the status of women (al-Rasheed, 2007, p. 4; 2013a, p. 113). Women in Saudi Arabia face various limitations in many vital aspects of their lives, and most of the reasons presented by the Saudi state are religious. The issue of Saudi women is very prominent in Saudi Arabia and the global media, and the Saudi discourse on women is mostly a religious one, thus leading to the assumption that the Saudi state and society are religious. Whichever side one is on, the fight over the status of women is fought on religious grounds. Religion is all over this issue, which gives observers and participants a feeling that religion shapes it one way or the other. Whenever Saudis discuss the previous ban on women driving, women's right to vote, their right to travel without the need of their male guardian's approval, or gender mixing, it is with reference to religion. This is not to say that religion is or is not the actual reason behind the restrictions to women's lives, nor to say which argument is stronger than the other, but rather that Saudis always invoke religion when discussing women's rights (Coleman, 2013). I will mention in some detail the demand to boycott supermarkets that hire female cashiers as a reaction from some Saudis to that issue. This reaction was based on religion and exemplifies the centrality of religious discourse when dealing with the issues of women in Saudi Arabia.

In Saudi Arabia, gender mixing is considered a grave sin and a path to corruption and decadence. In 2010, the Saudi state first allowed women to enter the workforce, and opponents of this decision used religious arguments. A fatwa was issued by the PCSRF prohibiting the work of female cashiers in a mixed-gender environment (Islammemo, 2010). According to the fatwa, this was prohibited especially because it would open the door for women to engage in illicit relationships with men. Some ulama considered it a landmark issue that they must resist lest this decision open the door to further corruption. One of the ways that the ulama opposed this decision was by calling for a boycott against the first supermarket to employ women as cashiers. Most notably, Yusuf al-Ahmad—an informal alim famed for his bravado in ordering virtue and forbidding vice—launched this initiative during a live Q&A TV program. A caller had complained that women were working as cashiers in supermarkets, which led to their interacting with men. The caller then asked whether boycotting Hyper Panda, the first supermarket to hire female cashiers, would be recommended in this case. Al-Ahmad answered by saying this was a prohibited deed and part of a Westernization project that seeks to gradually normalize unacceptable forms of female behavior. Al-Ahmad then expressed surprise that the management of Hyper Panda persisted in this policy, and asked whether they were secretly receiving American support. Finally, al-Ahmad recommended that the stores be boycotted based on the duty of *hajr al-mubtadiʿ*, or the ostracization of those who publicly commit sins (ch905, 2010e). The logic of al-Ahmad's fatwa is noteworthy. He emphasizes the intervention of foreign powers in a matter as trivial as women working as cashiers, and by doing so he transforms the issue from one of women cashiers to a jihad against the gradual infiltration of Western values into Saudi society.

Al-Ahmad's sentiments, arguments, and prescription were expressed by other ulama, most notably Nasir al-ʿUmar (b. 1952), who is very popular among the religiously strict, as they consider him an alim who has not compromised with the state's demands for modernization (Almoslim, 2010a; ch905, 2010b). It is important to note that both al-Ahmad and al-ʿUmar are not formal scholars employed by the state, making it easier for them to publicly criticize a state's decision. The boycott they called for was effective, and the supermarket ended up withdrawing its decision to hire female cashiers (Almoslim, 2010b). It was only months later that the formal religious authority took a clear position on the matter when the PCSRF stated:

It is prohibited for the Muslim woman to work in a place where there is mixing with men, and it is compulsory [that she] avoid [places] where men are present and look for permissible work . . . and when companies hire her in such work it is an act of support for her in a prohibited action, thus it is also forbidden [for companies to hire her to work in such a job]. (PCSRF, 2010)

But the Saudi state went ahead with its decision to allow women to work as cashiers, and women were hired by various outlets. Even Hyper Panda resumed hiring them within weeks of the boycott, and other supermarkets followed suit. It soon became very common to enter a supermarket and be served by a woman cashier. More changes that allowed gender mixing in work environments were soon to follow, especially after 2016, with the absolute disdain and disapproval of most Saudi ulama.

2.3. Sin and the Ambivalence of Religion in Saudi Arabia

Having mentioned two prominent and highly visible reasons for assuming that Saudi Arabia is a religious country, I now move toward my argument that it is ambivalently religious: that religion matters, but not to the point where the country can be considered religious. Most importantly, the order of social and economic life is not centered around piety. I show in what follows that religion is not central, and that religiosity is ambivalent.

In the remainder of this chapter, I show the degree to which sin is prevalent and institutionalized in Saudi Arabia within both state and social institutions. At the state level, I explore the institutionalization of major sins and the disregarding of the fatwas and the guidance of the ulama. What makes the state's religiosity ambivalent is that it seeks to co-opt the ulama, even when those same ulama accuse the state of acting against religion. I also explore some of the ways which informal ulama interact with sin even while not committing sin. Ulama's interaction with sin shows a degree of acceptance of the authority of sin over critical aspects of life, making it impossible, even for ulama, to live in isolation from it. It also leads them to oscillate between rigid religious opinions and accommodative ones. It also leads them to accommodate sin itself. Finally, I explore the way Saudi individuals deal with sin, and how they navigate between the need and desire to commit a sin and the guilt that comes of it. All of this is to show that Saudi Arabia presents us with a set of contradictions that raise questions about the assumption of the religiosity of Saudi Arabia, making it better to say that it is ambivalently religious.

2.3.1. Sin

Sin exists in most religious traditions, but its accurate meaning cannot be separated from a specific theology. In its simplest definition sin—with regard to Islam—"is a human breach of relationship with Allah" (Krötke et al., 2015). In the Quran, more than one word is used to point to "sin," each speaking differently about the act of disobeying Allah, such as *khati'a, dhanb, ithm,* and *sayyi'a* (Wensinck, 2015). It is, however, a complex and contested concept (Mitchell, 1984, p. 165), "the proper use of which inevitably involves endless disputes about their proper uses on the part of their users" (Gallie, 1955, p. 169). I chose such a complex concept because it directly challenges the perception of Saudi Arabia as a religious state and society. Sin presents us with many cases that contradict claims to the religiosity of Saudi Arabia.

While sin has a theological aspect, it is also a political concept, as it is always determined by particular religious or political authorities. The Islamic concept of sin states that only Allah has the authority to determine what is sinful, and that one of the gravest sins a human can commit is to claim that right (al-Fawzan, n.d.-e; IslamWeb, 2011; al-Qardawi, 1980). A Muslim, however, must determine what Allah willed to be sinful by interpreting the Quran and the Prophet's Hadith, and only ulama with proper credentials are allowed to determine this. It is this quality of being determined by a religious authority that matters to this research. When differentiating between one sin and another, what ultimately matters is not the theological meaning of sin or the validity of the argument that concludes that a specific action is a sin; rather, the central question is who has determined that it is a sin, and the religious authority of that individual. When an individual wants to understand which acts are considered sins, they turn to the ulama. When laypeople argue about whether or not a certain deed is a sin, they argue about the alim's credentials and credibility. In Saudi Arabia the previous bans on women driving cars and on cinemas was debated citing the names of ulama for or against this practice. Thus, the social existence of the definitions of sin is constructed of two main components: the principle of adherence to religious authorities and the process by which those authorities come to be considered authorities. This is made clearer by the fact that a person is considered to commit a sin if he/she does an act that is defined as sinful by their authority. So, to say a person is committing a sin is not taken from jurisprudence books, rather from a socioreligious relation of authority.

One aspect of sin relevant to this research needs to be clarified. Committing a sin is an act of disobedience, but considering a sin permissible (*istihlal*) is an act of *kufr* (heresy or nonbelief). The Muslim commits a sin and is still considered part of the Muslim community, but such a person is excluded from the Muslim community if he/she claims that such an act is not sinful (Manhaj, 2014, p. 6; PCSRF, n.d.-b). For example, if a person drinks alcohol he/she is considered to be committing a sin. But if he/she says that drinking alcohol is permissible, he/she is considered a heretic who has challenged Allah's monopoly on determining what is right and what is wrong. Many, if not most, Saudis depend on ulama to determine what is sinful (Asbar, n.d.), and while a majority do not adhere to the fatwas of Saudi ulama, very few would dare to commit the sin of *istihlal*. This tension between committing a sin and avoiding *istihlal* characterizes the complex nature of the ambivalent religiosity in Saudi society. It is a mixture of accepting the authority of the alim, the correctness of the fatwa, disobeying the fatwa, and insisting on the sinfulness of the act. A Saudi sinner must continuously acknowledge to him/herself the sinfulness of his/her actions.

2.3.2. The Institutionalization of Sin

For the purposes of this chapter I take the Islam that is recognized by the state to determine what is sinful. This can be identified by looking into the opinions of the ulama, which the state formally sanctions and incorporates in its institutions. We can assess the state's religiosity based on the degree to which it applies religion in accordance with the view of its formal religious ulama. And conversely, one can say that the state is not religious to the degree that it does not practice religion according to the religious ulama that it uses as a reference point. Moreover, we can say that the religiosity of the state is ambivalent when it continuously insists that it is applying Shari'a while at the same time consistently committing and institutionalizing sin. There are two ways of approaching this issue. The first is to compare the ulama's vision of a religious state with actual situations in Saudi Arabia. The second is to look for their explicit condemnation of activities that the state has done and still is doing and whether the ulama label these policies as sinful. I take the second route because it minimizes some of the ambiguities inherent in the position of the ulama when it comes to their opinion of the state.

As mentioned above, most analysts who examine the religiosity of the Saudi state focus on the religious deeds it institutionalizes and upholds. They look at the language of the state, the treatment of women, the banning of alcohol, religion-based courts, and legal action against people who openly criticize religion. Here I take another route and look at the "sins" that the state institutionalizes. I disregard sins committed but not institutionalized, such as corruption. I also disregard short-lived sins; that is, one-off actions undertaken by the state such as inviting of American troops into the country in 1990 after Iraq invaded Kuwait, which was deemed sinful by many ulama (Lacroix, 2011a, pp. 160–161; al-Rasheed, 2010, pp. 160–163). And I only focus on those "sins" that are ongoing, public and frequently targeted by the Saudi formal ulama. Most importantly I focus on those sins that the state commits while incorporating all the Saudi population in that same sin, this in contrast to sins in foreign policy, for example, where the population is not part of the sin. In addition to highlighting the way the state does not act according to religion as set by the ulama, I highlight the criticism of these acts by popular religious ulama outside the formal establishment.

2.3.3. Modern Laws

Ambivalence in the religiosity of the state can be seen from its early years. In the 1950s and 1960s the Mufti of Saudi Arabia, Muhammad bin Ibrahim al-Alshaykh (1893–1969), issued a number of fatwas warning against deviance and sins that were happening, particularly with regard to some of the modern institutions being created in the country. He issued the fatwas at a very early stage in the life of the modern Saudi state, when its religious origins were very much alive and oil was still in its early stages of production. The religious establishment was still small and its opinions still relatively unified. The modern Saudi state was less than three decades old, and memories of its origins were still fresh. Despite this, the state was already, according to the standards of its ulama, deviating from religion. The Mufti demanded that cars not be driven during prayer times (al-Alshaykh, 1979a, p. 132); prohibited music, including music aired on Saudi state radio (al-Alshaykh, 1979c, pp. 229–230); and prohibited playing and watching football (al-Alshaykh, 1979c, p. 118).

His most severe set of fatwas concerned the development of modern laws and institutions such as the establishment of committees that followed a specific ministry or institution to settle cases outside religious courts. For example, the Ministry of Commerce was given the right to deal with commercial and business disputes (Boshoff, 1986; al-Ghadyan, 1998), but the Mufti considered that all disputes should be judged by ulama. The wording of these fatwas was severe, accusing the state of taking steps against what Allah had intended and decreed. He considered settling disputes to be the jurisdiction of the ulama and not of legal experts (al-Jarbou, 2007).

> To consider any law and to issue ruling according to it even in the most least of the least is undoubtedly a rejection of the ruling of Allah and His Prophet and attributing to the rules of Allah and His Prophet imperfectness. (al-Alshaykh, 1979c, p. 251)

Al-Alshaykh sent his opinion to King Faisal, after which the law was superficially amended in a way that would make the committees not equal to the courts but rather to arbitration committees. Al-Alshaykh rejected this compromise because he claimed no one should be given the title of arbitrator (*hakim*) unless he was a learned scholar of Islam, and that Allah would consider such an action "rebelliousness" and "lofty" (al-Alshaykh, 1979c). Finally, the state made it optional to go either to the Shari'a court or to the arbitration committees. This was also considered sinful by al-Alshaykh, who said that the only action compatible with what he believed and what all scholars of Islam abide by was that the Chamber of Commerce must be canceled, and he was very critical of giving people the option to choose between religion and positive law, insisting that Prophet Muhammad's Shari'a is the only legitimate source of rulings (al-Alshaykh, 1979c, pp. 254–255). Nevertheless, the fatwas were effectively ignored by the Saudi state. The Mufti reacted by publishing a short treatise on the application of positive law which starts "Of the greatest and clearest *kufr* is to make the damned law on equal status with what The Honest Spirit had brought down on the heart of Muhammad" (al-Hawali, 2000, p. 6). Although he considered that the state's actions amounted to nonbelief (*kufr*), he continued to embrace the new sins of the state as it continued creating modern religious institutions, all the while complaining about those institutions he saw outside the authority of religion. He also issued various statements in which he said that the Saudi state practices Islam fully, saying that "our state by the grace of Allah is *Shari'iyya* [Shari'a-compliant], its constitution is the Book of Allah and the Sunnah of His Prophet" (al-Alshaykh, 1979c, p. 273). Today few Saudis know about such fatwas, and the institutions that were the target of these severe fatwas have become an integral and natural part of the Saudi state and a key source of authority for the ulama.

This particular religious attitude to the Saudi state in its early years is extremely telling of the essence of the relationship between the state and religion in Saudi Arabia. While there have been many changes in the country since then, this essence continues to inform the relationship today: the state decrees, the ulama complain, the state may or may not compromise depending on the situation, and the ulama abide, even if they express disdain. What makes the case of these fatwas special is that they were issued at a time when religion and the state were mainly local matters, and before the politicization of Islam in Saudi Arabia. Thus, we have a clearer vision of the actual dynamics between state policies and religious imperatives. The state here wants to balance two imperatives. On one hand it needs to present itself as a protector of the faith. Durkheim tells us that the state's "first and foremost function is to ensure respect for beliefs, traditions and collective practices" (1984, p. 66). And in this sense the Saudi state needs to take into consideration the demands of the religious ulama. On the other hand, the state knows that to do so fully would be to the detriment of the state. The founder of the kingdom, King Abdulaziz, used to criticize his predecessors in the first Saudi state formed in the 18th century, saying that their fatal mistake had been to listen to the "zealots" (al-Nogaidan, 2012, p. 17). Such a case is also exemplary of the state's consideration when moving forward in issues pertaining to its existence. The state has always insisted that it upholds religion but has acted in ways to contain the ulama and resist being governed by them. This case is also exemplary of the way the ulama react. While they do express dissatisfaction, even disdain, at the decisions of the state, they allow themselves to be embedded within it and benefit from it.

2.3.4. Banking

I move to another sin which is continuously and consciously felt by most Saudis: banking. Many Muslims consider that interest-based banks are sinful and consider interest nothing but a euphemism for *riba* (usury)

(Choudhury, 2015). While there are ulama who view interest as distinct from usury, such an opinion has not gained wide acceptance (M. R. Zaman, 2008). It is thus accurate to say that Muslims largely reject modern conventional banking. The whole model of the modern idea of Islamic banking is based on the view that interest and usury are one and the same; and subsequently a pious Muslim should find an alternative way of banking and financing. Indeed, the sin of interest-based banking is particularly serious: the only sins worse than this are polytheism and non-belief in Allah, the Prophet, and the Quran. Ulama continuously argue that the greatest sin is dealing with *riba* and that it is worse that drinking alcohol, adultery, and even homosexuality (Useem, 2002). Moreover, there is even a narration from the Prophet which goes as follows: "The Prophet, PBUH, said, 'A dirham of riba which a man receives knowingly is worse than committing adultery thirty-six times!'" (Chapra, 2006, p. 10). Thus, interest is no everyday matter.

Yet the Saudi state has always been implicated in such sinful behavior. The first bank to work in the country was the Saudi Hollandi Bank, which acted as a central bank until 1952, when the Saudi Arabian Monetary Agency (SAMA) was established (SAMA, n.d.). From the moment that interest-charging banks operated in the country there were many voices both critical and fearful; critical of the sin and fearful of the wrath that Allah may send down onto those who are silent about this sin. The ulama continually criticized the banking system, warning Saudis not to use the country's leading financial institutions (al-Weeam, 2014). As a result, many Saudis became wary of putting their money in interest-based banks lest its purity be compromised. For example, a questioner asked one of the most prominent Saudi ulama, Muhammad bin 'Uthaymin (1929–2001), about himself and a group of teachers who wanted to open an account in an interest-based bank so that their salaries could be automatically transferred to their respective accounts monthly instead of continually cashing checks. The questioner also noted the benefits of using an ATM if he had a bank account. Ibn 'Uthaymin, however, was unswayed: this prominent Saudi alim simply stated, "If you need to open an account you can, but if you do not need to, then you cannot." The questioner kept repeating the benefits of having an account in the hope that he would get a clear answer allowing him to transact via a bank. Ibn "Uthaymin however would not give one, and kept responding: 'If you need—is this a need?'" (al-Shaty, 2012). Our questioner was not asking about making a usurious transaction with the bank, rather about simply opening a bank account. He was worried about unintentional sin, and the only answer he could extract was that only necessity rendered such an action permissible. In other words, banks, according to the average Saudi who follows the fatwas of Saudi ulama, are a sin.

Yet, despite the gravity of the sin, the fatwas of Saudi ulama and the apprehension of many Saudis when transacting with banks, the Saudi state did not alter its banking system. It did, however, encourage economists to present arguments that highlight the difference between interest and usury, the former being a healthy beneficial financial transaction that Saudi banks apply and the latter being a sin which Saudi banks do not engage in (al-Fanjari, 2006). These opinions, though, had little impact. As far as many Saudis—as well as many Muslims of other countries—are concerned, interest is identical to usury, the Saudi banking system is usurious, and they need to continually repent so that Allah forgives them. While the country's banking system is seen as having an institutionalized sin, there was no strong backlash from society at large or from most ulama against what they consider deviant behavior on the part of the state. Even the Committee for Ordering Virtue and Forbidding Vice never went to banks to forbid their practice, despite the public nature of this sin. What persisted, however, was protesting against the sin.

2.3.5. International Scholarship Program

A different type of sin institutionalized by the state is the mass scholarship program for Saudis that was initiated in 2005 by King Abdullah bin Abdulaziz al-Saud (1924–2015). More than a hundred and fifty thousand students had benefited from this program, almost a third were females. While this program is hailed by most reformers in the country as an investment in Saudi human capital, many ulama castigate it as a means of corrupting Saudi youth through Westernization.

Saudi ulama have always warned about traveling to Western countries and the lands of the *kuffar*[3] (disbelievers) in general. In principle traveling to such countries is not allowed unless there is a legitimate reason for it. In a fatwa of Saleh al-Fawzan (b. 1933), a member of The Council of Senior Ulama, he answers some fatwas about traveling abroad, saying:

---

3. *Kuffar* is plural of *kafir*, meaning a disbeliever. The verbal noun is *kufr*, meaning disbelief.

It is not permissible to travel to the lands of the *kuffar*, because this poses a threat to one's creed (*'aqida*) and morals and because it involves mixing with the *kuffar* and living among them. But if there is a need to travel to their countries, such as seeking medical treatment for one who is sick that is not available anywhere else, or travelling for the purpose of study that is not available in a Muslim country, or travelling for business, these are valid purposes for which it is permissible to travel to infidel countries, so long as one is able to adhere to Islamic practices and establish Islam in their lands. That should also be done only to the extent that it is necessary, then you should go back to the Muslim lands. (al-Fazwan, n.d.-b)

There is also a fatwa about traveling to America specifically, which warns against going there and only permits it with the conditions of the previous fatwa (PCSRF, n.d.-e). And to date there is not one fatwa from the top formal ulama of Saudi Arabia that allows Muslims to travel to a *kafir* country without it being necessary for medical reasons or something of that type. Saudis still travel to such countries for tourism and other reasons not considered necessary by the ulama, but they either find more permissive fatwas or simply ignore the forbidding fatwas.

Saudi ulama warn of Westernization or "intellectual invasion" in sermons and books (al-Baddah, 2011; al-Khuzaym, 2012; mdawyu, 2008) and thus the scholarship program was considered particularly dangerous. The volume of students being sent was so high that they considered it one of the worst initiatives of the time, and even sent emissaries to the minister of higher education insisting that he revise the policy of sending students abroad. The emissaries would meet the deputy minister and emphasize the dangers of the program for the religious identity of Saudi Arabia, while the deputy minister would inform them of the benefits of the scholarship program (Twasul, 2011). One of those visits in 2014 attracted much attention after pictures of ulama were posted on Twitter under the hashtag #ziyarat_al-mashayikh_li-bayan_khatar_al-ʾibtiʿath (The emissary of the shaykhs[4] to highlight the dangers of sending students abroad).

Yusuf al-Ahmad attacked the king's scholarship project on the Bedaya satellite channel, quoting fatwas from the previous mufti Abdulaziz bin

---

4. "Shaykh" is an honorific title commonly used when speaking of men learned in religion. Not all shaykhs are ulama. It also used when referring to men of social standing.

Baz (ch905, 2010c). His attack was so harsh that it prompted the channel's management to deny any connection to the statement (Annahar, 2010). The Ministry of Higher Education did not respond to the accusations directly; instead, the state had other ulama in the Senior Council issue a statement that severely criticized al-Ahmad and described his criticism as fantasy (al-ʿUwayjan, 2010). Still, there was much resistance to the program, to the point that those opposing it were able to insert a chapter into the public school curriculum titled "The Scholarship Programme: Its Dangers, Rules and Etiquette," which includes warnings about the dangers of living in a deviant and corrupt society. The chapter goes on to say that people in the scholarship program have returned:

> filled with the spirit of the West, breathing with its lungs and thinking with its mind and repeating in their country the echoes of their orientalist teachers. (al-Qunayʿir, 2011)

After a year of debate, the content of the chapter was finally moderated yet retained the title (W. al-Ahmad, 2012). Warnings about the scholarship program happened through a state ministry, despite the fact that it was against a project that the king was personally behind. In reality there was nothing different in what that chapter said from what the ulama were saying, except that it was placed in the educational curricula as a last resort by the ulama to fight what they considered a grave deviance and a serious threat to religion in Saudi Arabia.

2.3.6. Celebration of National Day

The scholarship program is severely criticized because ulama assume that it will Westernize Saudi Muslims and lead to the loss of their faith and values. Another matter related to identity that was also considered a sin is related to national identity. Here the ulama claimed that promoting national identity will lead to the weakening of the Islamic identity of Saudi Muslims. Moreover, while the scholarship program only puts some Saudis at risk of becoming Westernized, promoting national identity has a wider effect. Here the Saudi state, according to the ulama, was permanently distorting the purity of all Saudis' identity.

For many decades after the establishment of the modern Saudi state the issue of national identity was not a matter of importance and the state did not actively pursue instilling a sense of national identity in Saudis. As far as the state was concerned, a weak Saudi national identity was not yet a problem, as loyalty to the royal family of al-Saud was sufficient. Moreover, in the face of Nasser's pan-Arabism project, which threatened the existence of Saudi Arabia as an independent state, the Saudi state could not confront pan-Arab nationalism with a local novel Saudi national identity. The decision to postpone developing and promoting a Saudi national identity came at a cost, as the consequence of that option was that the political loyalties of many Saudis would become vaguely defined. To make Islam the foundation of a political identity of Saudi Arabia led to blurring national borders and to confusion in allegiances. The legitimacy of sovereign borders between Muslim countries would become questioned in Saudi Arabia; in the same way, Arab nationalists were questioning borders between Arab countries. In the late 1990s, national identity was introduced as a subject to be taught in schools, but only after 9/11 did the issue of national identity became a matter of supreme urgency for the Saudi state, and subsequently a hotly contested subject in Saudi Arabia. Pan-Islamism had instilled in many Saudis loyalties for political figures outside Saudi Arabia. And while that was tolerable to a point at one time, after 9/11 the state considered it a threat. More attention was given to the subject of national education, but the more visible step was to start celebrating National Day, commemorating the establishment of the country.

There was an attempt at such a celebration in 1950, when some suggested that King Abdulaziz should celebrate the jubilee anniversary of his entering Riyadh. This celebration, however, was canceled due to opposition from ulama of the time based on the principle that Muslims should only celebrate the two holidays of Eid al-Fitr and Eid al-Adha (al-Zirikly, 1988). National Day was first celebrated in 2005 (al-Ansari, 2005) and, unsurprisingly, it faced ulama's criticism as a grave sin. After a petition for a fatwa directed to the PCSRF, it ruled that celebrating National Day falls into the category of innovations in religion[5] that should be rejected, and moreover it considered it to be imitating disbelievers, which in itself is a grave sin (PCSRF, n.d.-a). Patriotism in the political sense, in which one is supposed to belong to a people defined by modern political boundaries, is not permissible, and national identities are considered deviant and sinful (al-Ghays, 2008). Other ulama, though, took the state's position and

---

5. An innovation in religion here means religious deeds and practices that are not based on Quran and the Hadiths of the Prophet; i.e., are not derived from authentic Islam (Macdonald, 2015).

provided a legal foundation for this practice (AlnaserLedinAllah, 2012). Later, Mufti Abdulaziz al-Alshaykh (b. 1943) issued a fatwa decreeing that it is permissible to commemorate this day and that he saw it as a day to thank Allah for the blessing of having this country (al-Alshaykh, 2011), although al-AlShaykh warned against celebrating it in ways that are sinful (Albilad, 2008; AlnaserLedinAllah, 2012). Examples of sinful celebrations include using musical instruments or organizing celebrations where the genders mix, and expressing allegiance, rather than mere love, to the state. While the first two acts are commonly known to be sinful, Saudi ulama have always considered that one's political allegiance should be exclusively to Allah and His Prophet, and while one can love his country—only if it is an Islamic country—he should not give it allegiance in any way (bin Baz, n.d.-c, p. 317).

Other highly visible sins that were institutionalized by the state include the National Festival for Heritage and Culture at al-Janadriya, the most important cultural event held yearly in the country. Though it is sponsored by King Abdullah himself, fatwas frequently warn potential attendees against the gender mixing and corrupt entertainment that occurs at this festival. Indeed, none other than a previous head of the High Judiciary Council, Saleh al-Luhaydan (b. 1932), warned women against attending (Qanat tellme000, 2012). al-Fawzan answered a question on the matter saying:

> No by Allah! No by Allah! It is not permissible for women to go these celebrations and forums because it is full of sin and gender mixing and evils, and a person who is safe from that should stay in his home and thank Allah for that. (Dahab, 2013)

Nasir al-ʿUmar, a prominent Saudi alim and secretary general of the Muslims Scholar Association, described al-Janadriyah as an event "to spread evil and curb good" (al-ʿUmar, 2013). Football is another sin that the state endorses, finances, and institutionalizes. Football is not only a sin but is also believed to be part of the Westernization project that aims to distract Muslim youth and replace loyalty to Allah with loyalty to teams (ch905, 2010d; al-Khulayfi, 2011). I will not go into the details of those sins, as the three examples suffice to show that while the Saudi State places religion at the center of its self-definition it does not itself abide by basic religious rulings. The Saudi state is not religious; instead, it is ambivalently religious.

2.3.7. Saudi Society and Sin

Up until now I have focused on showing that the state's religiosity is ambivalent and that it is inaccurate to assume that Saudi Arabia is a religious state. I have also shown how the ulama of the country, formal and informal, respond to the sins that the state institutionalizes or protects, and even accommodate certain sins. Now I want to shift toward Saudi society, arguing that society's attitude toward religion is congruent with the state's ambivalent religiosity. Indeed, the state is, if anything, more conservative than Saudi society at large.

Among Saudis, 90% describe themselves as practicing Muslims and about 75% follow ulama's fatwas (Asbar, n.d., p. 7). Yet at the same time most Saudis engage in "sinful" behavior such as gender mixing, listening to music, watching satellite TV, transacting with banks, and shaving on a daily basis. This ambivalence in religiosity in Saudi is not all unique; instead, it is shared by all religious societies. The Saudi case, however, is distinct in the marked dissonance between religious language and religious practice. Considering the lack of quantitative studies on Saudi Arabia, it is useful to compare the Saudi case with a few studies of religious dissonance among non-Muslims.

These studies are based on two sets of theories: cognitive dissonance theory and naturalization theory. Both aim to explain the ways in which people cope with behavior that they consider immoral or unacceptable. Cognitive dissonance theories state that when a person behaves in a way that is dissonant with the beliefs he/she holds, that person works toward reducing the dissonance through one of three strategies: the person ceases to engage in this behavior; alters the belief that is dissonant to the behavior; or abandons the belief causing the dissonance, and in some cases even chooses to leave the society that keeps raising the dissonance (Mahaffy, 1996, p. 393). Naturalization theory states that one needs to justify the action being done to oneself by denying responsibility for the behavior; by claiming to be under the influence of something stronger; by denial of injury to anyone else as a consequence of the action; by denying the existence of victims; by condemning the condemners; or by appealing to higher loyalties; that is, stating that this was being done for a higher good (Dunford & Kunz, 1973, pp. 3, 4). Most of these techniques have been observed among people who commit acts that they consider a violation of their faith. Some Christian lesbians who experienced tension between their religious belief and their sexual practices tried changing their belief as a way of resolving the tension, engaging in selective reading of the scripture regarding homosexuality. Others decided to leave the church (Mahaffy, 1996, p. 398). Mormons who do Sunday shopping while believing it is a "violation of 'divine' law" also use these techniques, denying responsibility through the claim that they have no other choice (Dunford & Kunz, 1973, p. 2). Some even appeal to higher authority by claiming that they went shopping for a greater good such as to purchase groceries to cook for guests (Dunford & Kunz, 1973, p. 6).

These techniques are hardly alien to Saudi Arabian Muslims as religious and nonreligious individuals who seek to lessen the dissonance between belief and behavior. Some Saudis may choose to change their belief by deciding that music—for example—is no longer a sin, while others change their alim to better accord with their existing practices and preferences. Often Saudis flock to particularly "permissive" ulama such as ʿAdel al-Kalbani (b. 1959), who stated that music was permissible. This gained him wide popularity among many Saudis but at the same time attracted harsh criticism from senior ulama, to the point where Abdulrahman al-Sudyas (b. 1960), when he was the Imam of the Mecca Grand Mosque, demanded that he be declared legally incompetent (Alawi, 2010; Ch905, 2010a).

The technique of changing belief and/or denying responsibility by delegating it to an alim does not work in the case of grave sins such as illicit sexual relations or alcohol consumption. In such cases those who engage in such actions often defer judgment by saying "Allah is merciful" or "When I grow older I will stop" or "May Allah forgive us and also help us to stop committing these sins." Such statements are often made with the intention of changing the subject if someone raises the matter of the sin being committed, and at other times are made with the sincere intention of improving one's behavior in the future and asking for Allah's support. One popular technique is support for the pious by the impious; as a popular statement goes, ʾUhibbu al-Salihin wa Lastu min-Hum (I love the pious but I am not one of them). This whole statement is taken seriously, especially the part about hating those who trade in sins, and I discuss this further when discussing takfir in Saudi Arabia, as a significant number of people active in supporting the radical ulama are not religious. Sometimes Saudis invoke the jurisprudential rule al-Dharurat Tubih al-Mahthurat (necessity permits the prohibited) (al-Sabil, n.d.). This principle—which has a parallel in the Bible, "getting the ox out of the pit," is frequently used by religious people to justify committing sins (Dunford & Kunz, 1973, p. 6).

Although only a small number of excuses are usually stated, studies have shown that they are endless and depend to a large degree to the type of violation committed (Maruna & Copes, 2005, p. 296).

2.4. Conclusion: Religion as Solidarity

Religiosity is ambivalent in Saudi Arabia, yet the language that many Saudis use to legitimate their actions is religious. This may arise from limited training in secular modes of argumentation. One of my interviewees, Adnan, explained:

> We do not have other cultures, no other inputs. So you find someone who has alcohol in his hands speaking religiously: [it is because] religious talk is on our tongues. The bad person speaks of religion [and] also the religious person. You feel as if this society had nothing else. But when it comes to application to our lives, there is no religion. There is religion to show [that we are religious, otherwise] people are living their lives.

The moral language with which Saudis are brought up is a religious language. Everything is thought of in terms of *haram* (prohibited) and *halal* (permissible), praiseworthy actions and sin. As a result, Adnan sees that Saudis must use a religious language to justify their social/secular motivation. Which in turn makes the Saudi or observer think that religion is driving everything.

Moreover, there is more to religion that just belief or ritual practice. It has other functions that may make allegiance to it a matter of practical necessity. Durkheim's theory of religion as solidarity and an expression of society echoes the ways in which religion is seen by a segment of Muslims in Saudi Arabia. For many Saudis, a society without religion would be one in which chaos ensued, yet these same people seem to show limited interest in obeying divine law. In this context, religion serves as a shield to protect society from elements of social existence, and this belief is shared by state actors, individuals in the community, and religious elites.

Indeed, this theme frequently arises in prominent Friday sermons. For example, imams at the Mecca Grand Mosque frequently attribute the downfall of the Muslim Ummah to the sins of its members (al-Sudays, n.d.). The same theme is frequently emphasized at the Medina Grand Mosque (Multaqa al-Khutaba', 2013). Each sermon is attended by more than one million people and listened to by many more. Some ulama are specific and point to certain sins and even categories of people as causes of the disintegration of community. The very well-known alim Nasir al-ʿUmar invoked the theme of destruction and chaos when commenting on gender mixing which, in his opinion, is endorsed by the Ministry of Education. He even contrasted the efforts of the Ministry of Interior to keep peace and civil peace with those who commit sin, leading to chaos and dissent (m3zad, 2011). Another preacher focuses on the danger of secularists to the stability of the country because they seek to separate religion from politics and are content with the weakened situation of religion in the country (azazi911, 2008; Qanat Abu ʿUmar al-Daʾwiyyah, 2013). In the same way the state relates upholding the duty to command order to *tamkin* (enabling), as mentioned earlier, but without practicing it; so too, much of society relates upholding religion to *aman* (security) without practicing it. One of the very common popular prayers in Saudi is *Allah la yughayyir ʿalayna* (May Allah not change our situation), as Saudis believe that if they lose their connection to Allah society will crumble.

Saudi Arabia is a religious society in its appearance and language, yet its apparent religiosity says little about social practice. Instead, religion is ambivalent, and in this ambivalence one finds criticism of religion and religiosity. The next chapter focuses on some moderate and extreme criticism of religion, while the following one looks into some stories told by Saudis describing their experiences with religion and their disengagement from it.

3

Criticizing Religion on Twitter

IN THE PREVIOUS chapter I explored the ambivalence of the religious landscape of Saudi Arabia in a way that sets the scene for this chapter. As mentioned in the previous chapter, Saudi Arabia is widely depicted as a religious country. Accordingly, I first challenged this depiction, thus allowing me to more accurately trace the steps taken by individual Saudis as they criticize religion. What I wanted to show was that they were not as far from the religious landscape of Saudi Arabia as the prevailing literature would have us believe. The criticism of religion in Saudi Arabia is not taking place against the background of a religious community but against a background of diverse and conflicting attitudes and opinions toward religion. In this chapter I discuss some of the critical views of religion that have once found their way to the available public space in Saudi Arabia. I focus on criticisms expressed in public spaces only, rather than those articulated in books or closed private spaces. There are two reasons for this. The first is that I want to gauge lay opinion and not that of the intellectuals, as the former is more indicative of structural factors influencing the course of religion by changing the sensibilities of Saudis—such as the breakdown of Hervieu-Léger's (2000) chain of memory and the erosion of Berger's (1967) plausibility structures—while the latter expresses the individual experiences of a few. Also, I want to explore opinions that participate, even in a marginal sense, in the Saudi public debate on religion, and not merely those that Saudis believe, yet do not voice publicly. It is important at the outset to mention that Saudi Arabia has always had voices critical of religion. The rupture of the period between 2012 and 2014 is in the high volume and diversity of *public* criticism expressed on Twitter.

From the early 1950s to the 1970s Saudi Arabia had a very active leftist movement: Nasserite nationalists, Ba'athists, and communists (Matthiesen, 2014). The existence of leftist ideologies could be an indicator of the presence of criticism of religion, but it would be difficult to know the extent of this criticism and how public it was. Also, most of the activity was in the Eastern province, making it harder to say whether or not this criticism of religion was widespread across the kingdom. Not enough research exists on the Saudi left, and original sources are hardly available, since very few members wrote biographies and their publications at the time were not preserved. Moreover, since the left in Saudi Arabia was an underground movement, its debates would most likely have been in closed circles. It is safe to assume that they would have been keen at the time to avoid inciting the public against them by openly criticizing religion. As an example, one important group, the National Liberation Front, (*Jabhat al-Taharrur al-Watani*) "used the annual hajj to Mecca in 1958 to distribute leaflets to the pilgrims" (Matthiesen, 2014, p. 493). This could indicate that they did not present themselves as critics of religion; otherwise they would have lost much of their target audience.

Turki al-Hamad, a well-known Saudi novelist and a Ba'athist in his youth, states that most of the young men of his generation were influenced by leftist ideologies, but he also insists that this did not influence their faith, and only a few of the leftists he knew went as far as denouncing religion or becoming atheists (Qasim, 2009). Al-Hamad's trilogy, which was inspired by his own experience as a Ba'athist, includes many statements and discussions by his protagonist Hisham al-Aber that question religion and belief in Allah (al-Hamad, 2002, pp. 76–80, 136–138, 188–191), but he insists that they were creative tools and should not be taken as accounts of factual events. Al-Hamad has stated that he has never lost faith; yet he has also said that his belief—and that of other leftists of his youth—in the Prophet Muhammad was based on nationalistic sentiment rather than religion: "What protected us [from atheism] was holding on to the Prophet Muhammad from a nationalistic stance, and not from a religious stance" (Qasim, 2009). That is, they believed in him because they heralded him as an Arab champion and leader, and not because he was sent from Allah. This form of belief in the Prophet indicates that al-Hamad, and other leftists that he referred to, had, in their youth, abandoned a most fundamental tenet of Islamic belief: that Muhammad is a messenger sent by Allah. But the extent and process of this has not been documented, and more importantly their opinions are not cited by contemporary public critics of religion.

There were, however, prior to Twitter, public intellectuals who did publicly criticize religion and who were and are still frequently quoted. I mention here four such Saudi public intellectuals who contributed to the criticism of religion and who are widely cited and followed. Each presented a different angle on the criticism of religion but also differed in the harshness of that criticism. These figures are important for two reasons: they provide a baseline for pre-Twitter public criticism as well as a broader intellectual frame for the discussions that took place between 2012 and 2014.

The mildest—relative to the other three writers—religious criticism was that of Hasan Farhan al-Maliki. In the mid-1990s, al-Maliki pushed the limits of public and popular criticism of Saudi Salafism. He was born in a small village in the Southern Region of Saudi Arabia, and after graduating from high school went to study at the Imam Muhammad bin Saud Islamic University in Riyadh, the main center for Saudi Salafi training and education. He used his training in Islamic studies to write critical pieces for Saudi newspapers and books about the Salafi view of the history of the early years after the death of the Prophet; the three foundational characters of Salafism Ahmad bin Hanbal (d. 855), Ibn Taymiyya (d. 1328), and Muhammad bin Abdulwahhab; and finally the creed of Ibn Abdulwahab (al-Maliki, 2000a, 2000b). A second important contemporary figure is Ibrahim al-Bilayhy (b. 1944). Al-Maliki's criticism is of the authenticity of the Hadith attributed to the Prophet, while al-Bilayhy focuses on the mindset of Muslims, which he considers a product of inauthentic Hadith but also a contributor to its creation. He considers Arab-Islamic culture a main impediment to development and continuously sought to expose what he considered the destructive elements in that culture (Albleahy, 2012; al-Bilayhi, 2010). His sharp critical language has earned him the label "self-hating Arab" from some writers (al-ʾUmaym, 2012).

Both al-Maliki and al-Bilayhi's public criticism stopped short of touching the fundamental tenets of Islam. For example, neither challenged the belief in the Muslim monopoly of heaven after death or the belief that non-Muslims—unless ignorant—will suffer eternal damnation. By contrast, the third contemporary critic, Mansour al-Nogaidan, made this charge. He had grown up in Burayda, a city to the north of Riyadh, to become an extremist jihadist who abandoned modern life, even living in a mud hut for a short time. In his youth he firebombed video stores and a women's social service center in his home city of Burayda because he considered them centers of evil and sin. He was imprisoned for a few months and, after leaving prison, gradually began to change. Although a radical militant, he had also experienced doubts regarding his belief in Allah since he was 16 years old. His experience in prison gave him the opportunity to reflect on himself and the cruel behavior in which he had engaged. While he was in this reflective phase, al-Nogaidan accidently came across two books that had a marked effect on his life. The first was *Naqd al-ʿAql al-ʿArabi* (Criticism of Arab Reason) by the Moroccan philosopher Muhammad ʿAbid al-Jabiri (1935–2010), and the second was *al-Mihna* by the Jordanian philosopher Fahmi Jadʾan (b. 1940) (al-Jabiri, 2014; Jadʾan, 1989). These two books changed the way he thought about religion and opened the door for him to engage further in progressive thought.[1] Al-Jabiri in particular has a strong influence on many Saudi intellectuals and reformers (al-Khidr, 2010). After 9/11, al-Nogaidan called for the development of a relationship with Allah focused on inner beliefs rather than outward rituals. He insisted on the need for a new Luther who would have the courage and ability to reform Islam (al-Wasatiyyah, 2002). Focusing on morality, love, and toleration of all humans, al-Nogaidan wrote about the need to accept that Allah loves the faithful of all religions. He also spoke of a religion of humanity and the freedom to choose one's faith. His belief was simple: Allah simply wants us to carry the "flame [of faith] in our hearts," whatever the faith (al-Nogaidan, 2000; Rubin, 2004).

The fourth and most extreme critic was Abdullah al-Qasimi (1907–1996) (Wasella, 2011). Al-Qasimi died in 1996, and most of his books were printed prior to his death, yet one can consider him part of the contemporary public discourse because of the fresh interest in and revival of his thoughts. Specifically, his ideas have become a symbol for dissent and alternative ways of looking at religion. He was a native of the al-Qasim region, the heartland of contemporary Salafism, his education was religious, and he became a prominent alim. Yet al-Qasimi turned toward militant atheism and began strongly criticizing religion, the Arabs and Islam. Saudis from the generation of the 1960s and 1970s acknowledge his influence on them, and his influence continues today, as his name and books are cited in various discussions and forums on religion and politics

---

1. In a personal communication, 2014, Dubai, UAE.

and his books are widely sought-after (Kersten, 2015; al-Muhayni, 2007; Whitaker, 2014).

These four voices illustrate the diversity of religious criticism in Saudi Arabia. Al-Mailiky was a critic of the religious interpretation of scripture, yet was also keen on retaining the sanctity of the Quran, emphasizing the Muslim contribution to human civilization in the past and its capacity to contribute once again in the present. Al-Bilayhi, on the other hand, categorically criticized the Muslim mind, considering it to be the cause of the Muslim Umma's ills, and called for the assimilation of Western modes of thinking. Along similar lines, al-Nogaidan criticized the idea of institutional religion and to some degree the Prophecy, but still believed in deity and sought to retain spirituality as a foundation of morality. Finally, al-Qasimi was a critic of the idea of deity itself and everything that stemmed from it, instead seeking to dismantle religion altogether by showing its absurdity. We will see in the popular criticism of religion that I discuss in what follows such a difference in the critical approaches to religion, as well as a discussion of many of the themes that these four writers discussed.

3.1. Heresy on Twitter: General Overview

In what follows I examine Twitter hashtags that criticize religion. I specifically explore hashtags that originated in Saudi Arabia, or were at least popularized and widely used by Saudis, that center on criticizing religion. In any given hashtag there are many irrelevant tweets, but is in itself a developing narrative created by the tweets. Hashtags, though, should not be considered a collective dialogue but rather "multiple dialogues" with limited sociability (Jones, 2014; Ross, Terras, Warwick, & Welsh, 2011). A participant in a hashtag is not talking directly to other participants in the same hashtag but rather indirectly engaging through commenting on the same topic. In this case I considered a Saudi Twitter hashtag a set of statements on one particular theme, made by individual Saudis to other Saudis, each expressing his/her opinion on the matter. The statements do not talk to each other as much as to the theme of the hashtag. Participation in the hashtag is not for the purpose of Saudi-to-Saudi dialogue but rather for the purpose of expressing one's own conclusions on a theme where other Saudis are doing the same.

Based on these considerations, my focus centered on popular hashtags that criticized religion and I discuss specific tweets within those hashtags that presented various forms of religious criticism. Some of those tweets are easily understandable, while others need contextualization. Sometimes I mention more than one tweet criticizing the same aspect of religion, if the approach of the criticism was different. My purpose here is not only to show that there is criticism of religion but also to show some examples of the issues being criticized and the various critical approaches.

Drawing on hashtags to construct a critical narrative of religion, I explore the emergence of a new intellectual scene in Saudi Arabia. Many of these hashtags focused on the so called "inauthenticity" of religion as practiced in Saudi, with others highlighting the perceived unfair treatment of women in so-called Saudi religion. Additional key topics included the way religion neglects issues of politics, economics, and society in favor of what are considered by some trivial questions of female modesty and purity, as well as the overdependence of the state on ulama and relegating scripture to a secondary status. There were those who criticized the intensive prohibition in what they called *Saudi Islam*, while others criticized the conformist demands of religion and the rejection of dissent and ostracization of dissenters. There were also, as I show, more fundamental forms of criticism set against religion, some reaching the point of atheism. In these criticisms I was not looking for complex arguments, nor for Saudi intellectuals or experts in religion or philosophy; instead I wanted to capture the way a lay Saudi would articulate his/her criticism of religion. Indeed, the less sophisticated the argument, the more it demonstrates the influence of structural factors in the disengagement from religion in Saudi Arabia.

There were, of course, ethical issues to consider here, most important of which was whether or not I should use tweets without the consent of the tweeters. I decided that since they were in the public domain they could be used without requesting informed consent from their authors. It is worth nothing that many of the ethical concerns about the use of Twitter are inherited from the early Facebook era and are not applicable to Twitter (Priego, 2014). Posts on Facebook can be either public or restricted to one's friends depending on the settings one uses. Thus, Facebook posts cannot be considered part of the public domain by default. That I can access someone's post because he/she befriended me on Facebook does not give me the right to share that content with someone who is not a friend of that person, unless that person's post were made public. Twitter is different. On Twitter, accounts are either public or private. Tweets on a public account can be seen by anyone, while tweets on a private account can only be seen by individuals who are accepted by the account owner. The fact that a tweeter has the option to make his/her account private means that a public account is a public domain by virtue of surrendering the option of privacy.

Having said that, I understand that Tweets may have been made impulsively then forgotten, yet would be regretted if brought back to light. Tweeting is a highly spontaneous activity, and many tweeters simply react to an existing tweet or an ongoing hashtag without considering the consequences of their tweeting. Thus, out of concern for the privacy of the tweeters I imposed on myself a number of rules. First, I avoided using extrasensitive tweets if the tweeter was using his/her real name. Second, I differentiated between posts on a tweeter's own timeline from those posted in hashtags. The former I considered personal reflections shared to followers while the latter were intentionally tweeted as a contribution to a public discussion, thus I restricted myself to using the latter type with the exception of benign tweets. Third, I mainly used tweets that had been retweeted, as I consider retweeting an indicator that the tweeter does not object to sharing with audiences beyond his/her followers, otherwise the tweeter would have deleted the tweet after being circulated in that fashion. Fourth, I excluded from my references links to the tweets and did not mention the full user name of the tweeter. However, I kept links to the hashtags for reference to the overall discussions that went on.

3.2. Saudi Religion Versus Islam

I start with a very prominent hashtag, "Saudi religion vs Islam," which includes harsh criticism of religion in Saudi Arabia. In this hashtag one observes a long discussion that contrasts these two categories as *distinct* religions, thus belittling so called "Saudi religion" by virtue of the suggestion that it is distinct from authentic Islam. The claim is not that Saudi Salafis have their own interpretation of Islam or even a distorted Islam, but that they have created a new religion altogether.

One tweeter in this hashtag said, "In Islam one is supposed to think [independently], while in Saudi religion one should not think in order to preempt corruption, and one should always have a *mutawwiʿ* between himself and hell" (@El, 2012a). This tweet highlights a number of issues such as the value of independent thinking, the way that "Saudi religion" undermines critical thought, and the related challenge of exaggerated dependency on the ulama. The tweet is based on the perception of the tweeter—and many other Saudis—that ulama demand that Muslims not think independently when it comes to understanding religion; rather, a pious Muslim should always ask the learned ulama and follow them. This perception is not without foundation, as there are many popular fatwas to this end (IslamWeb, 2009). Even junior ulama are required to have their opinions supervised by more senior ulama in order to ensure that they are correct (@naseralomar, 2015). Many Saudis today, however, question this premise and call for the democratization of religious interpretation. As I have said, it is difficult to give an exact assessment of the statistical representation of such a view, but it is enough for my purposes here to show that this is an issue that is being openly raised among Saudis, especially since it is highly relevant to the course of religion in Saudi Arabia. Ulama authority is a major constituent of any religious order, and once that authority starts to erode, so too does that of the religious order more broadly.

A second theme in this tweet relates to accountability. She says in her tweet that Saudi religion demands placing a *mutawwiʿ* between the individual and hell. This commonly used metaphor is invoked to suggest that the only way to save oneself from hell is by seeking the opinion of an alim before taking action. The *mutawaʿ* is someone who is pious and learned in matters of religion, and by asking him one rescues oneself from accountability before Allah. If on the Day of Judgment Allah asks one about his/her deeds, then that person could reply that he/she based them on a fatwa, saying, "The mutawiʿ told me so," and the claim of some is that such a response is a basis for justifying the deeds. The tweeter is critical of this view, even though it shifts the accountability from her to another person. She prefers to be independent and accountable to being dependent and unaccountable.

One of the repeated themes when criticizing Saudi religion is the issue of prohibitions. According to many Saudis who criticize religion on Twitter, Islam seems to be solely focused on prohibitions. One repeated criticism in this regard uses the jurisprudential principle common to many Muslim jurists which states that all things are permissible unless there is evidence of their prohibition (al-Duwayhi, 2007, pp. 39–58). If applied, this principle would limit the number of prohibitions in Islam in contradistinction to "Saudi religion," which according to our tweeters centers on prohibitions. One tweeter mentions this principle, stating that it represents authentic Islam. In actuality, many Muslim jurists do not accept this principle, but the tweeter is not a scholar of religion and is apparently deciding what is authentic Islam and what is inauthentic Islam based on her own sensibility of how Islam should govern her life and that of others. She is implicitly assuming that Islam should not have many prohibitions, and this assumption is guiding her thinking when assessing claims about Islam. Then she says that in "Saudi Islam: the principle is that all things are prohibited to pre-empt facilitators" (@Af, 2012). Here she is referring to another jurisprudential principle *sadd al-dharaiʿ*, or preempting conditions that might facilitate sin (preempting facilitators). Women driving is a good example of how this principle works: many Saudi ulama state that while women driving is not prohibited in principle, women driving in Saudi Arabia leads to gender mixing and women going to meet their boyfriends. Thus, it is best to prohibit their driving (Um al-Qura University, 2005).

Many Saudis are becoming fed up with this principle, as they feel that it is being used to constrain them and limit their ability to live as they wish. In the words of one tweeter, "Saudi religion used [the principle of] preempting [facilitators] to create an assumed religion to block life itself" (@Al, 2012). This tweeter not only speaks about the consequences of the principle but also implies that the original intention of the ulama is essentially to hinder the lifestyles of Saudis and that principle is their tool for this. This anger about the intentions of the ulama is repeated in many other tweets, one of which was quite popular and was retweeted over 250 times. Here the tweeter says that the real purpose of this principle is to ill-treat worshipers and suppress them (@Se, 2013b). Following this line of criticism, another tweeter complains that Islam came to make life easier while Saudi Islam is making it harder (@iF, 2012). This sense of difficulty posed by Saudi religion is widespread and seems to be increasing, leading to the sense that Islamic prohibitions and duties—or at least many of them—are insignificant. This is an important change in attitudes toward religious decrees, as in Islam prohibitions are characterized by ulama as beneficial, and according to them only the degenerate and corrupt describe Allah's decrees as a burden (al-Jawziyyah, 1991). Here we can see traces of Luckmann's tension between newly acquired sensibilities and existing religious beliefs, a tension that can lead to disengagement from religion.

The principle of *preemption* is criticized not only for its consequences but also because of the way it is applied. Some Saudis seek to delegitimize it by demonstrating its fickle relationship between ulama and their interests. Some Saudis claim that some things were banned at a certain point in time because they were judged facilitators of sin, but then these very same things became permissible at a later time when the ulama found it in their interests to allow them. I later mention a few examples of sins that were once permitted by ulama, but here I quickly point to one example that I previously discussed. Satellite television receivers were once prohibited under the principle of preemption because of their so-called degenerate content, only to be permitted later. Some Saudis critical of the principle of preemption claimed that the change in the fatwa about satellite channels did not happen because of a fundamental change in the content that they broadcast; on the contrary, they still air the same degenerate content, if not worse. Instead, tweeters charge the ulama of manipulating fatwas to suit their needs rather than the interests and needs of the community. Here one tweeter says, "whatever they cannot do they say is *harrrram* and [they] curse [who does it] and look how they present criticisms and they philosophize and after a few years they do it as long as circumstance helps them" (@lo, 2013). This tweeter focuses on ulama's access to novel modes of technology and argues that their changing position on the latter's religious status is directly linked to its capacity to serve their professional interests, in this case their visibility in the media. This growing awareness of the manipulation of religion by the ulama discredits them and pushes Saudis toward a more individualistic religion, or away from religion altogether.

Another issue widely criticized and framed as Saudi religion or Saudi Islam is prohibitions that are exclusive to women. The issue of women is repeated time and again whenever the subjects of religious reform and criticism are raised. In this hashtag, one woman expresses her frustration at the prohibitions under which women live. But her criticism focuses on the contrast between what is prohibited for men and what is prohibited for women, and concludes that Saudi Islamic prohibitions are exclusive to women. According to her "Saudi Islam is to be practiced by women alone, while Islam is to be practiced by everyone" (@sm, 2012). Here she demands an egalitarian religion whose demands of both genders are identical. For this tweeter, egalitarianism is a value that Islam, and any other religion, must appropriate. The logic presented in this tweet is that, since religion must be egalitarian and Saudi religion is not, one must conclude that the defect lies with Saudi religion. Islam, on the other hand, is a "proper" religion, therefore it must be egalitarian. This is striking, as we see here that a modern sensibility has become the standard for the legitimacy of religion. This tension between modern sensibilities and religion also invokes Luckmann's theory about the effect of the tension between changed sensibilities and religion, which has had an impact on the status of religion in many Western societies.

Such criticisms of religion are significant insofar as they reveal the deep frustration of many Saudis with religion as practiced in Saudi Arabia, as well as religion in general. The many angles of their criticism reflect the complexity of religious criticism that is developing. It is worth mentioning here that by attacking Saudi Islam, some of these critics are also defending Islam. They want to say that Islam in itself is without problems, and that the problem is with one form of it, namely the Saudi form. We see other critics much less sympathetic to Islam specifically and to religion in general. Another point that we should keep in mind as we go through the other tweets in this chapter is that the basis of much of the criticism in these Saudi tweeters is not religious scholarship but rather the modern sensibilities against which religion is measured. The tweeters are not arguing against a certain religious interpretation by countering it with another religious interpretation; instead, they are countering the religious interpretation that they reject with a modern value that they have assumed; that is, a sensibility.

3.3. Dissonant Religiosity

Another criticism of religion in Saudi Arabia focuses on the way that Saudis practice religion. Many Saudis' criticisms of religion start by highlighting the dissonance in religious practice or in the way Saudi lay people understand religion. While the previous tweeters focused on how Saudi religion is theorized and presented by the Saudi ulama, other tweeters are concerned with how the average Saudi understands and practices religion. This dissonance—as far as our critics are concerned—shows that religion, or the particular form of religion that they practice, is dysfunctional. One of the hashtags dedicated to this is titled "The Saudi concept of religiosity." One specific tweet in this hashtag was retweeted more than 50 times, and I found it expressive. The tweeter does not say anything explicitly; rather he quotes what a hypothetical Saudi is supposed to have said. The full tweet is:

> *Heeyyy can I send you a direct message?*
> *You slut the Hay'ah is the crown of your head*
> *Don't forget to read the surah of al-Kahf*
> *What's your origin you Tarsh?!*
> *We awake and the universe is always Allah's. (@Fr, 2013)*

The tweet includes a number of short statements supposedly said by this hypothetical Saudi. The tweeter does not comment on these statements, but those living in a Saudi context can immediately grasp his intention. The first statement "Heeyyy can I send you a direct message?" introduces us to this person. He wants to flirt with a woman on Twitter by opening up a direct and private communication with her through Twitter messaging. This initial statement frames our view of the person, an average Saudi who is not particularly religious and is looking to interact with a woman. Then comes the second statement, where the same flirtatious Saudi is now defending the Committee for Ordering Virtue and Forbidding Vice. "You slut al-Hay'ah (the Committee) is the crown of your head." Here, this Saudi clearly considers the Committee an important institution, most likely because in his view it upholds Allah's mandate. But in this statement we witness the first dissonance between being flirtatious and also defending the Committee. He wants to flirt with a woman through direct messaging on Twitter, yet also wants to defend the Committee, which seeks to combat flirtation. Still another tension remains: this person uses profanity to defend a religious institution. It is as if he is saying, "You slut, you should be polite." Use of profanity when upholding the authority of the ulama and institutions is common on Saudi Twitter.

Then our person goes on to say, "Don't forget to read the surah of al-Kahf." Now the same person is offering religious advice, and quite specific advice at that, by recommending a specific surah in the Quran—al-Kahf, or the Cave—which is usually read on Fridays by those who want to do voluntary deeds. The advice implies that he is a pious person, seeking to exceed his ritual obligations. After giving his religious advice, the person turns and asks, "What's your origin you Tarsh?!" "Tarsh" is part of a phrase "tarsh bahr," which literally means "the sea's vomit," and refers to people whose families originated outside the Arab Peninsula and arrived through maritime migration. Sometimes people say "Hajj leftovers" to mean the same thing, implying that these people came to perform their yearly Hajj duty but then decided to stay. The phrase is used with racial undertones as a way to belittle and humiliate Saudis who cannot trace their origins back to the country's tribes. Such behavior is rejected because, according to this tweeter, Islam judges people according to their deeds and not their origin. Yet the person who was just defending the Committee and advising reading the Quran is now calling someone *Tarsh*. Finally, that same imagined person, having belittled and sought to humiliate a fellow person, says, "We awake and the universe is always Allah's." Religiously observant

Muslims say such words of glorification to Allah when they awaken to emphasize their ongoing awareness and gratitude toward Allah, and this person is doing it to imply that he has Allah in mind all the time.

Our tweeter illustrates the paradox of Saudi religiosity. By collecting these statements and placing them in one tweet, this tweeter highlights the extreme dissonance between religiosity, good behavior, and ethics that is prevalent in Saudi Arabia. He does not need to make any comment. He simply collected the statements and put them together, and the Saudis who read it understood his meaning.

Another tweeter posted a cartoon by the Saudi cartoonist Abdullah Jaber[2] (@jabertoon) published in a Saudi newspaper that illustrated this point neatly. The cartoon is of two drug addicts, one asking the other, "What's your opinion of the girl who puts the ʿabaya on her shoulders?" (@Ah, 2014). The ʿabaya, a piece of black cloth that women in Saudi Arabia are supposed to wear in public, can be placed over the head or over the shoulders. Many ulama are critical of women who place it over their shoulders, based on the claim that this practice reveals the woman's figure and could lead to illicit sexual acts. Placing the ʿabaya over the head, by contrast, is appropriately modest. As this tweeter notes, the corruption of drug dealers hardly stops them from attempting to monitor others. Along similar lines, a second tweet describes an individual who "holds a glass of vodka even as he tells his friend to be careful because the meal contains pork" (@s7, 2012). Although consuming alcohol is considered a grave sin, many Saudis drink it, even as the same individuals warn against the "sinful" consumption of pork.

One tweeter sums up what Saudi religiosity is by saying, "Let your beard grow, follow al-ʿUrayfi and curse the Shiʿa, divorce your wife with a Fatwa from al-Mutlaq and take her back with a fatwa from al-Fawzan,[3] and go to a shaykh to recite over you against the evil eye!" (@ra, 2013). The purpose of this tweet is to ridicule the authority of the ulama and delegitimize it. The tweeter's first suggestion is to grow a beard. He does not mention love of Allah or morality but rather a superficial marker of religiosity that Saudi ulama consider a duty, such as not shaving (bin Baz, n.d.-f), which the tweeter believes is far more important in Saudi religion that other fundamental issues of what a good life constitutes. While the

---

2. https://twitter.com/jabertoon/status/429573404564656128

3. Muhammad al-ʿUrayfi (b. 1970), Saleh al-Fawzan (b. 1933), and Abdullah al-Mutlaq (1954) are three prominent ulama in Saudi Arabia.

ulama focus on superficial acts, they ignore the sublime and the sub-stantial. The tweeter then goes on to recommend following the teachings of al-ʿUrayfi. This is a marker of religiosity because a religious person should follow an alim, but not just any alim. A famous one is better to follow. He goes on to point to another marker of religiosity, which is curs-ing the Shiʿa, something Saudi Salafi ulama are accused of doing and condoning. But then he gets to the core of how many Saudis understand ulama authority, which is to practice selective fatwa. In Islam certain types of divorce cannot be retracted except with religious legitimation. Also, certain forms of divorce are condoned or even required by certain ulama, such as divorcing a wife who does not wear a hijab. So, if a man does divorce his wife but then regrets it, he needs to go an alim who can tell him that the formalities of the divorce were not legitimate, and thus the divorce is retracted. Finally, going to a shaykh to recite the Quran points to the ulama's claim to supernatural authority. A person goes to an alim who will recite the Quran over him to ward off evil supernatural powers. This tweet underscores religiosity as it manifests in three central issues: appearances, hating the "other," and submitting to the ulama on matters of life and the supernatural. This depiction of religiosity is meant to ridicule religion as practiced by Saudis.

3.4. The Exclusivist Nature of Saudi Religion

One of the consistent criticisms of Saudi religion is that it is exclusionary in that it considers Wahhabism the only valid form of Islam. One tweet reads, "Islam: you have your religion and I have my religion." This ref-erence to a Quranic verse in which the Prophet counsels acceptance of other religions is then contrasted with the remainder of the Tweet: "Saudi Islam: I have my religion and you have no religion" (@Mu, 2012). That is to say Saudi Islam claims a monopoly on the truth, and all those who ap-proach Islam differently are *kuffar*.

At times dark humor makes its way into these discussions. A hashtag with the title "Bring out the Salafi in you" was popularized as a means of motivating tweeters to imagine what they would write if they were Salafis. But there is another meaning here, which implies that everyone raised in Saudi Arabia has been affected by Salafism because of its immense cul-tural imprint. One of the tweets in this hashtag posts a cartoon without commenting on it. In the cartoon there is a very short dialogue between a Muslim and someone else. The Muslim says, "Whoever wants to believe can believe and whoever wants not to believe, can." Here, the reference is to the Quranic verse "Whoever wills—let him believe; and whoever wills—let him disbelieve" (Quran: al-Kahf, 29) and is usually quoted to illustrate the Quran's insistence on freedom of faith. The person responds and says, "I choose not to believe." Then we are shown that the Muslim cuts off the head of the other person, saying, "You chose wrong."

This same cartoon can be found in more than one place in hashtags criticizing radicalism or religion in Saudi. In this case, it is referenced to conjure up the violent nature of Salafism according to this tweeter (@mn, 2014). Salafis claim that there is freedom of faith, but according to such tweeters it is the freedom to choose Salafism alone.

These tweeters also emphasize the sensibility of tolerance and contrast it with claims to a monopoly on understanding religion. Here, one tweeter interprets what it means to have such a monopoly on understanding religious scripture, analyzing a statement in which an alim says that one needs certain credentials in order to understand religion. The tweeter tells us that what the alim is saying is, "I am the only one who is able to communicate with Allah! And I am the closest creature to Him! Worshiping in a different way is innovation" (@al, 2013). While Salafis do not make this claim, this tweet is significant precisely because it equates the demand for credentials to interpret the Quran with a claim of a unique privilege vis-à-vis Allah. The implication of this tweet is that since no one has special access to Allah, everyone is equally entitled to interpret the Quran. Once again, we find an egalitarian sensibility at play, as the tweeter demands that ulama and laypeople be on an equal footing when trying to understand Allah's words and decrees. In these tweets we again find a tension between modern sensibilities and religion as understood by the tweeters.

3.5. Preoccupation with Women

Another important theme in the criticism of religion in Saudi Arabia is the preoccupation of Saudi religiosity with issues related to women. As in the tweets already discussed, it is not just the criticism that matters but rather the way that this type of criticism emboldens Saudis, men and women, to criticize religious authority and religiosity. In turn, such tweets open the doors for more advanced criticism of religion in itself. One tweeter expresses this criticism through an image she posted of a man whose appearance and dress are stereotypical for a religious man—bearded and with a *thawb* that only extends halfway down his legs[4]—and in the background a group of men and women. The man is shown to be screaming with all his lungs, "The Hijaaaaaab."

While the man is primarily concerned with the hijab, the background speaks to additional, far more pressing, challenges including poverty, unemployment, housing, human rights, health insurance, education, bread, and inflation. This man's screams, however, are limited to women's dress and drown out those of the people around him. Although his fervor is greatest, the issue that he advocates is the most trivial.

The picture was probably first used by Tunisians to ridicule Islamist political parties, and it was used by some Saudis to ridicule religious men and their mindset while accusing them of an obsession with female behavior. The concern with women's rights is a modern concept, and it is thus no surprise to find that Saudis consider this value to be in tension with Islam as it is articulated by the ulama. The comment by the tweeter is, "The Saudi religion's axis of rotation is women. But other issues are totally disregarded" (@1m, 2013).

A related image is that of a man drawn with exaggerated features associated with religious people. The man is down on his knees, keenly writing a fatwa while looking at a picture of the lower part of a woman's body. Behind the man, other individuals hold banners for major social issues: human rights, women's rights, embezzlement, bribery, and corruption. The message is the same as in the image before, but here the point is driven home more extremely. The religious person is obsessed with female sexuality, rather than women's welfare or the broader welfare of Saudi society (@ej, 2013).

Another tweeter adds, "'The woman' is a creature that suddenly dropped from the sky, and so they were confused about her, and everyone sees himself as more knowledgeable about her issues." This comment is followed by a number of fatwas and edicts that bear directly on women, whether prohibitions of gender mixing or of posting pictures of females publicly. This was also a popular tweet and was retweeted more than 130 times (@IS, 2014). The message is unmistakable: men claim the right to decide all religious issues that pertain to women, yet these men do not understand the women whose behavior they seek to regulate.

---

4. According to Salafis, a pious person is expected to wear a short thawb that does not extend below the ankle.

3.6. Wahhabism

Another hashtag, titled "I learned from Wahhabism," is similarly dedicated to criticizing religion as practiced in Saudi Arabia, and frames itself as a confession. Instead of the tweeter criticizing Wahhabism, he/
she is lamenting past experiences as a Wahhabi, underscoring the ways
in which former Wahhabis understand and reiterate their break from
Wahhabism. Under this hashtag we also see criticism of the monopoly
of religious truth claimed by Salafis in Saudi Arabia and expressions of
regret at having accepted this claim. But my main interest is in the tone
of regret and the implied break with the Wahhabi—and sometimes the
Islamic—chain of tradition. Being a Wahhabi, or a Muslim in general,
requires one, according to Hervieu-Léger (2000), to be connected to the
Wahhabi or the Muslim chain of tradition through memory. Here we see
many Saudis regretting those memories and subsequently breaking away
from the chain of tradition that is supposed to sustain their belonging to
Wahhabism or Islam.

One tweeter recalls that when she was a Wahhabi, she believed "that
real Islam is in Saudi only. And it is pure and clean if it is in Najd[5]" (@
sa, 2013). This tweeter now realizes that there are religious visions beyond
Wahhabism and beyond Najd. Another tweeter sums up a number of
values common to Wahhabism in Saudi Arabia and his days as a Wahhabi.

> When I was a Wahhabi, I was taught that he who does not follow
> us is an innovator[6] and a disbeliever and a heretic . . . they taught
> me that the "meat of scholars" is poisonous and that one should not
> argue with them and obey them and obey the guardian "rulers." (@
> Om, 2012)

This tweeter includes a number of themes that are presented critically. The
first is the monopoly on truth: Wahhabis have the Truth, and anyone who
does not follow their teachings is misguided and will go to hell. Hence
the tweeter claims that the labels of innovator, disbeliever, and heretic,
serious accusations against the integrity of his faith, were applied unfairly
by these who disagreed with him.

---

5. A region in the center of Saudi Arabia where the Wahhabi movement was born.

6. Someone whose religious practice is not derived from authentic Islam.

A second theme concerns the authority of the ulama. When the tweeter says, "the meat of scholars is poisonous," he is referring to a metaphor in Arabic. Eating someone's meat is a metaphor for speaking ill about someone. But since the ulama have special status, bad-mouthing them is not merely eating their meat; it is also about eating poisonous meat. The origin of the metaphor is the Quranic verse "Do not spy on or talk maliciously about each other. Would one of you like to eat the flesh of his dead brother?" (Quran: al-Hujurat, 12). Additional themes relate to the duty to obey the ulama and accept their views without question, as well as the religious obligation to obey the king (albaderi6, 2013; al-Fawzan, n.d.-d). Here in one tweet some of the main themes common in Wahhabi culture are presented in a critical and rejectionist tone. Saudis are breaking many taboos when it comes to religion and religious authority. That Saudis criticize the ulama and the authority of the alim is not a simple matter in a culture that considers the ulama the main path to understanding the laws of the Quran and gives them a status that makes them exempt from criticism by the layperson.

Salafis, like many Muslims, claim a monopoly not only on Truth but also on heaven. In this hashtag former Wahhabis expressed their criticism of how they thought heaven was reserved for them while hell was set aside for *others*. "Others" could be people of other sects or religions, or simply those who do not adhere to the standards of religiosity set by Wahhabi scholars. Another tweet recalls, "When I was a Wahhabi, the [correctness of the] Islam of everyone who is non-Saudi was doubtful" (@oa, 2012). Here is another aspect that some tweeters related to Wahhabism—religious nationalism, where Wahhabism and Saudi nationhood become one and the same (al-Rasheed, 2013a). As I have said before, these ideas may not actually reflect the Saudi Salafi ulama's interpretation of Islam, but this is not what matters here. What is crucial is how those who embraced Wahhabism remember their experience of it and how they have subsequently criticized it. Here someone else focuses on how he used to belittle and disrespect the intellectual conclusions of non-Wahhabis: "I used to think we were the ones who practiced Sharia while everyone else was deluded" (@Je, 2012). And:

When I was a Wahhabi I used to think that all followers of other religions and sects were stupid [and] believed their ulama without thought, while assuming that we were very clever and do not sanctify men. (@es, 2013)

In this last tweet the tweeter not only criticizes the Wahhabi attitude toward others but also highlights a contradiction within Wahhabi practice: while Wahhabis criticize the sanctification of ulama by fellow Muslims and non-Muslims, they do not apply this criticism to their own religious hierarchy.

This hashtag not only criticizes the ideas one carried as a Wahhabi but also invokes personal memories of Saudis, and most of the time invokes negative memories about being a Wahhabi. One girl says that, when she was a Wahhabi, "If I saw a girl not wearing the hijab I would label her as a disbeliever (*kafira*) and a grave sinner (*fasiqa*[7]) . . . and if I saw a young man without a beard, I would assume he was secular. May my Lord forgive me" (@LA, 2014). The issue was not the claim that the hijab was obligatory, but this girl's tendency to label those who neglected religious law harshly. Despite their severity, these two judgments are quite common among Salafis when dealing with people who commit even slight sins. Having such a negative attitude toward someone committing a slight sin such as not wearing the hijab influences social relations between practicing and nonpracticing Saudis, and Saudis who had walked away from that mode of thinking felt, like this tweeter, that a new opportunity for bonding with others had been created.

The level of these ex-Wahhabis' reflection and self-criticism reflects the regret felt by many Saudis for their previous religious choices. Frustration is indeed a frequent sentiment in criticism of Wahhabism or religion in Saudi Arabia. But it is not only frustration due to the negative perceptions they had of others who are different but also frustration due to the sense of a hijacked life, as the next example shows.

While the consensus among Wahhabi scholars forbids taking or keeping photographs of a human being or animal other than for official requirements such as passports (Lajnah al-Daʾimah Li-l-Buhuth al-ʿIlmiyyah wa al-ʾIftaʾ, al- [Permanent Committee for Scholarly Research and Fatwa, or PCSRF], n.d.-d), many ex-Wahhabis regret the sacrifices that they made as strict followers of Wahhabi teachings. These regrets extended to the most basic of memories: "When I was a Wahhabi I used to put a line on my neck in [my] photographs, and after I heard a cassette [lecture] by a shaykh about the prohibition of photography I tore up my picture. The irony is that the same shaykh now goes on satellite channels" (@Ey, 2012). Still others who have become more pious decided to tear up

---

7. *Kafira* is feminine of *kafir*. *Fasiqa* feminine of *fasiq* meaning one who committed a grave or major sin such as murder or adultery (M. Q. Zaman, 2015).

their photograph albums or burn them. One tweet on this was retweeted almost 17,000 times, reflecting its resonance with the sentiments of many Saudis:

> My mother told me "I burnt a collection of rare pictures twenty years ago in response to the fatwas of ulama whose pictures I now find everywhere!!!" (@al, 2011)

There were Saudis who adhered to the sinfulness of photographs but instead of destroying their pictures reverted to an opinion circulating among lay Muslims that advises drawing a line across the neck of living beings in the photograph. The line is supposed to render the living being dead, thus making the photograph permissible. This opinion is not accepted by Salafi ulama (Abu Zahr, 2008). Many people were thus shocked when they saw many ulama using their own photographs to promote themselves in the media or appear on satellite channels after they used to prohibit it. But it was not just a shock: there is also the sense of a lost life, a lost memory that was not necessary.

Another popular hashtag in which Saudis criticize the Wahhabi establishment is titled "What has Wahhabism offered Arabs and Muslims?" The content is similar to the previous hashtag, but the framing of the discussion and the conclusions that various tweeters draw differ. Here, tweeters argue that the whole system of Wahhabism offers nothing of value to Muslim or Arab civilization. This brings us back to the theme of a dysfunctional religion and the ways in which people turn away from it. One tweeter notes that Wahhabism "eras[es] the unique cultural identity of each region in Saudi Arabia and mutilate[s] it by enforcing the ugly and depressing Wahhabi thought upon it." She points to the frustration of many Saudis with the Saudi state regarding the neglect of their cultural identities and histories (@Al, 2013b). According to a number of Saudis, Wahhabism has sought to enforce the culture and values of Najd across all of Saudi Arabia and to detach people from their cultural roots.

3.7. The Authority of the Ulama

The criticisms in the tweets here were mainly about ulama authority and less so about divine commandments. This, in principle, is less heretical than criticizing Allah's commandments, yet leads to the development of personalized forms of religion where individuals choose what is right or wrong based on their own sensibilities rather than on an authority.

Probably the most popular Saudi Twitter forum criticizing authority of the ulama is a hashtag titled "It was haram, now it is *halal.*" The immediate purpose of the hashtag is to list things that the ulama used to consider prohibited or *haram* that, with the passage of time, have become *halal.* But its underlying purpose is not a jurisprudential discussion but rather to ridicule the ulama and highlight the way they change their religious legal opinions based on whim or political interests. The tweets do not argue the logical structure or the scholarly integrity of the fatwa, they only wonder or laugh about the change, which seems to them funny and ridiculous. This hashtag became so popular and its effect so serious that it was covered by the al-Arabiyyia news channel, which emphasized the shift in the way that individuals think (Ibrahim, 2013). Indeed, this hashtag touched a nerve with prominent figures: the prominent columnist Khalaf al-Harbi posted in the hashtag a link to one of his older articles entitled *Yasriqun ʾAʿmarana Thumma Yaʿtadilun* (They steal our lives, then they become moderate). The purpose of the article was the same as the hashtag: al-Harbi argued that ulama made Saudis feel guilty about what they did or convinced them of the prohibition of certain deeds. Yet as soon as their interpretations were implemented the ulama moderated their views and, suddenly, what had been wrong was now right. The tweet that carried his article was retweeted almost a thousand times, and the article itself was already a very popular one in Saudi Arabia (@khalaf_h, 2013).

One tweeter is blunter in expressing her frustration. She says "We ought to say it was *halal* and then prohibited by those sons of dogs and we exposed them" (@No, 2013). Here she asserts that matters that were prohibited were never sins in the first place; but the ulama—toward whom she shows clear disdain to say the least—prohibited them. This tweeter considers her efforts and those of others in the hashtag as a campaign to expose ulama so-called hypocrisy. The anger in the tweet underlies many of the comments in this hashtag and reflects the eroding legitimacy of religious authorities and the sense of empowerment that Saudi tweeters feel in exposing the contradictions of ulama claims to authority. A more sarcastic take on changes in fatwas comes with a tweet that says, "The rule says that everything is *haram* until someone with a beard uses it, and then it becomes *halal.* The beard is the first source of legislation" (@Ne, 2014). Islamic legislation is based on sources, the primary and secondary of which are the Quran and the Hadith (Usul al-Fiqh, 2015). The tweeter here is ridiculing religious authority that has become independent of religious scripture. According to this tweeter, the only requirement for ulama standing has come to be a long beard. Another point the tweeter highlights is the perception shared by Saudis that everything is prohibited unless an alim makes it permissible. This tweet was also popular, with more than 200 retweets. One tweeter sums up the tone of many tweets under this hashtag regarding previously prohibited items "Radios, television, satellite receivers, insurance, banks, Bluetooth, ballot, wearing a hat, trousers, abaya on shoulders, education of girls, women in the shura council. etcetera." (@Mo, 2013). Once forbidden, they are all now permitted. In this tweet we are faced again with a statement implying that religion is dysfunctional and forbids basic aspects of modern life.

A more critical hashtag on religious authority was about funny fatwas (#fatawi_mudhhika). Tweeters listed fatwas that they considered laughable, many of which had already been mentioned in tweets in other hashtags, but the framing is different because the hashtag title generates a different context for discussing them. One popular tweet here says, "'The mother of all' Funny fatwas the prohibition of the Pokemon" (@He, 2013). Pokemon is a Japanese cartoon that was prohibited by some ulama in the early 2000s after it gained wide popularity among Saudi viewers (al-Jazirah, 2001).

Another way of mocking religious authority is placed in a hashtag titled "Sacred Comedy." The focus here is to mock religious utterances that, according to the tweeters, make no sense. Images are used here more than words: in one tweet there is reference to a report on the sexual harassment of women and an image that says that the country that came first was Afghanistan, followed by Egypt, then Saudi Arabia and Yemen together taking third place. The tweeter's comment was that most women in Afghanistan wear a *niqab* (face cover), most women in Egypt wear a hijab, while most women in both of Saudi Arabia and Yemen wear a *niqab*. Under the four images of women representing the four different countries is a laughing donkey stating "Harassment is caused by women's dress." In Saudi Arabia, as well as in other places, the solution to harassment is considered to be more modest dress. If enforced modesty is supposed to protect women, social reality, the tweeter argues, begs to differ (@3a, 2014).

Such attitudes and statements about religion and fatwas have been present in the past, but their presence was restricted to small social circles. On Twitter, by contrast, open and harsh criticism of previously undiscussed issues has surfaced. Moreover, the critics are not scholars, nor they do they base their ridicule on scholarly knowledge; instead, the foundation of the criticism is sensibility.

One tweeter replies to the topic of the hashtag by saying, "Oh you flock who don't understand except via an explanation on the blackboard" and then posts this image of scientists and what seems to be ulama or religious individuals. Under the image of the scientists is written "discovering antibodies for the corona virus" and under the image of the ulama, "discovering the name of [Prophet] Muhammad [written] on an egg." (@ al, 2014). The latter refers to ulama's claims that a miracle has happened after allegedly finding the name of Muhammad on a fish or an egg or a tree. He implies that the followers of the ulama are sheep, ridiculing them as uncritical followers who may even follow their shepherd to their slaughter. This tweeter mocks the ulama, while offering the authority of science as an alternative.

Another tweeter is more explicit in this regard. He posts famous picture from the 1927 Solvay Conference on Quantum Mechanics Physics that includes some of the most prominent scientists in the 20th century, such as Erwin Schrödinger, Werner Heisenberg, Niels Bohr, Max Planck, Marie Curie, and Albert Einstein. The tweeter comments: "When they are like these, who we learn and benefit [from] we [will] sacralise them and respect them" (@21, 2014). These two tweets indicate the role of science in reshaping the view of religion and religious authority. It is becoming difficult for many Saudis to ignore the outcome of scientific work when assessing the claims of religious authority.

3.8. Criticism of Obligations and Prohibitions

While the previous hashtags and tweets reflect a high level of criticism of religion and religious authority, as well as emotional frustration and anger against both, the overall tone was still within the basic boundaries of Islam. These criticisms did not imply a rejection of religion, nor a cry for a dramatic change in the tenets of Islam, and most of the issues criticized are in alignment with the criticism of religious reformers. Implied in these criticisms is the assumption that religion per se is good, but the way it is applied—that is, by Wahhabis—is bad. This is still significant and is indicative of a change of attitude toward religion. Of course there are tweeters in these discussions who categorically oppose religion, but they are very much in the minority; as importantly, the hashtag titles create and frame the narrative within them, and those titles imply a quest to alter or reform particular forms of religion. Yet also we find hashtags that criticize religious obligations and prohibitions in ways that are outright heretical.

There are two approaches to challenging obligations or prohibitions. The first is to argue against the scriptural argument that led to their imposition, while the second is to argue against the prohibition itself. For example, when discussing the prohibition of interest-based banks, the first type of argument would say that usury is wrong but it does not apply to the interest that banks give. Here the argument concedes that usury is sinful, but argues that interest-based banking does not qualify as usury. The second type of argument would claim that the very prohibition of usury itself is unjustified, thus rejecting the commandment itself. The first type of argumentation is accepted as legitimate by the ulama, provided that those arguing have the credentials to make these claims. By contrast, the second type of argumentation is considered heretical because it constitutes *istihlal* and a rejection of what is known by necessity. Criticism of both types is common on Twitter, but the relevant type for this analysis is the latter. There are more and more Saudis criticizing religious commandments rather than merely the arguments that lead to them. Here, we see forms of criticism that, if we apply Salafi—and even non-Salafi—orthodox standards, border on heresy if they do not constitute outright heresy.

With these two approaches to challenging obligations or prohibitions and the difference between them in mind, I now explore hashtags that criticize religion as a general category to the point of challenging foundational belief in Allah. I start with the hashtag "What has the hijab deprived me of?" This hashtag is a criticism of religion per se, and already a significant criticism. To speak of the things that Wahhabism has deprived one of is to criticize a form of Islam, but to speak of the deprivation caused by a Quranic injunction is to criticize Allah, even if indirectly (al-hawali, n.d.-a; bin Baz, n.d.-a). Muslims are required to believe that all of Allah's decrees are for the good of humans, and that one must always believe that there is goodness in them no matter how they may appear. In an Islamic cultural context, to say about something that Allah decreed that it "deprived me" is already a form of blasphemy, as it implies that one does not submit to Allah's wisdom, that one's inner compass does not align itself with Allah's Will, which is deemed beneficial for humans (bin Baz, n.d.-d). The title of the hashtag, "What has the hijab deprived me of?," challenges not only the hijab but also the very idea of binding Islamic legislation. Muslims who do not abide by Islamic rules usually do so while acknowledging the wisdom and necessity of such a law.

In the previous chapter, I discussed the stance, "I love the pious but I am not one of them," by which one aspires to adhere to all Islamic teachings even while frequently falling short. I also spoke about the concept of *"istihlal,"* in which one commits a sin without believing it to be sinful, itself a serious form of blasphemy (Manhaj, 2014). The title of the hashtag here already presents a statement against the very wisdom of the hijab. Instead, the hijab is positioned as a burden, as something that has deprived a woman of a proper and natural life. The discussions in that hashtag underscore the degree to which many Saudis are willing to push the criticism of religion to the limits of heresy.

While the tweeters are often highly critical of ulama's authority, they also struggle with the heretical leanings of this particular hashtag. I use these tweeters to show that even the harshest critic of Wahhabism and religious authority may find it troubling to criticize a Divine injunction. One tweeter states:

> The problem is society: if it had looked at the woman in a hijab as a natural human being who can go wherever she wants and do whatever she wants, this hashtag would not exist. (@to, 2013)

This tweeter does not criticize the hashtag directly, but rather the reasons that led to this particular expression of dissent. Reference to frustration and society is the tweeter's tactic for balancing harsh criticism with protecting the sanctity of the injunction to veil. The claim here is that if women were not frustrated because of uninformed social practice they would not be critical of the hijab. The tweeter does not want to accept that the hijab per se is not welcomed by many women and that the hijab in itself makes some women feel deprived, frustrated or not. Another tweeter who is often critical of religion as practiced by Saudis says, "Take it off, tear it, burn it, it is up to you what you do, but do not attempt to legitimate taking it off and do not shame those who wear it or despise it, for it is a rule in all religions" (@Se, 2013a). And then she adds pictures of women of different faiths such as Sabian, Sikh, Orthodox Jew, Druze, Catholic, Amish, Orthodox Christian, Hindu, and Muslim, all wearing one form of veil or another. The hijab is considered an obligation by many Muslims, and while many Saudi women do not wear it they would not question this obligation, as that would constitute *istihlal*, which is a particularly serious form of *kufr*. So this tweeter is telling women not to be critical of the hijab, even as some of them choose not to wear it and even to burn it. One tweeter who is careful not to criticize hijab as a general obligation focuses her criticism on the downsides of face-covering *niqab*: "Since I am a Saudi I am forced to wear the veil and cover the face, yet my face is my identity and erasing it leads to the loss of many of my rights" (@Al, 2013a). This form of criticism is acceptable because this woman is criticizing a form of the hijab and not the hijab itself. And when she says that covering her face can lead to losing her rights she means in courts, as women cannot show their faces in front of a judge, which can lead to impersonation. This issue was resolved in 2014 by the Saudi state when it enforced fingerprint identification for women. Women would still not reveal their faces to identify themselves, instead they would use their fingerprints to do this (al-Sharidah, 2014).

Most of the tweets that appeared under this hashtag were produced by women and men who considered the hijab fundamentally wrong or oppressive. We cannot be sure about the motivation behind these tweets, but they share a claim that the harm of the hijab lies not in how women are treated but in how it impacts on their sense of self. To criticize an Islamic duty based on this is a very individualistic and modern way of approaching religious duties, taking us back to Taylor's (2011) discussion of the self as the standard for believing or not believing. Also this form of criticism, which is ultimately based on mere preference or discomfort at an Islamic duty, is considered *kufr* (PCSRF, n.d.-e). One tweeter declares: "It nullified my existence." And with that she posts an image that includes the following text:

Windows are banned in homes: so the shadow of a woman is not glimpsed. Cars are shaded: so no one knows if there is someone inside them. The matter is not hijab: rather it is the abolishment of existence (wujud). An exile in a moving coffin. (@zo, 2013)

Here the tweeter rejects the hijab, going as far as saying that it erases her very existence. According to this tweet there is no possibility of considering the hijab as a just rule that is misapplied. This form of criticism is considered heretical in a traditional Islamic framework, as it suggests that Allah is committing the evil deed of erasing women from existence, social or otherwise. Along similar lines, another tweet about the hijab states, "It deprived me of showing my humanity and made me like this," and the tweeter posts an image of two women in a black veil near two binbags (@sh, 2013). Here she is saying that the hijab degraded her to the point where she saw a resemblance between her appearance and that of a black binbag. Allah's command hardly appeared divine for this tweeter. Another tweeter takes aim at the practical implications of the hijab. For this woman, the hijab limited her lifestyle choices: "And the beach? I see most Saudis and their likes who go to the islands of the world to see its malls!! Because nothing is possible for them at the sea[side] #damn" (@ No, 2013). Although this statement would have been benign had it been said independently, its placement within a discussion of how the hijab has deprived women extends its scope for questioning divine prescription. Another tweeter makes the same point through an image of a woman enjoying the beach wearing a swimsuit, and under that image is a frown from the tweeter (@sa, 2013).

3.9. Individual Religiosity

Criticizing the authority of the ulama takes a more serious and direct tone in the hashtag "Bringing down the Guardianship of Clerics." But here the emphasis is not merely on criticizing the ulama but rather on calling for an individualized religiosity whereby one does not need to seek the ulama's guidance. One very well-known Saudi writer explains:

> Most of the problems in the Muslim world are because of men who claim that they have a special role in leading the faithful, and they profit from this. (@ma, 2014)

Along the same lines, another says:

> They use us to profit, take advantage of our ignorance to vent their malice, make us renounce life and then they embrace it, and they make us desire death so they may live. (@Ri, 2014)

It is important to note the subtle difference between these two tweets: the former is critical of Saudi religious authority in principle while the latter is critical of the current structure of religious authority. Both are important indicators with regard to Saudi attitudes to the ulama, and both play a role in promoting a discourse of criticizing religion, but this difference is relevant because the conclusion of the former is to erode all forms of religious authority and not merely to reform it, as the second tweet aims. A tweet similar to the second one mentioned here elaborates on the need to reform religious authority: "It [reforming religious authority by eroding the authority of incompetent ulama] is a religious duty since in the third millennium they still think that the earth is flat and not a sphere" (@ga, 2014). This tweeter is referring to a popular accusation that the previous Mufti Abdulaziz bin Baz claimed that the earth is flat, which he denied (bin Baz, n.d.-h). But nevertheless, many Saudi ulama still believe that the sun rotates around the earth, and the purpose of this tweet was to ridicule those who can believe such ideas, which contradict scientific observation, using the pretext of scriptural evidence (Dearden, 2015; OmarHater, 2012). Here, the tweeter is not calling for the destruction of all institutions of religious authority but rather for the removal of those that are not competent enough to understand the basic principles of science. More importantly, this tweet suggests that challenging the ulama's authority is a *religious* act in which pious individuals should engage, not because that authority has committed a sin but rather because these ulama reject modern science. Science, according to this tweeter, is the standard by which to measure religious statements; it is even a standard by which to assess the competency of the ulama. This tweeter accepts the principle of religious authority but as long as its competence is measured by the standards of modern science.

This next tweet is significant because it argues that religion should be a question of individual choice. As the tweeter explains:

> Religion does not need ulama who guide you. The Quran is not a foreign [language] so that it is necessary for someone to read it on your behalf and dictate legislation according to his understanding or his personal interests. (@re, 1994)

This meaning is repeated by another tweeter, who laments:

> They play the role of a telecommunications company between Allah and humans, they see themselves as agents of Allah on earth, topple their guardianship so that there is no guardianship (*wisaya*) in religion from the outset. (@Wi, 2014)

Again, we see the stress on the individual nature of religion and the ability of individuals to understand Allah's will. Another tweeter gives a practical angle to this call by offering a rationalist methodology for understanding the Quran: "to be liberated from them, read the Quran rationally without going back to their exegesis . . . you will find the right Islam which came

down from Allah, praised be He" (@Na, 2014). A fourth tweeter emphasizes the personal nature of the relationship with Allah:

> Allah does not need a mediator between Him and His worshippers,
> so he said "Pray to me and I will reply," a direct and clear relation
> between the worshiper and his Lord. (@SA, 2014)

There is no legitimacy for ulama's interpretation of the scriptures; instead, the relationship between Allah and His creation should be intimate
and private. Such public expressions of individual religiosity are novel in
Saudi Arabia; that they come from lay people is an indicator that a new
attitude or sensibility has emerged by which religion is evaluated. One
rarely find among these tweeters sophisticated arguments presented by
reformist Muslim philosophers of religion such as Fazlur Rahman (1919–
1988), Abdulkarim Soroush (b. 1945) or Muhammad Arkoun (1928–2010)
(Arkoun, 2004; Rahman, 1984; Soroush, 2009). Instead, they rely on in-
tuitive statements to challenge the existing religious hierarchy.

3.10. Questioning Religion

Criticism is not limited to Islam or Wahhabism; it also extends to religion
more generally. I begin this section with a hashtag titled "This is a logical question, no one better accuse me of non-belief," which has amassed
many thousands of tweets. The title of the hashtag frames the discussion
by introducing the position of skepticism and uncertainty and seeking to
legitimate its public expression.

What is most interesting about the all the hashtags discussed here is
the lack of intellectual engagement with religion based on scholarly knowledge. While some Saudis may consider this an indication of the insig-
nificance of what was going on in these hashtags, I saw this "this lack
of depth"—to use the words of one critic (@al, 2013)—as an indicator of
changed sensibilities. Saudis are now willing to discuss Islam without
being learned in religion; we are not witnessing Saudis speaking against
religion because they are misinformed about it, rather we are witnessing
Saudis whose sensibilities have changed to the point where they criticize
or reject basic tenets of religion because these tenets no longer, to use
Taylor's expression, speak to them.

The thousands of tweets in this hashtag reflect the mundane and the
deep questions many Saudis have about religion. The tweets in the hashtag

are not all in the form of questions; but the question in the hashtag was sufficient to turn the statements in it into a question. Rhetorical questions are a complex sentences and have been attributed with various functions, sometimes contrasting functions, enabling the speaker to make a more convincing statement or to soften the strong effect of a statement (Frank, 1990). In the case of the hashtag it would be impossible without knowing the full context of the tweets to know what the tweeters wanted: to be more convincing or to be softer, but given the legal and social consequences of making such an assertion the greater possibility is that the hashtag was used to soften the statement. Thus very bold questions and/or statements that were close to heresy were made, but framing them as rhetorical questions allowed people to state them. It is one thing to voice an opinion as a statement and another to make it in the form of a question, even if a rhetorical question. The former could lead one to being accused of heresy while the latter can at worse lead one to being accused of utter ignorance. Stating ideas in the form of a question protects the tweeter from any legal consequence.

One tweeter tweeted a picture of the seal of the Prophet. In the seal there three words from top to bottom: "Allah," "*rasul*" (messenger), and "Muhammad," with the word "Allah" at the top. The words are supposed to be read from below as "Muhammad rasul Allah," or Muhammad is the messenger of Allah. This tweeter tells us that "most of the time I read it as Allah rasul Muhammad" (@sa, 2012), meaning that Allah is the messenger of Muhammad. He is saying that Allah's word expresses the will of the Prophet, rather than the other way around. To say that Allah is the messenger of the Prophet raises the issue of the human construction of religion and deity or casts doubt on the sincerity of the Prophet when attributing the Quran to Allah. This is outright heresy, but because it is framed as a question it easier to voice it. A more direct question on theodicy is posed in this tweet: "Is it reasonable that all these [scientists] are in hell despite the inventions they have provided that make human life easier and better?" (@Ab, 2013). Although his point was to ask a question, he made it an assertion, as if to shock the reader. Under his comment he used the picture of scientists from the 1927 Conference.

The tweeter may be expressing doubt that these men of knowledge go to hell; alternatively, he could be stating that if they did go to hell it would be unjust. To doubt or question a non-Muslim going to hell and being eternally damned and deprived of heaven is heresy, as is casting doubt on the justice of the decision to send them to hell. That only Muslims go to heaven is a basic belief even of very moderate Muslims. This tweet thus raises a very serious question, but does it not based on any rereading of the Quran, rather by a new sensibility. Instead of faith being the criterion for going to heaven, the tweeter is using the criterion of the benefactor; these who benefit others should not be punished. This is a critical development in the sensibilities of some Saudis.

Another question on the mercy of Allah asks, "Does it make sense that Islamic religion, the religion of mercy and forgiveness, has the *hadd of rajm*? Stoning a man to death???!!" (@no, 2012). The traditional stance toward divinely decreed punishments is to accept them without questioning, since they are decreed by divine wisdom. In this instance the tweeter is criticizing such an approach and questioning how a religion that claims to be merciful can actually have such a decree. Stoning is the punishment decreed in Islam for adultery (Frolov, 2015), and there have of course been some Muslim reformers who have criticized it, but they presented their argument in the form of jurisprudential argument claiming that there is no evidence in either the Quran or the Hadith for the punishment of stoning (shaikhAdnanIbrahim, 2013)—but here the tweeter is not referring to any of that. She is merely disdaining the nature of the punishment and rejecting it on these grounds. Her concern is personal sensibility, not scholarly argumentation.

One tweeter writes, asking, "Why did Allah create a universal religion for all mankind that depends heavily on the understanding of 1 language?" (@hi, 2013). Here the tweeter indirectly questions the insensibility of the claim that Islam is the only true religion and the sole path to salvation. How, he wonders, can this be when everyone needs to understand the original language of the Quran, something which is undoable? Another tweet simply says, "Young boys made eternal!!" In heaven Muslims are promised many pleasures, of which one is the service of eternally young boys (Quran: al-Waqi'ah, 17) and the implied statement in the tweet is that pedophilia is a pleasure in heaven. Such a statement cannot be made explicitly, of course (@Ab, 2012). To have explicitly wondered whether or not the Quran condones pedophilia in heaven would cause him much trouble, so he decided to frame it as a question. Another example here is a feminist outlook on prophecy: "Why are there no women prophets or messengers—why are they all men?!" (@sa, 2012). Once more we see a modern sensibility being used to criticize matters of faith, even criticizing divine decisions to only send male prophets.

Some of the questions in this hashtag were based on simple inconsistencies between science and the Quran, like:

If the evening of Qadar is one evening and it came upon us in Saudi Arabia it will be in other countries day light in other countries. do they have another evening after our evening? (@mo, 2012).

Muslims believe that the evening in which the Quran was revealed is with cosmological significance and it is called: "the evening of decree" based on the Quranic verse "We sent the Qur'an down during the Night of Decree" (Quran-al-Qadr, 1). So he is asking about the sense of this verse, considering the spherical nature of the Earth. That is when the Quran was revealed it was evening in Mecca but day time in other place on earth. The question seems simple, but it does indicate the role of scientific understanding in problematizing the Quran, and more importantly the degree of sensitivity to anything that no longer makes sense. A similar question was, "If the biological and psychological qualities change, then who is going to heaven?" (@al, 2012). Again science is brought in to problematize the understanding of theology. Science is also brought to question miracles. A tweeter asks:

Why is there not one credible scientific source that gives evidence to the splitting of the moon? Even though they were able to know its gaseous and rocky surface and the power of its gravity? (@Fa, 2012)

Many Muslims believe that the moon was split to present the unfaithful of Mecca with evidence that Muhammad is indeed a Prophet. Some Muslims have claimed that NASA affirmed this as a fact (mbc.net, 2014), although NASA has denied it (Bailey, 2010). But there is of course no evidence of that, and this tweeter is using this lack of evidence to question a miracle stated in the Quran. He could have asked the same about the parting of the sea for Moses or Abraham being saved from the fire of Nemrod. The point is that he invokes scientific evidence rather than faith, and this itself is a significant development.

Other tweeters look into the internal contradictions within religion itself. One contentious issue is the relationship between the Quran and the Hadiths ascribed to the Prophet. This is becoming a popular topic among many critics and reformers of religion such as Hasan al-Maliky, mentioned earlier.

Many of the questions in this hashtag are about contradictions between historical facts and articles of faith. For example the Quran says that the Ummah nation is the greatest, but as this tweeter says, "if we were really the greatest Ummah that Allah raised, then why are we the most underdeveloped in all domains" (@El, 2012b). This contradiction is quite relevant in creating a space for questions. The contradiction between how Muslims ought to be and how they are is a repeated theme in Muslim discussions and has been intensified by the increase in Muslim terrorism. But more relevantly, the fact that she uses development as a standard for being better is significant; having Muslim faith alone is not enough for her to be the best Ummah.

One tweeter raises a question with a hint of sarcasm saying, "since 1400 years ago [we hear] 'The hour is coming I am almost hiding it' where is it?" (mh, 2012). The "hour" in this context is the Day of Judgment and the tweeter is referring to a Quranic verse that says "the Hour is coming [it is so close] I almost conceal it" (Quran: Taha, 15) meaning that the Day of Judgment is close. But after 1400 years the tweeter here wonders.

Another tweeter wonders why miracles stopped appearing 1400 years ago (Ra, 2012). This wonderment could be taken as to cast doubt on miracles themselves. It is as if he were saying: if miracles are real they would have continued, but we no do not see them, thus they are not real. Of course the tweet could be a mild protest at the current absence of miracles, since they had played an important role in preserving the faith of believers. A tweeter also asks, "why do we hear of miracles but not see them?" (El, 2012). Here she is implying that they never existed. A final example from this hashtag asserts the right to doubt and be skeptical. She asks, "Why did Allah not be angry with Abraham when he asked him to prove his divinity and he gets angry with us?" (Ma, 2012). In the Quran it is mentioned that the Patriarch Abraham had doubted the existence and abilities of Allah, and Allah's response was to show him proof for both issues. She is saying if doubt in itself was prohibited then Allah would have punished Abraham rather than indulge him with evidence. The tweeter seems to wants to condone doubt yet is worried from the backlash if she did, thus she placed it in the context of a rhetorical hashtag.

3.11. Atheism in Saudi Arabia

The public discussion on religion in Saudi Arabia went to another level when a report on global atheism was discussed on Twitter. The report was published in 2012 and received some attention among Twitter users, and became a topic for discussion (@Ala, 2012; Gilani, Shahid, & Zuettel, 2012). The report's main points include the finding that 5% of Saudis describe themselves as atheists and 20% describe themselves as not religious. Conceptualizing a demographic of atheists or disbelievers has methodological challenges, particularly problems of definition, as the words "atheist," "disbeliever," "religion," and others can mean different things to different people even from the same culture (Zuckerman, 2007, p. 332). Nonetheless, one can still state that a significant number of Saudis are shifting from belief to nonbelief. This led to a number of discussions on satellite channels about atheism in Saudi Arabia (Khalijyyah, 2013; al-Layth, 2014). The points in these discussions, as on Twitter, ranged from denying the accuracy of the report to analyzing the reasons behind that high number of nonbelievers.

One of those hashtags had the title "Atheist Saudi Arabia." Some of the tweets here considered atheism a natural phenomenon that does not warrant surprise, and others explained the rise of atheism as a reaction to Saudi religion. The relevance of the first set of tweets is that they show how some Saudis are not concerned about fellow Saudis who commit the gravest sin, and more importantly are not threatened by their existence. To understand this stance it is important to remember that many Saudis consider atheism a threat to the social fabric of society, and in 2014 it was classified as terrorism by the Saudi state (WAS, 2014; Withnall, 2014). Many Saudis were shocked by the report because they could not conceive the idea of a Saudi atheist, and we see in chapter 5 the way in which many Saudis responded to what they perceived as the spread of atheism in Saudi Arabia. A few hashtags were set up and became active in response to that report. The relevance of the second set of tweets, which explain atheism as a reaction to Saudi religion, is the way in which they reveal the dysfunctional nature and even destructive function of Saudi religion. This second set of tweets are mostly by Saudis who want to defend Islam and say that only one form is corrupt—the Wahhabi form—and that had Saudis been exposed to other moderate forms of Islam they would not have become atheists (@a7, 2012). There are, however, Saudis who explain atheism by saying that it is not Wahhabism that presents a distorted religion but rather the Quran itself presents a set of distorted facts that lead sensible people to reject it altogether. One female tweeter explains:

He who says it is the shaykhs who distorted religion . . . I say to him
it is enough to read the Quran and you find scientific mistakes and
moral and human abuses. (@za, 2012).

According to her, Islam itself carries the seeds of its own rejection. One
tweeter takes this idea further, claiming that to "be a Saudi does not neces-
sitate being a Muslim." He goes on to say that "this deep rooted assumption is wrong, who becomes a Muslim is for his own sake and who is not
[a Muslim] is the same" (@i7, 2012).

Some tweeters who accepted the results of the report blamed the situation of religion in Saudi Arabia as a reason for that high number of
nonbelievers. He says the reason is that "we demand executing the atheist
instead of engaging him in a dialogue" (@al, 2012). He is here referring
to the way ulama and their followers react to those who openly profess
heresy. His view is that people who have doubt should be allowed to speak
up, as that may lead to finding answers, but since they are not allowed
the conclusion would be that they would dismiss religion altogether. This
same idea is expressed in another tweet that dismisses the fruitfulness of
discussing the report, saying, "to discuss a topic like this in an environment that totally lacks the basics of freedom is like Don Quixote games
with windmills." (Wa, 2012).

Another hashtag with a similar line of thinking is titled "Why do they
leave Islam?" This hashtag also explores the reasons leading many Saudis
and non-Saudis to leave religion, and its content is similar to the content
of the previous hashtag. One interesting tweet here emphasizes the role of
social media in empowering these with subversive views. She says:

Yesterday they used to behead he who criticised them. Today the
Face[book] and the Twitter opened the door for critics to demolish
their fables and the minds of people were opened. (@as, 2013)

It is as if she is saying that there is an inherent problem in religion itself but authority has inhibited and scared people, and now with social
media people are able to speak out and express their real attitudes toward
religion. She was not explaining why people left religion but rather why
people are not able to express their views against religion.

One of the tweets here comments on the process of acquiring faith as
opposed to the process of leaving it:

Let us admit that religion has become a nationality you are born to bear it you did not choose it you did not believe in it you did not understand it rather you are initiated its love since childhood and that it is the absolute right. (@Mo, 2013)

This is quite a significant view of religion that some Saudis are now echoing. Religion according to this view is not something one has chosen but rather something one was born into. And this line of thinking trivializes the whole question of why some people leave Islam, because, according to this view, those people never really were in it. Such a statement is subversive and challenges the Muslims' claim that they have the monopoly on Truth, and more importantly it stresses that the belief one follows is the outcome of chance, and not of conviction based on intellectual contemplation or spiritual experience.

Another hashtag, titled "letter to an atheist," reflects Saudi attitudes toward atheism. The content of this hashtag was advice to the atheist to repent and redeem him/herself. Such advice would come as no surprise. But the surprise was to find, again, more and more Saudis accepting the right of the individual to leave his/her faith, and their only request was that these individuals respect the faith of fellow Saudis.

your belief is one of your rights, but it is not a prerequisite of atheism to assault other religions!! you can be an atheist without contempt for others!! (@e3, 2013)

Instead of asking the atheist to go back to faith, the message here was that he/she should be a moderate atheist who does not reject the right of others to believe. This sentiment toward atheists was not uncommon. Another important tweet says:

If you are an atheist for real, do not make Allah the cause around which all your talk rotates, keep busy with other useful things and leave Allah for those who believe in Him. (@iA, 2013)

This was retweeted more than 150 times. This tweet normalizes the presence of atheists, rather than seeing them as a threat to the social fabric, and simply asks them to avoid ridiculing religion openly.

I conclude this overview of the criticism of religion on Saudi Twitter with the hashtag "a letter to Allah." Here we also find much criticism of religion and faith; but the tone is different. Those participating in this hashtag are not speaking to the ulama, or highlighting the way religion is manipulated or misinterpreted; rather they are sending a complaint—or rather tweeting—directly to Allah. Most of the hashtag reflected people who still believed yet were critical of some aspects of belief; but there were those who were cynical unbelievers and also those who were dogmatically faithful. Most of the issues discussed above were repeated here, but framed as a tweet to Allah rather than as a discussion on religion. For example we find here complaints about the authority of the ulama, such as this tweet:

> Those who speak in your name want us to worship you out of fear of your tormenting punishment . . . they do not allow questions and they cut the throats of those who question; all I want is to worship you out of love and deep conviction. (cr, 2014)

Here the tweeter is seeking a direct spiritual relationship with Allah, and complaining about the current way religion was tailored in a way where the ulama control the channels of communication with Allah. There were many similar tweets reflecting individualistic attitudes to religion and the desire to move away from a faith that was based on the ulama's interpretation of scripture to one that is based on a personal relationship with Allah.

3.12. Conclusion: Contours of Criticizing Religion

This chapter has explored some of the critical discussions of religion that had once occurred in Saudi Arabia on Twitter, demonstrating the breadth and depth of the criticism. The few tweets that I have discussed are just a small sample selected from thousands of similar tweets critical of religion in general and Islam specifically. In these tweets one sees that all aspects of religion of different degrees of theological centrality are subjected to criticism. The examples I have cited show Saudis criticizing the wisdom of Allah, the monopoly of Muslims on heaven, the benefits of Quranic commandments, the ulama's authority, the legitimacy of a layperson's interpretation of the Quran, and tolerance of atheists and apostates, among other issues discussed earlier. Saudis are indeed criticizing religion. Almost no detail of religion is immune from criticism and almost no detail is accepted without doubt or taken in absolute blind faith.

The limitation on public space which I discussed above and the criminalization of certain statements critical of religion limits the extent of the development of a discourse of religious criticism. For now, we can only observe sporadic opinions developed through personal experiences and discussions among small groups. Yet we can at least claim that the grounds for that critical process exist. Today, I cannot speak of a discourse, as what I observe on Twitter are statements and the rationalization of those statements, and the limitations of space on Twitter as well as fear of legal repercussions limit the dialogue.

More important than the nature of these opinions critical of religion are the intellectual and scholarly credentials of those making these criticisms. These critics are not philosophers, nor scholars of religion, and are certainly not ulama. Their criticism is not founded on a deep understanding of religious scripture, nor on methods of modern reinterpretation of the Quran. Most of the opinions above do not cite a Quranic verse or a Prophetic Hadith in order to legitimize their claim. These opinions are founded on a tension between their sensibilities and their understanding of religion. It is not possible to understand from Twitter how these sensibilities had developed, but one can assume that they are part of the modern way of thinking that is embedded in the lifestyle of most Saudis. Modernity has not just affected the institutional structure and consumer behavior in Saudi Arabia; it has also affected the way they think. The least effect one can see from these tweets is that it desacralizes the authority of the ulama, allowing Saudis—at least potentially—to think independently when it comes to religious matters.

One can also glimpse in these discussions the factors that are accelerating this process of criticizing religion, particularly the perception that religion impedes worldly comforts and the increasing legitimacy of modern science. The success of science and the sense of gratitude to scientists are being contrasted with the way that religion impedes daily life and the frustration that many Saudis feel with the ulama as they compare scientific discoveries and the Quranic worldview. A third factor is the difficulty in continuing to embrace traditional Muslim theology as Saudis question whether only a fraction of the world's population goes to heaven. This unease with theology seems to be in proportion to the degree to which the Saudi is exposed to the goodness in the nonbeliever. This is why we mostly see it reported when making queries about scientists, who will supposedly burn in hell. These scientists provide tangible benefits for many Saudis, and thus one can say they are exposed to their goodness. We also see this with Saudis who have actually interacted with "infidels" and are perplexed by the view that such people go to hell. The breakdown of the chain of memory is also apparent in some of these tweets, although to a lesser degree, and the erosion of the plausibility structures does not stand out clearly here. Of course without in-depth interviews with a large number of Saudis it would not be possible to discern the subconscious factors that are leading Saudis to disengage from religion and to the emergence of the criticism of religion. The coming chapter is based on interviews with some Saudis, where I further explore the impact of the factors stated in the theories on changing Saudi sensibilities and on disengagement from religion.

4

Religious Disengagements

THE TRANSFORMATION OF the relationship between the self and religion is a complex phenomenon involving different processes that lead to
change from a state of religious belief or experience to an alternative set of
beliefs, whether toward other forms of religions or religious experiences
or a worldview separate from religion altogether (Johnson-Miller, 2005;
Lawrence, 1998). In this chapter I explore in detail some of the stories of
Saudis who underwent changes in their belief system, specifically changes
away from the basic fundamental precepts of Islam.

The individuals whose stories are presented here are from diverse
social and economic backgrounds, as well as varying educational experiences and home lives. The dominant views in the homes of the people
whose disengagements I discuss range across religion, some Sufi others
Salafi, some indifferent to religiosity, and others fundamentalist. Some
of those individuals could be considered learned in religion, while others had a superficial knowledge mostly based on primary and secondary
education, limited self-education, and the mass media. The level of nonreligious knowledge also differed among them; though all were educated,
only a few could be considered intellectuals. Even their awareness of
Salafism and Salafi religious symbols and characters differed greatly from
one to another. The ways they changed are also different, as are the issues
that triggered the change and the outcomes of their changes. I do not attempt to extract a pattern, as the sample I used is too small for that, and
moreover I am trying here to explore multiple stories with multiple factors. More importantly, I do not give more explanatory weight to the similarities, as this is not a statistically representative sample; instead, I take a
qualitative approach that seeks to highlight an underexplored social phenomenon and some of its contours. Although each story is separate in its

own way, I present the collectivity of the stories as one short introductory paragraph in the story of criticizing religion among Saudis.

While I knew the background of my interlocutors, they also knew my background. They were familiar with the multiple identifications rightly or wrongly assigned to me: Saudi—Yemeni—Zaydi[1]—Shi'i—Mu'tazili[2]—secular—liberal—heretic. I understand that the salient identification from my interlocutor's perspective influences how he/she perceives me and what is said to me or how a memory is constructed or a situation interpreted. It was not possible to predict my exact position at the outset, nor to discover it through the process of interacting with them. All I could do was to be aware that my relative position continuously shifts from person to person with a possible effect on the outcome of the research.

The chapter centers on the stories of my interviewees and is thus rendered in narrative form. I want as much as possible to allow the reader to "relive the experience through the writer's or performer's eyes" (Humphreys, 2005, p. 1), because Saudis experiencing such disengagements have not had the chance to be voiced, and I attempt to do that here. Giving Saudis a voice is especially important in the initial phases of understanding the criticism of religion in Saudi Arabia, which is the ultimate purpose of this study. In any study one always needs to use analytical categories that have been used in different social settings, and these categories have the potential to obscure one's understanding. By giving more voice to the Saudis I am interviewing, I am in a better position to develop analytical categories from their own voices, which could be more relevant to understanding them. Through detailed description, I explore key causes behind the process of religious criticism in Saudi Arabia. While the Twitter discussions of the previous chapter underscore the extent of this phenomenon and the breadth of the issues being raised and challenged, this chapter focuses on the life stories of people who undertook this process of religious criticism and the factors that drove this shift.

Having said that, I acknowledge that I am not merely giving voice to those whom I interviewed; instead, the interlocutors' responses were elicited and influenced by my questions and also by my explanation of the

---

1. A school of thought influenced theologically by the Mu'tazilism and politically by Shi'ism. Many sources consider it a branch of Shi'ism. Sunni sources consider it the closest of the Shi'a to Sunnis (Madelung, 2015).

2. One of the most influential Muslim theological schools of thought in the 9th–10th century whose main starting point was the belief in the primacy of reason over religious scripture.

goals of the research. All knew that my research would center on how Saudis understand, debate, and criticize religion and Islam. I told them that my research project sought to understand the way Saudis generally criticize religion, and more specifically the opinions on religion that they share, and the issues that they question. I told them that my aim was to understand this phenomenon, which exists widely but had not been studied before, and they knew that I had selected them because they had expressed such opinions before, either in writing, blogging, or tweeting or through open conversation. They knew how I would use the material I collected from them. They also knew the confidentiality policy that I would follow, in particular with regard to keeping their identities secret, which in itself may have influenced how they presented themselves. Although they trusted that I would keep their identities safe, the presence of a recorder and my mention of confidentiality would almost certainly influence them (Belson, 1967; Bucher, Fritz, & Quarantelli, 1956; Joinson, 2001; King & Horrocks, 2010). The final product from our conversations was also influenced by my interlocutors' perceptions of me and by how they wished to present themselves to me.

Moreover, the selections I extracted from each interview were influenced by my own biases and preference for what seemed to me most relevant. Also the order in which I organized the material and the themes I extracted were all done by me. Finally, my comments accompanying the narratives influenced how they would be read by the end reader, and these comments were influenced by my own experience with each interlocutor. As I moved from one interview to the other, I noticed that I myself had changed in how I discussed the goals of my research and how I presented the details around the research. I was not expecting that change in me to happen when I first started, but I noticed it happening beginning with my third interview.

Luckily I had not listened to the recordings of the first two interviews, so when I noticed the change in my presentation of the issue I made the decision not to listen to any interview before I had completed them all. It is also important to acknowledge that my own interpretation was influenced by reading the transcripts and listening to the interviews. I say this to emphasize the weight of my presence in these interviews. Thus, while I did want to give a voice to the interlocutors, I understand—following Cary and Lewis—that I served as a filter and that the stories presented here are not in the pure context of the interlocutors; rather they have been partially contextualized by me in a way that could potentially alter or distort the voices that I aim to present. Thus I should not overrate my role in giving a voice to this Saudi segment of critics of religion (Cary, 1999; D. Lewis, 2008). What I present here is in the final analysis my interpretation of the accounts that I recorded, which was an interpretation and reconstruction of the memory of the lives of my interlocutors.

I did not probe to find our whether historical facts or memories were factually accurate, I was rather looking for the interlocutor's presentation of these facts and the clues it offered me about their past. What actually happened did not matter to me as much as how it was recalled and how it was articulated.

There are many ways to represent life stories as a written narrative. I decided to follow Goldman et al., who when using this method sought to "discover common generative themes amongst the varied group of inter-locutors" (Goldman et al., 2003, p. 566). The narratives here are divided into three sets. The first covers the childhood of my interlocutors, the second, the transformation toward religion that most underwent, and the third, the disengagement each experienced and the different reasons each presented. Moreover I divide the experiences of disengagement according to a theme that was a central milestone in influencing the disengagement from religion.

First, though, I begin with one story, that of Alaa, which encompasses many of the themes to come but also presents a different twist in that the key theme in this story is her unsuccessful attempt to transition back to religion after swaying away from it. Alaa's story serves as an introduction and provides the reader with a sample case of disengagement. The stories that follow are not all presented as one complete narrative but rather as parts of different stories woven into one. There is also another reason I mention her first, which is that she was the first person whose interview I reviewed when I started my analysis, and thus casts light on my analyt-ical process as well. By mentioning her story first, I try to place myself and the reader on partially equal footing in terms of relating to the other stories.

Alaa was born in the 1980s into a middle-class family in a rural city of Saudi Arabia. Due to her father's career, she moved around Saudi Arabia frequently and did not settle in one city. She said that her father was not religious but her mother was. He was a believer, but did not practice the obligations of Islam nor restrict himself from its prohibitions. He did not even fast in the holy month of Ramadan, which is usually practiced even by nonreligious Saudis who do not otherwise practice other rituals. Her

mother was a big fan of Muhammad al-ʿUrayfi, the famous alim mentioned before, but she did not try to impose any of her religious values on
her children.

So Alaa grew up without practicing religion at all, and early in her
childhood—aged around 12, she said—she stopped believing in anything. This particular point on lack of faith at an early age is something that other interlocutors mentioned in passing, but none of them
were as clear as she was in asserting her loss of faith as a child. She
remembers that this was an indifferent form of lack in faith. It was not
something she adopted or tried to speak about; instead, she actually
avoided all religious discussions at school as she did not want to get
into trouble. The reason as she recalls for her loss of faith was that she
had questions—about the existence of Allah, the afterlife, and the duty
to obey Allah—that were not answered convincingly by her teachers,
whom she used to ask. Another thing she recalls is that whenever she
asked a question they responded in a condescending tone. The answers
were dictated in a way that implied that she should simply surrender
to them. She now explains it by saying that she was a stubborn child
and such a tone repelled her. That she neither had a religious home nor
lived within her network of relatives may have played a part in shaping
her faith, albeit in an indirect way. There was an absence of religious
nurturing in her family life, which would have normally played an important role in her religious development.

The questions she asked as a child were the kind of questions many
other children ask about Allah and religion. She would ask, for example,
"Where did Allah come from?" This is a very common question that almost every child asks at one point. But the questions that she described
as more significant to her at that age had to do with the Prophecy and theology. "Why," she would ask, "would Allah talk to one person only? Why
does He not talk to all of us?" More concerning for her was "Why did He
create people and then make some free and others slaves?" There was another thing that troubled her much more than the issue of slavery, and this
concerned nonbelievers going to hell. Her family had a "pagan foreign
maid"—"*wathaniyya*," to use her own expression—who was working for
them, and it troubled Alaa that this person would go to hell. She was not,
as she recalls, thinking of hell conceptually, but rather in concrete terms of
real people that she knew and loved, and who were supposed to go there.
"Why should she go to hell? It was not her fault that she was created in a
country of pagans!" she would think at that early age. She said that after

not getting answers she simply decided not believe, and stayed like that until she got married.

Alaa was married before her eighteenth birthday, quickly became preg-nant and soon underwent a transformation. Now she wanted to believe again. She said "I wanted to believe in some meaning to make sense of the child growing inside me." She needed to believe to give life meaning, the life of her coming child.

> When I was pregnant I felt very lost, and I was afraid I would bring this burden to this poor creature. I needed something to contain me, me and this creature, something with a meaning, for me and the baby.

She felt that there was something missing. So she tried to pray, to read the Quran, but she felt nothing. She finally decided to stop trying and stop asking questions and accept that there are no answers, and that one should simply live life as it comes. Gradually, she developed a justifica-tion for her lack of belief, which is that one should not "believe in some-thing which will cause harm" as she would say. By that she meant one should not believe in a deity that would punish people for not believing properly. After deciding not to believe, she read some books that would give her rejection of faith some intellectual justification. But that did not help her either.

Alaa was simply an indifferent nonbeliever. She did not find reason to believe, but she also did not actively seek to destroy her belief. In the process of seeking a justification for her lack of belief, she read books and articles by atheists such as Richard Dawkins, Daniel Dennet, and Sam Harris, all of whom are popular advocates of militant atheism and critics of the very idea of deity and religion. Most of what she read was avail-able on the Internet or had been brought into the country from abroad. She also followed many of the debates between the faithful and nonbe-lievers on YouTube. She said that the main things she learned were not refutations of religion and deity but rather the categories of nonbelievers, such as atheist, agnostic, or areligious, and she tried to see where in these categories she would fit. But then again she tried to believe once more. So she read two books by Mustafa Mahmud[3] (1921–2009), a well-known

---

3. All of his books and articles can be found on the Mustafa Mahmoud Electronic Library website at http://mostafamahmoud.net/

Egyptian physician who tried to present faith and religion in a popular style, while also using argumentation based on the miracles in nature as proof of Allah's existence. That did not convince her, so she went back to her previous position. At the time that we spoke she had concluded that religion is something that organizes people's lives. It gives them meaning, direction, and a set of instructions. But religion, according to her, is also a way to redeem and relieve one's conscience. "People do wrong things and then," she said, "they believe they can delete it by doing something else." She finds this idea disturbing. "They think they can do something wrong, hurt someone and then go and delete it" by asking for Allah's repentance. But she developed no position for or against religion. She thought religion and religious experience too complicated to be judged in terms of either good or bad. "Perhaps both," she told me, "it is good because it makes them comfortable, and it is bad because it allows them to delete the bad."

Alaa's story presented me with a few surprises which, I must acknowledge, may have influenced my later style of interviewing. It not only challenged my perception that most Saudis grow up with some commitment to religion; it also raised questions about the nonlinearity of religious disengagement and its direction. The assumption I had started with was that Saudi individuals grow up to be religious or at least with some kind of faith, then go through a disengagement from religion. Here was a disengagement that started when she was a child, which cannot be looked at as a serious disengagement since it happened at such an early stage in her life, at a point when one is not making informed rational decisions on abstract matters of faith. Then the second and genuine conscious disengagement was to return to religion; to transit from nonfaith to faith. But this second transition was due not to the presence of proof but rather to an emotional need. Despite these exceptional aspects, her story presented some of the general themes that we see in most of the other stories: a family whose members are either indifferent to religion or to the religious practices of its members, questioning from an early age, an understanding that one cannot be open about one's convictions, a personal quest for faith, and a loss of faith.

4.1. First: The Childhood and Growing Up Phase

In presenting the stories, I begin by showing the way my interlocutors spoke about their religious life as children. Most of the interviewees were from families for whom religion was significant, yet the role of religion differed within these families. Some attempted to impose piety on the child, other families were religious but did not attempt to impose piety on the child. For still others, religion was not a significant matter at the parent's level, and some families were not religious at all.

4.1.1. Religious Families Who Impose Religion on Their Children

The way three of my interlocutors—Adnan, Ibrahim, and Abdulrahman—spoke about the imposition of a religious lifestyle on them was somewhat similar and also not very surprising to me as one who grew up knowing many such families. There are of course relevant differences in their stories. One main difference is the urban background and level of education of each family. Adnan was born in the 1980s into a middle-class family in a village in the south of Saudi Arabia. He grew up without electricity in the village, and people there had to use electric generators. For him, access to television in his childhood was a luxury because of the challenges of accessing electricity. Ibrahim was born in the 1990s in a lower-income family in a suburban setting. Abdulrahman was born in the 1990s into an upper-middle-class, highly educated family in the United States. The level of education of the three families was significantly different. Adnan's father had an elementary education, which was quite advanced compared to the other people of his peers, who Adnan said were mostly illiterate. Ibrahim's father had an elementary education, while Abdulrahman's father was a science professor educated in the United States.

The way each family imposed religion in the household was similar, which is not surprising, as they were following one religious norm: Salafism. Two similarities stood out: the first was the limitation on entertainment and the other was the limitation on interaction with society. With regard to the former, music, for example, was strictly forbidden in each of the three homes. Adnan told me that the first time he had ever listened to a song completely was when he was about 11 years old. Prior to that, he would listen to bits and pieces from passing cars. His father not only banned music in the house but also prevented Adnan from collecting musical cassettes or listening to music in secret, and when Adnan was caught listening to music his father broke the cassette player and destroyed the tapes. Adnan, of course, did not stop listening. Ibrahim said that the only form of entertainment allowed in his house was a computer game, and it was only later that he was allowed to watch television at home, and even then this was limited to football matches and religious channels. Abdulrahman's home was even stricter, and did not have television at the time I interviewed him at the end of 2013.

With regard to social interaction, out of the three the one who experienced the strictest parenting was Abdulrahman. His father would discourage him from interacting with his extended family because, in Abdulrahman's words, "of their lack of religion, since they listened to music." This form of restriction from family was unthinkable for Adnan and Ibrahim's families, whose restrictions were limited to avoiding neighborhood friends, unless these friends were religious. The way each of the three recalled these restrictions differed. Adnan and Ibrahim did not describe them in a negative way. They remember that it was mainly a normal parental measure to protect them from bad habits that one can pick up in the streets. But Abdulrahman reported that he grew up feeling estranged from everyone, often feeling that he was a person on the right path among people committing wrongs and sins.

Of the three, only Adnan mentioned having questions about faith as a child. He recalled that his first existential question was "What does Allah benefit from our worship? Why do we pray?" He was 13 at the time, and to question praying is common in the early teenage years, but the way he framed his question was less common. He would say:

> Well, ok, there is someone who lets others work for him, so they produce, so he makes money, but why do I pray? What does Allah benefit from my prayers, what is the exact benefit? Or is it just like this?

Here his underlying logic was not merely tackling the duty of praying; rather it was related to the whole concept of religious duty toward Allah. For Adnan, to command someone to do something must have some benefit for the commander, otherwise it would be a futile command. Although his questions would later come back, Adnan reported that this form of questioning did not last long nor keep him up at night. Indeed, he would soon find himself fully immersed in a religious lifestyle, as we shall see.

4.1.2. Religious Families Who Do Not Impose Religion on Their Children

Not all religious parents imposed religion on their children. The interlocutors here—Lina, Uthman, and Yasir—experienced no restrictions to entertainment or limitations to social interaction. Two issues here were mainly brought up by my interlocutors. The first was limiting those who wanted to impose religion on the household, and the second was coping with a life made up of piety and sin.

Lina was born in the 1970s into a wealthy family, and she grew up in a cosmopolitan environment. Lina's family was not religious during the early part of her childhood, although her extended family was extremely religious; some of her female cousins never went to school, as it they considered it a sin. She grew up neither praying the five obligatory prayers of Islam nor seeing her father pray; a most grave sin according to all Muslims (bin Baz, n.d.-g). She even said that the very concept of the mosque did not even exist in her mind, as it was not a part of her life as a child in any way. She used to celebrate Christmas with her Christian neighbors[4] and wore a swimsuit in mixed pools and at private beaches; all un-Islamic practices. But when she was about 14 Lina's older sister turned to religion and she influenced the home. The father started praying and soon became very religious, even memorizing the whole Quran by heart. Lina said the father, however, never imposed religion on her, and the only tension that grew in the house was from her sister, who tried to enforce religiosity on everyone in the household. The father wanted Lina to be more religious, but he did not press on this and reprimanded his religious daughter.

Uthman was born in the 1970s into a middle-class family in a large city. He grew up in a traditional environment, but his father never imposed religion in the home, nor did he allow others to do so. His father is a Bedouin and, Uthman said, was more concerned with social behavior than religion; with "the knowledge of men" or "ʿulum al-rijal," as they call it; that is, the social etiquette that a man should know when interacting with other men. The father would never allow any of his religious relatives or neighbors to give religious advice when there was a social event at their home; instead, he was concerned with telling and hearing stories.

Yasir was born in the 1980s into an upper-middle-class family, and grew up in an environment that was cosmopolitan and traditional at the same time. One of his challenges growing up was navigating between both settings.

Lina did not feel that she needed to struggle with the coexistence of piety and sin in her life, because she herself was never religious. Yasir

---

4. This was and still is possible for some of those who live in gated communities.

and Uthman, however, spoke of this as a problem that lasted from early childhood to young adulthood. Both decided to become religious because it seemed to be the right thing to do. Uthman was more explicit, saying that he became religious because people respected religious young men, and he wanted to be respected. Yasir said that from his early childhood he saw his father mixing sin and spirituality in a way that made it almost natural, and to some degree guilt-free. Yasir summarized this when saying, "My father listens to al-Shuraym when going up to Mecca . . . and plays Abu Bakr Salim when going down."[5] This image of listening to the Quran when going to Mecca and then to music when coming back conjures the contradictions that many Saudis see in their personal religious experience. For Yasir, the contradiction was in being able to maneuver between sin and obedience. His father commits sins in his life, but at the same time respects religious symbolism. So when he is driving to Mecca to pray at the mosque or perform the ʿUmra, he listens to the Quran. If the father is driving to Mecca without the intention of performing a ritual, such as to visit a friend, he listens to music. The father believes music is *haram*, but he likes to listen to it and he does it in a way that minimizes his sense of guilt. This was Yasir's situation.

Uthman grew up as religious boy, not because his father or mother pushed him toward it but because he wanted to be a good boy, and the meaning of a good boy was to be religious. The drive here was in a way an attempt to conform in the hope of getting social approval. I later discovered from my interviewees that conformity was a major driver toward religion for many of them. But Uthman was never either extreme nor fully observant of religious mandates. Instead, he would listen to music and watch television, both of which are sins that always made him feel guilty. With Yasir's family, navigating between sin and guilt was considered the norm, but this did not occur in Uthman's case.

4.1.3. Nonreligious Families

The details of the religious experience of my interlocutors whose families were not religious at all were sparse. They had no religious experience in their childhood homes to talk about. In the cases of two of my

---

5. Saud al-Shuraym (1964–) is a famous alim who leads the prayers at the Mecca Grand Mosque, and his Quranic recitals are widely distributed because of his appealing voice and style, while Abu Bakr Salim (1939–) is a famous singer of Yemeni origin.

interlocutors, Rakan and Ahmad, the central feature was the absence of a religious life and hatred of the *mutawwiʿ* (pious people). No one forced them to be religious, they did not live the tension between believing that an act was sinful while committing it at the same time, and there was no significant family member who was religious and trying to preach.

Rakan was born in the 1990s into an upper-class traditional family in a major city. His father was openly nonreligious: he neither prayed nor fasted, and was open about this position in a society that preferred discretion when committing sin. His father would sometimes mock religion although, Rakan said, he was still a believer.

In Rakan's case, the hatred of the *mutawwiʿ* stemmed only from his father. Other members of his family respected them but did not want to be like them. But Ahmad's family was different. He was born in the 1990s into a middle-class family and grew up in a major city. He told me that of all his immediate and extended family only one person became a *mutawi*, but even that person changed back to being "normal"—"*adi*," in his own words—after having a bad experience with the Committee. By normal he meant that they were indifferent to the religiosity of others and that they practiced their rituals without zeal.

The three types of family and the key issues that my interlocutors brought up do not say much about their transformations toward religion or away from it, and that is precisely why their narrative was important. Some of them grew up with much religious restriction, others were totally indifferent to religion, and still others were concerned with religion but navigated between it and sinful practices. There were families who respected piety and those who detested the pious, all of which is part of the lives of many other Saudis. There is one question that I need to ask here and then answer in the conclusion of this chapter. In the cases of people like Ahmad and Lina, who were never religious, could one speak of disengagement?

4.2. Second: Turning Toward Religion

The turn toward religion seems to be a common trait among many Saudis regardless of their religious experience during childhood. This was certainly the case with my interlocutors, most of whom had experienced such a turn, albeit with different individual details. Perhaps the reason has to do with the fact that being religious is considered a positive trait among a good majority of Saudis. One of my interlocutors, Muadh, born in the

1990s into a middle-class urban family, whose father was not religious, told me that when he turned toward religion his father was happy because of the prevalence in his community of the concept of *"al-walad al-salih"* (pious offspring). That is the belief that those who have pious offspring will ultimately be better positioned on the Day of Judgment. The central characteristic I found among their stories was the "group." Most of them became religious through previous membership of a social group, or became part of a group after turning to religion. I consider this central to their change due to the way they discussed belonging to the group. As I went through the interviews I noticed that multiple interviewees repeatedly noted the role of the group as a central factor in the progress of their transformation toward religion. It was not a cause of that transformation, according to their descriptions, but without it—according to them—the process of change may have not started or moved in the direction that it did. There were, however, those who turned toward religion without any form of group belonging. I start with these individuals.

4.2.1. Individual Transformation

Lara and ʿUthman's turn to religion were individual. Lara's home, like Uthman's, was religious but did not impose religiosity. Another common trait in their homes was that the parents did not seek fatwa for every small religious detail. Lara said that if her father considered music *halal* then as far she was concerned it was *halal*, even if the prevalent fatwa among Saudis was that it was *haram*. She also remembered her father telling her that it was best to take fatwa from Egyptian ulama rather than from Wahhabi ulama, as he considered the former more moderate and rational in their fatwas.

ʿUthman's father was religious, but, ʿUthman said, "in an independent way." He explained it by saying that although his father was illiterate, he made his own religious choices in matters of jurisprudence. For example, when it rained, the father would pray at home instead of praying at the mosque, even though praying at the mosque is considered by Wahhabis a duty for any Muslim who lives within walking distance (WAS, 2010). Another choice his father made related to fasting; during Ramadan, Muslims are supposed to stop eating once the call for Fajr prayer is announced. But the father would allow his children to eat until the call for prayer ended and for some minutes after. The examples that ʿUthman mentioned relate to minor religious issues, and there is room for differences of opinion in them among Muslim ulama; yet they are still significant. The father was making religious choices without the credentials to do so: credentials set by tradition and emphasized by the ulama (IslamWeb, 2009). This behavior seems to express independence from religious authority and hints at some limited form of individual religiosity, all the more notable given the father's illiteracy.

The turn of both of them to religion was through individual experience. Lara said it was a result of reading books written by Muslim mystics such as Abu Hamid al-Ghazali (c.1056–1111) and listening to some of the popular preachers of the 1990s, such as Amr Khalid (b. 1967), Ali al-Jifri (b. 1971), and Tariq al-Suwaydan (b. 1953). Subsequently she started attending religious sessions led by female preachers. But the preachers she knew were focusing more on the spiritual aspect of religion. By spiritual she meant an emphasis on loving Allah rather than a more ritualistic or legal focus on duty to Allah.

ʿUthman had grown up religious, as we saw earlier, because he wanted people to praise him. His transformation was toward a more intense religious experience. When he was at secondary school the whole neighborhood changed; this was around 1984, during the peak of the activities of the Salafi Islamic movement in Saudi Arabia—*al-Sahwa al-Islamiyya*, or the Islamic Awakening. *Halaqat al-Tahfidh*—seminars for memorizing the Quran—increased, and religious summer camps multiplied. Even his father turned to religion, ceasing to listen to music, though he did not force ʿUthman to do so. During this time ʿUthman's religiosity increased: "I remember at that time I would listen to music and afterward feel guilty . . . I would cry . . . I would masturbate and feel great guilt and cry." He found comfort in praying as it gave him a sense of purification. He said his life was like a cycle of self-inflicted impurity and then purification through praying. His increase in religiosity was in restricting himself from the actions he believed were sinful. But he said there was no commitment on his side to the authority of the ulama; it was a personal relationship between him and Allah and he did not want the ulama to intrude.

4.2.2. Transformation with Group Belonging

Most of the people I interviewed experienced religion through belonging to a group, and the main difference in their stories was the relationship between belonging to a religious group and being religious. Qasim and Rakan wanted to be religious, and being part of a group was a way to support that. Adnan and Muadh, on the other hand, wanted to be part of a group, and being religious was their way of sustaining that belonging. But whatever the reasons for joining the group, this social structure imposed itself on each of them, influencing how they behaved, their access to knowledge, and their sense of well-being.

The groups to which my interlocutors belonged emphasized control over exposure to unsanctioned knowledge. Qasim was born in the 1980s into an educated upper-middle-class urban family. He told me that when he was between 15 and 16 years old he found it problematic that none of the books he read in science had any mention of Allah in them. He would wonder how nature and physics could be explained without resort to a deity. At the same time he also began to ask, "Why is there a god?" During that time he coincidentally came across a book that sought to establish a link between science and Allah. "Today," he said, "when I read it I find it a normal book, but at that time it silenced my questions." He recollected that he was reprimanded by one of the supervisors in his religious group for reading such a book as it was considered too complicated for his age, and he was told that he should not concern himself with issues of theology. In any case, he said, for a time that book answered his questions:

Whenever I would get questions I remind myself of the book. Though I would not remember the contents it was enough for me to say, "this has been answered."

This statement is quite interesting in that it reveals that his confidence in his faith was not based on his own personal understanding, but rather on the confidence that someone else understood. He himself told me that he wanted to mention this particular story because it exemplified his relationship with belief: he was believing because others whom he considered authorities also did.

Qasim, whose family was religious but not imposing, came to religion through his participation in extracurricular school activities during his high school years, yet he was not very committed to the group and soon found himself practicing religious rituals alone. He spent long hours in the mosque and sometimes the full day praying, contemplating and reciting the Quran. These practices, he said, created a deep relationship between him and the mosque in which he spent so much time. Today, he said, although the mosque is no longer a sacred place for him it is nonetheless a site of fond memories that he visits to relive. He said, "If they change the mosque's structure I will not go any more." Rakan's experience was similar. He said that he was genuinely and deeply pious. He went through two phases in his relationship to the Islamic group to which he belonged. The first was simply preaching and teaching, whereby he participated as a disciple in religious seminars and various activities such as sports, group pilgrimages, and the theater. The second phase was when he became a member and was given extra duties, such as supervising activities or making efforts to attract fresh recruits. He used to attend the group meetings in both phases secretly, as his father hated *mutawwiʿs* and did not want his son to mingle with them.

Rakan added something important. He said that the groups "filled our time with activity: intellectual discussions and entertainment." Indeed, part of his pleasure from his membership was derived from the sense of belonging to a group and the sense of self-importance it nurtured in him. He added that by belonging to these groups he developed a "sense of place in this world . . . a sense of mission." So piety was not the immediate appeal for him when belonging to these groups, even though he soon found himself moving in that direction. He became very pious and would not sleep before he had spent time listening to religious lectures from various ulama. He considered leaving home because the household members in his view were not ritually observant. He even became a *muʾezzin*[6] in a neighborhood mosque and realized that this made him more socially respected.

Adnan's initial motivation to join a religious group was loneliness. A very close cousin of his had died and he needed company. Oddly enough, he joined a religious group while having religious doubts. The death of his cousin made him ask questions such as, "What the heck is Allah doing?" Nevertheless, he went ahead and joined a local religious center, where he found people with whom he could have fun, as he described it, "I wanted to fool around but I could not leave home," as his father would not let him go anywhere he deemed unsafe. His father was comfortable with the religious centers, so he let his son join them. He comments on this saying, "We had nowhere to go except these places . . . no safe haven for young individuals . . . where you are valued." For Adnan, membership of

---

6. A person who recites the Muslim call to prayer.

this group was not about religiosity per se but rather about finding a so-cial group and building self-esteem. He said that he was especially excited to be treated as a peer by people whom he saw at that age as important people. He then decided to put his questions aside and become more reli-gious. Adnan was very clear about the social motivation of his religiosity: it was about belonging to a group. He even said that many members of the group were not religious and committed various grave sins such as prac-ticing homosexuality, but that did not matter to him. He soon became the imam of a mosque near his home, which would fill up with people to listen to his recital of the Quran.

Adnan said that once a friend of his who had become a member of the Committee invited him to volunteer with him in "forbidding vice"; that is, to drive around in the Committee car and reprimand or even detain anyone committing a sin. His friend was not religious but he enjoyed the authority that came with the position. Adnan accepted the invitation and used to patrol the streets calling on people to pray. "We had such a sense of authority." His friend, not being religious, was not particularly strict, even allowing unmarried couples who were "caught dating" to stay together instead of reporting them. Adnan's experience was one in which religion was mixed with self-interest, claims to authority, and pressure to conform. He did not describe religion as an inner experience so much as a process of group identification through the observance of particular norms and behaviors.

Muadh also emphasized the role of the group in his religious experi-ence. He went to a school that included in the curriculum memorizing the Quran—known as *madaris al-tahfidh*. Such schools gave out stipends to their students to encourage more enrollment (al-Jarid, n.d.). Following his enrollment he noticed that his local community treated him with higher regard because he now appeared to be more pious. But he also found in the *madaris al-tahfidh* a place to express his talents. Like Adnan, his turn to religiosity meshed with his interests: the stipend served his financial interests, social respect built his self-esteem, and the opportunity to use his talents produced personal satisfaction. He said that he decided to leave the *madaris al-tahfidh* when he was in 10th grade. He wanted to create new friendships with nonreligious people. "I wanted people like me . . . but I did not want to go astray . . . I still had a strong religious impulse." Here he was clear about the effect of the group. He wanted friends, but could only find friends in his original religious group, so he went back to them. There was no religious motivation for him to remain in the group.

"It was not like you can either go to an Islamic group or instead go and learn music!" He said that there were no alternative youth activities, and even some of the nonreligious people he knew encouraged him to attend activities organized by religious centers because they were thought to be important for one's personal development.

Like Adnan, Muadh spoke of the attractiveness of power and authority. Sometimes when they were studying with an alim their teacher would tell them to go to a "*shisha* [hookah cafés] to forbid the sins." *Shishas* are considered places of sin, even more when they show films on television or play music. He went on to say, "We would go and everyone would listen . . . they would turn off the television. . . . I started to feel like I was a soldier." Like Adnan, he was clear that the sense of belonging was stronger than the sense of spirituality. "The bottom line for [the group leaders] was that we attended the class; the bottom line for us was the football match afterwards." Even his view of what was sinful was defined by the group:

> The things that we forbade were determined by those from above . . . we did not forbid a bank because no one told us to do so . . . if we were told, we would have gone . . . we were soldiers.

He was specific about the sins to which they paid attention. He said that they were not all grave sins but rather those that the group leaders focused on. The sins that he remembered focusing on were fornication (*zina*), homosexuality, satellite dishes, and shaving. He explained it by saying that the group associated these practices with sin, while other sins such as *riba* were not part of his focus. He once passed a video store with someone senior from the group. That person told him to spit at the store, and he obeyed and spat. "They made us feel different . . . important." They would also reprimand anyone in the group who ate at a local restaurant, as one should not sit among less pious people. Instead, he would order his food and eat out on the pavement.

The six experiences discussed with regard to the turn to religiosity are distinct in one main way: the effect of the group in the experience of religiosity. We can see that religiosity was performed not only for purposes of piety but rather to conform to a group that could provide various forms of benefit for its members. In the case of those who belonged to a group, this dynamic is clear, yet one can also argue that 'Uthman's piety had a broader social value as he wanted to be perceived as a good boy. Moreover, the turn to religion was not always made through a group; it often occurred through individual learning such as reading. Finally even those who said they became religious for purely utilitarian reasons reported a genuine experience of piety.

4.2.3. Disengagement from Religion

The experiences so far discussed are quite ordinary, whether they are stories of childhood or of subsequent turns to Islam. Crucially, however, all of the individuals I mentioned earlier, and others I speak of later, underwent various forms of religious transformation to something that was less apparent in a Saudi context; that is they detached themselves from religion. I want to say at this point that I did not see this ordinariness at first. Even after I transcribed and summarized my interviews with them I was still looking for something exceptional, for something that would indicate their future change and make the stories of their childhood and their first experiences with religion more exciting. Yet none of them experienced epiphanies or dramatic spiritual experiences, nor did many become religious after a deep and intense intellectual experience with theology or spirituality. Their levels of knowledge varied, but it was not a main factor in their experiences at that point.

Another thing I came to notice somewhat later was the individual nature of the disengagement that all of them underwent. Each one was disengaging from religion alone, so to speak; only one case emphasized the role of dialogue—Nura—in crystallizing her ideas. There was no public discussion going on criticizing religion that influenced them, nor were there public salons where those interested in religious criticism could attend and in the process change. Those who had belonged to a group emphasized leaving the group as a critical milestone in their change but not as a central driver of that change. Just as importantly, although each person acknowledged from the outset that the change had happened gradually, all of them when discussing their stories mentioned one critical milestone, but not one mentioned a specific turning point. That milestone did not create the change itself, but it oriented each one of them to a new course in their religious thinking and made them much more receptive to the ideas critical of religion to which they were later exposed. In what follows I will mention the key milestones that played a marked role in the religious disengagement of interlocutors.

4.2.3.1. Near-Death Experience

Lara's change can be characterized by a state of indifferent belief promoted by a near-death experience due to eclampsia, a condition that effects pregnant women and can sometimes lead to death. After she had recovered she asked herself, "I was close to dying, should I now live piously or enjoy what remains of life? I chose the second without a second thought." Her choice was peculiar in a religious culture where one would be expected to choose piety after facing death. She even wondered about her choice, saying, "One is supposed to be grateful" and thus one should choose the path of piety, but she felt that life is too short and she wanted to enjoy it. Initially she only withdrew from religious activities and reduced her ritual practice, stopping praying although she continued to fast throughout Ramadan. This situation of indifference to religiosity continued for many years.

Her disengagement entered a new phase when, by coincidence, she watched a program about atheists who had turned religious (al-ʿAwadhi, 2012). The presenter of this program, Muhammad al-ʿAwadhi (b. 1959), is a very popular Kuwaiti preacher who focuses on atheism, particularly since 2011 after the news that it was spreading in Saudi Arabia. In this particular program, al-ʿAwadhi was trying to prove the validity of religion by presenting the reasons individuals left religion and then returned to it. His purpose was to vindicate religion, but for Lara the effect was different. The reasons he presented for their leaving religion were more convincing to her than the reasons that led them back to it. Moreover, it opened her mind to ideas and questions she had never considered before. Prior to that, her most serious theological question had been about hell. She could not comprehend the idea of people burning in hell regardless of their sin, let alone fathom why some people would burn because of personal actions that hurt no one such as fornication, not wearing the hijab, or listening to music. Now she was listening to ideas about the very existence of Allah and the validity of the Prophecy. This, she said, made her come "out of the box and look from the other side." Now, as she explained, she was able to see new details of religion that she had not paid attention to before.

Following that experience she came across Hasan al-Maliki, the Saudi scholar of religion mentioned earlier, who is very critical of the traditional historical narrative about the era of the Prophet and the first two centuries after. His intention in critiquing that era is to reform Islam, but the effect on her differed. Part of al-Maliki's method depended on discrediting many of the key figures in the formative period of Islamic history who in his opinion played a role in distorting the authentic Islam of the Prophet. While many of his readers found this helpful, Lara said, "I saw the ugly picture in history . . . the perfect picture I had of that generation collapsed" and this was, in her words, "the first stone to roll." Her faith was premised on the purity of many of the figures al-Maliki discredited.

The final straw for Lara was "Rashid the Christian," a Christian polemicist of Moroccan origin who has a show called "Daring Question" that is posted on YouTube (Brotherrachid, n.d.; Rachid, n.d.). The program aims to show the falsity of Islam by exposing historical facts about the Prophet and the influence of Christianity on him. Rashid also presents theological arguments that criticize some of the theological tenets of Islam. Lara said that she came across him by coincidence. She was looking on YouTube for material on the Prophet's Celestial Ascension (al-Isra' wa-l-Mi'raj). Rashid the Christian had one episode on this matter that came up in her search, so she listened to it. thinking it would be an explanation of the event. Instead of someone explaining the event, however, she found a program that traced the roots of the story back to legends in other cultures (al-Hayat TV, 2013). This partially discredited the Quran for Lara and instilled doubt in her faith.

Then she moved on to the stars of atheism on YouTube; Richard Dawkins, Daniel Dennet, and Sam Harris. She said she also found them by coincidence while doing various searches for different lectures on religion. She did not read any of their writing, confining herself to listening to their debates with religious people. This experience on its own further decreased her confidence in the idea of religion.

This all happened to her very quickly in less than a year. But it was all happening to her on her own. She never participated in online discussions, nor spoke about it to anyone. She did want to speak with others who shared her doubts, but did not find anyone whom she could trust with sharing such thoughts. She went through various emotions of anger and anxiety. She was angry because she felt she had been deluded by the ideas that she had previously believed. She wondered about the consequences of her change and the influence on her life. She had nightmares, and some nights she could not sleep. But that did not last long. She soon relaxed and told her husband. He was not happy with her change, but he only made it a condition that their children should not hear such ideas from her. She was not a militant atheist and was not keen on preaching to anyone, even to her children, so she accepted his condition. Moreover she wanted them to grow up and make their own decisions.

4.2.3.2. Resolution of Guilt

Yasir's change was precipitated by his search to resolve the seeming contradiction he felt between his sinful life and his desire to be pious. He said this feeling of dissonance gradually grew in him until it overtook him and even to the point that he felt tense reading a novel written by an unbeliever. He would enjoy the story and then he would tell himself, "But he is a *kafir!*" His peers, who were also religious, did not experience this tension, and he wanted to resolve it. Accordingly, he turned to the history of early Islam, particularly the story of the third caliph 'Uthman bin 'Affan (577–656), who was murdered by some companions of the Prophet. People usually read stories about the Prophet's companions to gain religious inspiration, but for Yasir the story actually made him live better with his sin. The story of 'Uthman bin 'Affan erased his image of the perfection of that era and helped him to improve his image of himself. Previously he would tell himself that the Companions of the Prophet were saints, role models that a good Muslim should aspire to be like. This changed when he started seeing them as normal people who committed all sorts of sins. "If the closest companions of the Prophet committed grave sins," he would tell himself, "then I should not be too hard on myself when I commit sins."

Yasis continued seeking a resolution to his sense of guilt, while aspiring to find happiness through religiosity, but he said nothing worked for him. This depressed him, as he had grown up believing that the only path to happiness was religion, and he became suicidal. So he tried Sufism; he thought that its spirituality might provide him with the happiness that he sought. He enjoyed the Sufi rituals; they were "beautiful . . . artistic," but he soon felt that they provided him "with no logical answers."

He then attended Harmonious Being sessions, where he felt comfortable with his questions about faith. At one of these sessions he listened to a discussion about a story mentioned in the Quran, which describes a pious man who saw a dead animal and wondered if Allah could bring this animal back to life. Allah, according to the story, put the man to death for a hundred years and then brought him back to life. When he had risen from the dead, the man became certain of the power of Allah to revive the dead (Quran: al-Baqarah, 259). Yasir said that from this story he derived the lesson that Allah would not punish him for questioning. "Even you Yasir, Allah will not pick on you. This is a guarantee card! Go and search!" he told himself. He decided to leave the country for a couple of years and enrolled in the Saudi scholarship program, choosing to move to a Western country. There, he became comfortable with his questions. He would say that in Saudi Arabia you are:

> in a big club . . . with twenty million people. It is, you know, too frightening to leave that . . . to say that only I am right and all of them are wrong . . . it is not easy.

Being in a Western city meant for him that he had joined a new club, and was fully free to think differently from the members of his previous one. That new city, in turn, contained all kinds of ideas and beliefs. He could now choose whatever he saw best without feeling different and with the confidence that he was not alone. I pointed at the end of chapter 2 to some of the coping strategies religious people followed when they found themselves in a situation where their religious teachings contradicted their behavior. Some ceased to engage in their behavior, while others chose to abandon the belief that deemed their behavior unacceptable (Mahaffy, 1996). Yasir's resolution was to abandon his belief.

4.2.3.3. Tension Between Islam and Sensibility

Nura was born in the 1990s into a very educated middle-class urban family. She grew up in a moderately religious house and she herself was quite religious in her teenage years. She traced her disengagement from religion to her first experiences at the age of 16, when she recognized the tension between her inner moral values and particular Islamic legislation such as the historical practice of slavery and the social standing of women. The first she knew of through reading history books of early Islam, and the second through her personal experience as a woman growing up in Saudi Arabia. She was disgusted by the practice of slavery and asked her teacher about it. She could not fathom that the Companions of the Prophet, a generation she had grown up to hold in reverence and respect, would enslave people. Her teacher tried to convince her, though she said "I think I was convinced . . . or I wanted to be convinced . . . I needed to be convinced."

Nura noted that the situation of women in Islam, especially in Saudi Arabia, had more impact on her than the issue of slavery. Slavery was detested, but it remained for her a distant and abstract idea, while the status of women was an immediate everyday experience. "Let me tell you, the situation of women is very much connected to the causes of atheism." Her deep rejection of that situation would evolve into a rejection of the religion that in her view allowed ill-treatment of women to continue. "I think for women this influences [their relation to religion] . . . perhaps not men because they don't feel it." It was clear that she was facing tension here between a religious sensibility and a religious culture. Her sensibility rejected slavery and the treatment of women in Saudi, while her religious culture accepted both.

Coinciding with these doubts, she came across The Liberal Saudi Network while browsing the Internet. The written discussions she had with Saudis from different parts of the Saudi cultural and religious spectrum helped her to develop her ideas. She said that the first change she recognized in herself was when she consciously acknowledged the legitimacy of other opinions, no matter how heretical they sounded to her. Before that, she had considered different opinions as "mere whims without any solid intellectual foundation, produced by people who want to justify their lustful behaviour." Liberals and some religious reformers in Saudi Arabia—and other Muslim communities—are often accused of wanting to liberate themselves from the prohibitions of Allah on certain pleasures. After interacting with different books and people, she gradually changed. While this may seem trivial to an external observer, it was a major step for her because she was deeply convinced that there was only one version of Truth, and it was the version in which she believed.

After entering college, Nura said, bigger issues surfaced and she engaged with fellow students in philosophical discussions concerning metaphysics and morality. But the one issue that had the deepest impact on her was that of moral relativism. "Those debates made me reach a break-off point not only from Islam but even all religions." She said that moral relativism was used by some of her apologist friends to justify Islamic legislation that is not accepted today such as slavery. Muslims had been justifying the continuity of slavery in Islam in various ways. The main justification was that Islam had improved the treatment of slaves, limited the means of acquiring slaves, and encouraged the freeing of slaves (Alwan, 2004; Usmani, 2013). Such justifications could be true and have been attested by Western scholars of Islam (Clarence-Smith, 2006; Lewis, 1992), although not for the purpose of justifying slavery or defending Islam for having assumed the practice. These justifications were not always accepted, so some of her friends resorted to moral relativism, claiming that slavery was an accepted practice in the social context of Islam 1400 years ago, which is why Islam assumed it and did not eradicate it completely. But that did not help her to accept that a moral religion such as Islam would accept an immoral act such as slavery. Moral relativism instead convinced her that there was no hope of reforming religion. Her conclusion was that religion itself is relative, and thus should not be expected to play a role in modern times, as the values of individuals have fundamentally changed.

Nura's experience highlights the factor of being a woman in her disengagement. Unlike the case of Lara, her gender activated in her a set of underlying morals that had no religious basis. Had her moral sensibilities been developed by religious precepts, she may have not experienced this tension. Unlike some of the other the individuals I have discussed earlier, Nura was an intellectual, and her process of change was based on reading and discussion. She needed a solid foundation for her new course.

4.2.3.4. Tension Between Islam and Islam

Hana was born into a middle-class educated suburban family. She grew up in a very religious house that imposed expectations of religious belief and practice on its members. She became quite "extreme"—in her own terms—to the point that she used to consider Shi̇ a unbelievers and would wonder why they were not simply "exterminated." She also despised those who listened to music and women who wore trousers.

Hana traced her transformation to a discussion on *hijab* that revealed what for her was a tension within Islam. She was brought up to believe that there was only one correct opinion in Islam and that no two opposing opinions could be equally valid or legitimate. So when it came to the hijab the only correct opinion was that of veiling the face by way of the *niqab* was a duty, and that proceeding unveiled was wrong. When she was 14 years old, she heard for the first time that there were credible Muslim scholars who believed that covering the face was not compulsory. For her, this came as a pleasant surprise. "This for me was something very beautiful . . . for the first time I realized that there is difference of opinion in religion." When she discussed the matter with her father, who was a teacher of religion, he dismissed it and firmly told her that there was no such thing as a difference in opinion in matters of religion and that there was only one right opinion. She left the matter at that, but a year later she read an online discussion on music. The discussion, in her words:

> really changed me . . . it showed me that religion is not as we had thought . . . that not everyone is simply wrong . . . this also shook my confidence in what my father said . . . and I felt I had been tricked.

For the next 3 to 4 years, Hana continued to ponder differences of opinion within religion. This was a disorienting matter for her, as she had never thought that such an aspect existed in religion. Her sense of being tricked had the effect of discrediting religious authorities to whom she had previously listened, and during that period she came across a book that was circulating online as a PDF, *Wu'adh al-Salatin* (The Sultans' Advisers), by Ali al-Wardi (1913–1995) (1995). This book, which detailed the corruption of religious ulama who provide dictators with religious justification for their actions, had a significant impact on Hana. 'It made me doubt the holiness of people. . . . I would see people through their interests and greed." This desacralization extended to the Companions of the Prophet. She was surprised by the normal way the author spoke about that generation, which she had grown up revering. The mere fact that the author discussed their lives as normal people was an eye-opener for her. Saudis, and perhaps most Muslims, are used to speaking about the Prophet and his Companions as suprahuman, or at least with deep reverence. Their lives were not presented as the lives of normal people who can be criticized, but rather as the lives of saintly people who are to inspire us and guide us.

She was also deterred by the hate that was required to people of other faiths. In Saudi Arabia the concept of *al-Wala' wa-l-Bara'* (loyalty and disavowal) is deeply rooted in the religious education of Salafism and the educational curricula of Saudi Arabia (Khalijyyah, 2012; al-Qahtani, 1992; Shavit, 2014). Its essential requirement is that one should hate nonbelievers and impious people. Yet Nura asked, "Why should I hate everything that is different? . . . it exhausted me." Her comfort came when she realized through Twitter that there were many people who thought like her. She was at first surprised to find that many other Saudis thought like her, and she started contacting them directly.

Her faith was now shaken, and the more she read the more doubt she had. She said "For a long time, I asked Allah to guide me to the right way, wherever it was." She would go and sit alone on the roof of her home, think, and ask Allah for guidance. She was afraid, but she felt she could not return to her old religiosity or her previous religious convictions. Her final step was that she started reading philosophy, where she found the material worldview more convincing. At that point she decided to cast doubt on religion but she retained her faith in Allah.

4.2.3.5. Seeking an Easier Islam

Ziyad was born in the 1980s in a middle-class suburban family. The starting point for Ziyad was different, as he sought faith in a different form and ended up criticizing its roots. Ziyad grew up as a religious person with a religious family and belonged to a religious group, yet he had questions during his teenage years. For example, he would ask himself about the validity of Islam, and wonder if Christianity was more valid. But he would quickly dismiss such questions and say to himself this was the devil trying to mislead him, and he would curse him; in response, he would engage in activities that could reaffirm his faith such as watching videos that sought to show that the Quran reveals scientific facts that were only discovered in the 20th century, the conclusion of which is that the Quran is indeed the word of Allah, for the Prophet would not have been able to know such facts in the seventh century (al-Najjar, 2006). While he was in 11th grade he decided to become religious and he befriended a religious group. Ziyad had a car, and the group assigned tasks that needed driving to him. This gave him a sense of importance and he quickly rose in their ranks until he became the supervisor of the group's cultural programs, staying with them for 3 years.

At this time he became aware of the opinions of religious scholars who considered listening to Islamic songs permissible. Music is prohibited and is considered a very serious sin by Saudi ulama, as I have mentioned, but I want to add here that the main reason for prohibiting music is musical instruments. If a song is played without instruments, it is considered permissible to listen to it, and that is what Ziyad used to do. But then under the influence of non-Saudi religious activists the opinion spread that one can listen to songs with musical instruments if, and only if, the lyrics are religious and the associated music is not too heavy, such as heavy metal; and these were called Islamic songs (Otterbeck, 2014). This opened up much discussion among the religious youth in Saudi Arabia: Ziyad found himself convinced by the argument that allows "Islamic songs." At the same time he was also introduced accidentally to the concept of the "modern Islamist," which was exemplified at the time by Tariq al-Suwaydan (b. 1953), the famous Kuwaiti preacher mentioned before, who had presented himself in a modern appearance and used the vocabulary of self-development to promote religiosity.

Ziyad liked the easy model that al-Suwaydan presented, and he soon trimmed his beard like Suwaydan, listened to Islamic songs, and wore a long *thawb*. He told me that these issues were very significant in determining one's religious position and more importantly they signaled the shift of allegiance from to one group or another. Religious groups, he said, are "circles of ideas, and with each idea you adopt you move into another circle until you reach the outer limit." He looked at religious disengagement as a process whereby one moves from one group to another as one's ideas change. His change became too much to tolerate for the last group to which he belonged, so he was expelled from it. Although he was upset, this provided Ziyad with an opportunity to explore other groups and other ideas more closely. He said that from then on it was a matter of exploring new ideas one after another, and with each exploration he moved a bit further from where he had been prior to that. Soon he considered it permissible to listen to all types of song, which in his view was a fundamental shift in his religious practice. Then he stopped preaching religiosity and turned his attention to intellectual debate. He attended Harmonious Being sessions and was influenced by the style of the open debate on religion. He also participated with some of his friends in setting up a philosophical reading club, which was a fundamental step away from his old religious self, as philosophy is considered heresy in Saudi religiosity, and reading books on philosophy and even logic is prohibited (al-Fawzan, n.d.-c; IslamicoVideos, 2012).

4.2.3.6. Anger at Allah

I have mentioned that Adnan had had serious questions since his early childhood, but he had insisted on believing. He said that when he was 15 he decided to stop believing until he found answers to his questions, particularly relating to evil and the reason Allah requires us to worship Him. He said that he once went into went to a mosque and then left, deciding not to pray until he found answers. But he retracted and started praying, as he was afraid of not believing. This fear was not based on an intellectual conviction. The way he described how he was at the time made it sound as if continuing to believe or not was a decision that he consciously made. Knowledge or evidence, according to him, seemed to matter little. He had no knowledge and no evidence, but he finally decided to hold on to his faith. Actually, knowledge seemed to him to be a problem for his faith. He used to attend lessons on creed at a mosque, and when the teacher started saying things that seemed nonsensical to Adnan he stopped attending the class. One of the things he recalled the teacher saying was that once while the Prophet was praying he saw some grapes, so he reached out and ate them. Adnan thought the story was ridiculous: "Where did the grapes suddenly come from? And how can the Prophet eat while performing a prayer?," he would ask. Hearing such "nonsense"—to use his expression—made him fear for his faith, and he left the teacher and stopped attending the class. Adnan was consciously holding on to his faith, despite the questions he had and the "nonsense" he heard. Indeed, he added that he was not religious at that time; he simply loved Allah and the Prophet and did not want to hear things about them that did not make sense. He had what he described as "a rural religiosity": a simple approach characterized by a personal relationship with Allah and indifference to the complex theological and jurisprudential language of scholars and the ulama.

Adnan's insistence on believing is significant here. He had consciously sought to doubt Allah and then willingly made the decision to retain his faith. Moreover, Adnan had a strong allegiance to his religious group, which happened to be an extremist one; that is until the terrorist attack against the Saudi traffic police which claimed the lives of many officers (MacFarquhar, 2004). Adnan had approved of targeting Americans and foreign embassies and considered killing them legitimate, but when the attacks killed Saudis he changed his attitude to radical violence and left his group.

Now without a group, his doubts surfaced once more, although he still considered himself religious. Soon he graduated from high school and went to a religious university. In the summer of 2004 his 4-year-old sister, to whom he was particularly close, became seriously ill. He would sit near her and cry from grief over her. That was, according to him, the worst phase in his life. His grades plummeted, but also the big questions he had considered for a long time resurfaced forcefully. He said the suffering of children was always the most confusing matter for him: "Why would Allah allow it?" In the past, when that matter surfaced, he would not allow himself to go beyond the question of "Why?" and then he would dismiss the question and curse the devil. But this time it was personal, and he asked himself, "What the heck is Allah doing to my sick sister?" His sister was eventually left blind by her illness, and at that point Adnan decided to cease suppressing his doubts: he blamed Allah for his sister's predicament and his confidence in Allah ended. He repeatedly asked himself, "How is she at fault?"

A few months after his sister's illness he went with a friend to buy novels from a bookstore that sold books banned in Saudi Arabia. There are not many such bookshops in the country, the main such one being *al-Maktaba al-Turathiyya* in Riyadh. While he was looking for novels he came across Friedrich Nietzsche's book *Human, All Too Human* and, thinking it was a novel, bought a copy. He amusingly calls that "the unlucky day." He spoke a lot about the influence of Nietzsche on his religious disengagement. "The danger in Nietzsche's books and the important quality," Adnan said, "is that Nietzsche said what you cannot say, and he said it forcefully." He learned from Nietzsche that humans had invented Allah. He said that he remembered reading, perhaps in one of Nietzsche's works, that "if Allah knew about the idea of Allah he would have laughed at it." Regardless of the source of the statement, Adnan said he agreed with it and adopted it. Reading Nietzsche helped him to articulate a sentiment that he had previously lacked the language to express.

Nietzsche, according to Adnan, spoke to him. He was at the time very angry with Allah and enjoyed reading anything critical of Allah. He said it was odd that he was not afraid of reading such blasphemous works: "I didn't feel fear when I read it . . . no shock . . . it seems I was in a very vengeful state." He said that he was unlike some of the people he knew who were angry at Allah yet feared mocking Him, even if they had decided to disbelieve in Him. Soon enough, he rejected the idea of Allah, became an atheist and even publicly advocated this view. His rejection of Allah was firm, and not even a near-death experience changed him. He had a car accident that almost claimed his life yet he never considered faith an option. "It crossed my mind but I felt silly about it . . . nothing from Allah has happened before . . . so why now?" Allah had meant nothing in his past, and the only Allah he would return to would be that same deity. He thinks that such a firm rejection of Allah was related to the way he had learned about Him; "[Wahhabis] trivialized the idea of Allah . . . they made it so silly . . . this Allah whose job it was to hold you to account for trivial actions but would leave the grand issues." This position regarding Allah after a near-death experience differs from that of Lara, whose choice to not return to faith had more to do with wanting to live life to its fullest. For Adnan it was a philosophical position from the very idea of Allah which he did not want to return to. He also thought that his extreme position against Allah was due to the influence of Nietzsche. Adnan mentioned the influence of the many other angry Saudi atheists that he had met during his college years. They had spent nights talking about the insensibility of faith and ridiculing the idea of Allah. In one phase of his anger to Allah he even refused to say His name socially. For example when someone is asked how he is was doing, the answer is usually "Thanks be to Allah, well." There came a time when he rejected such phrases, but eventually accepted its use. "If you see an atheist who uses the name of Allah then he is in a very mature phase . . . these who are extremely angry don't use it at all."

But Adnan's anger did not last long, as one of his acquaintances introduced him to Bertrand Russell. Adnan said Russell's coolness in dealing with the idea of Allah tempered his anger; Russell's ideas taught him to equate the assumption of Allah's existence to the assumption of His non-existence; and that for him was one central idea which cooled his firm rejection of Allah. Soon he looked at the positions of both faith and nonfaith as equal and he gradually developed an indifference to the whole matter of faith. Adnan said that he had made peace with his faith of the past. He tried to remember the image of Allah as he knew it in his childhood before he was indoctrinated by the religious groups that he joined. He said "I had a nice relationship with Him then. He wasn't like what He became later in our lives . . . that cruel god."

4.2.3.7. The Problem of the Good Kafir and al-Qasimi

Two of the people I interviewed, Muadh and Rakan, stated that a key milestone in their disengagement was being exposed to good *kuffar*. When Muadh entered college he gradually became less religious. He said it had started with him distancing himself from the group to which he belonged. It was not deliberate, he said, more an unintended consequence of neutral decisions. For example, he said that being in college itself limited his daily interaction with his religious group because each of the members had different classes. Then he needed a job, and the demands of the job also limited his ability to spend time with them. But he added that the job itself became a milestone in his change. One of his assignments was to write reports on the content of the liberally oriented Saudi forums that were mushrooming in the early 2000s, and this experience changed him significantly. He said it was the first time he heard the terms "liberal" and "secular." Moreover, he would read in these forums about Western philosophers such as Socrates (c. 469–399 BCE), Baruch Spinoza (1632–1677) and Voltaire (1694–1778), and he was attracted to some of their ideas. He intensified his online reading about philosophers and modern ideas. In his own words:

> From there on I started reading everything from all sites. I had no decision, no direction, no name, no categorization. I just wanted to read and read and read as if to make up for lost time. My brain was like a burst pipe. Unconsciously, I was saying "This is right."

After this experience he withdrew from his religious life, but he said his ideas did not change. All that had happened to him was that he had become, in his own words, "like the average Saudi." At this point he still believed that Saudi society was an ideal society and that Islam was the most perfect of religions, and when he listened to music he still felt that he was sinning and prayed to Allah to forgive him.

In 2005, Muadh decided to continue his studies abroad in a Western country, and he stayed outside Saudi Arabia until 2009. This experience exposed him to people living a lifestyle totally different to that which he knew. He said that the greatest influence on him was Western society. He was touched by the treatment of animals, the insistence on the right to be happy and the tolerance of others who are different. His interaction with people influenced him in a very deep way to the point where it influenced his theology. Before he left Saudi Arabia he had held the belief that all non-Muslims would go to hell. But 6 months later he was unable to give such an answer. He knew non-Muslims from close up and could no longer comprehend that they deserved to go to hell merely for not believing in Allah.

His ultimate disengagement with Islam was when he came across books by Abdullah al-Qasimi. He said "His books hit me at the roots; ʿal-Qasimi's audacity and criticism of everyone was especially intriguing. His courage to criticize Allah appealed to me." With these books, Muadh's whole faith eroded. He believed that his faith eroded too fast but that this is natural for Saudis because in his view, they do not have an intellectual foundation for their faith and thus it crumbles at the first serious challenge.

Muadh sometimes laments squandering the best years of his life due to his religiosity. He regrets the pleasures that he did not enjoy and the negative feelings toward the nonpious that burdened his emotions. But now he is trying to make up for this, although he has not yet made full peace with his religious past. He is happy that he changed at a young age, and wonders how it would have been had his change come much later. As a result, he said, he understands the basic impulse of militant atheists who take it upon themselves to continually mock religion and religious people:

I've been through this phase. Those that I see are in the early phase. There is a phase of feeling that you've been tricked. The phase when after thinking you are the best and the most stable you realize how fragile everything is.

He himself underwent this phase, and it lasted more than year. He lost faith in everything and hated his society; he even hated being an Arab.

4.2.3.8. Surprise from the Saudi Kafir

Rakan's change also happened in a Western country. When he left Saudi Arabia, he was still very religious. He was even worried about being lured into sin by what he described as the "decadent lifestyle" of that Western society. He would say his daily prayers in a local mosque and he became popular among those who attended the mosque. But questions would soon rise. Like Muadh, his first issue was with good *kuffar* he met. "I met this great kind old lady and I would ask myself 'Can she go to hell?' . . . So I tried to make her excuses." Many Muslim ulama say that if a non-Muslim does not know Islam in its proper form he/she will be excused in the afterlife and may have a chance to go to heaven after all (almuslim1994, 2010; TheFhad555, 2012). Rakan's sense of morality could not fathom how someone kind would be punished in hell. But this was against his religious conviction, which taught him that kindness is irrelevant in the afterlife and that what ultimately matters is faith.

He held firm to his faith and tried to silence his questions until he discovered Paltalk. He would go to some of the Paltalk rooms listen and talk with other participants. In one room he found someone whose talk was all against Islam and from his accent he realized that this person was a Saudi. "This was a shock to me because he spoke with my own accent from my region." The discovery that another Saudi would lack faith was shocking for him, even more shocking than the content of these talks. He would listen to him, then read further about the topics being raised. He was trying to refute his arguments against religion, but when they engaged in debate Rakan would sometimes feel that the Paltalk Saudi atheist had a point. His religious behavior did not change as a result, but his faith slowly eroded. Although Rakan managed to convince the person to return to faith, he himself had lost confidence in his own faith in the process.

Rakan said that he went through a deep crisis of faith. Doubt was increasing in his mind and heart. He was exhausted by it, even in its early phases. His absolute conviction was now eroding. He wanted to believe and tried to hold on to it as much as he could. He was afraid of not believing, yet his mind was pulling him the other way. He tried to read religious books that provided answers for skeptics, but this did not help him to restore his conviction. He eventually fell into a deep depression, started to hate those around him, and stopped eating except to survive. He would sometimes go to isolated places and scream and cry and ask Allah to give him a sign. He would even curse Allah, angrily blaming Him for his situation because He was not providing enough evidence for faith. He met ulama who were famous for debating with atheists, but dismissed them as silly people with weak ideas; indeed, they even made his doubts increase, and so did his depression. After much reading he made the decision to leave Islam: "It was a hard decision and the most important in my life." After making this decision he went to a Muslim country. While he was there he heard the call to prayer and his body started to shake. He could not believe the state that he had reached, and felt very sorry for himself. He went to a mosque and prayed, and he said that the experience of praying at that time was very spiritual. After he prayed, he sat in a corner of the mosque and decided to spend some time reciting the Quran. He was once more in such a perfect state of faith that he thought that Allah was finally sending him the long-awaited sign. In the back of his mind he thought that the sign would come through the Quran. So he opened a random page to see which verse his eyes would fall on first:

> I opened the Quran waiting for Allah's message and I saw the verse "And be moderate in your pace and lower your voice; indeed, the most disagreeable of sounds is the voice of donkeys." (Quran: Luqman, 19). And I said to myself . . . is this a god? Is it logical that a god speaks to us in this way? Allah? Allah who is so great? Who created this universe?'

Reading that verse ended his whole emotional state of perfect faith and he left the mosque with the firm belief that he was no longer a Muslim.

4.2.3.9. Philosophical Investigations

'Uthman's change was almost purely intellectual, or at least that was how he chose to present his story to me:

> For myself, I had a debate with religion first from a metaphysical stance . . . I engaged with the world view its offers. Of course by religion I mean Islam, and to be honest, I mean Saudi Islam.

This started after he read Rene Descartes's (1596–1650) *Discourse on Method.* It turned everything around for him, and he applied Descartes's method to religion. He asked himself whether the answers that the Quran provides regarding the universe make sense or not. Another issue he debated with religion was ethical. Specifically, he extracted the moral position of Islam on various issues such as slavery and jihad and then asked himself questions such as, "Is such a deity moral or immoral?" He would ask, "How does this deity resolve issues? How did He solve problems? Was He able to solve the problem between Adam and *Iblis* (Lucifer/Satan)? Was evicting Iblis really a solution? And why deal with this problem in this style?" The stories in the Quran of Allah's punishments were also problematic for him. "Why," he asked, "would Allah bring collective punishment to the people of *Lut,* many of whom were children? Why destroy everyone in the time of *Nuh* (Noah)?" His thoughts and questions led him to think that "the deity offered by religion does not seem to me a good deity deserving of worship." But the issue of theodicy was the greatest challenge for him:

> If he is a good deity then why is this world full of evil and full of pain and suffering . . . pain and suffering that is not justifiable whatsoever? . . . Like a baby born with a handicap.

His conclusion was that the image of Allah in the Quran is no different from any dictator: when He is angry He commits crimes, and when He is happy He is merciful. For him this is an erratic deity not bound by any set of fixed morals.

4.2.4. Summary and Synthesis

The themes I have mentioned as milestones have an important dimension to them, in that they were within my interlocutors. While their transformation to religiosity was affected in one way or another by their context, their change away from religion was reported as an individual act. None of them reported the influence of someone else in their disengagement, nor were there financial incentives for moving away from religion nor societal (respect) benefits. One of the traits common to all of my interlocutors was their high degree of independence and sense of individuality. When I asked them about the effect of their change on their relationships with their immediate family, all of them without exception stated that this was their personal choice which those around them had to accept. They were all in agreement that they would not go public with their views, but this was only due to fear of the legal consequences and societal ostracization.

This is not to say that having this trait leads to this same path, but it is worth considering as an important condition for those who decide to criticize and change their beliefs and religious belonging. Being an individualist does not necessarily mean that one also has the courage to accept or reject the established faith or act in accordance with his or her sensibility.

Most but not all of my interlocutors were influenced by religion in their childhood. Most of them became religious at a point in their lives, albeit for different reasons and with different effects. Some sought piety, while others sought belonging. In turn, all of those who had become religious went through different experiences that pulled them away from religion. The ideas on religion that they came to adopt varied and, more importantly, do not seem to be related to the specific experience of each. And these variances were in fact the result of the individual aspects of their change. I could not predict the nature of the conclusions any one of them would adopt based on knowing their religious background or their disengagement from religion.

Some stopped believing in Allah, such as 'Uthman and Adnan, but in different ways. 'Uthman still sought faith and found it in the commonality between him and religious individuals. He did not characterize himself as a nihilist who says, "This universe is a machine and the only logic of life is that of survival of the fittest," to use his own words. Adnan, on the other hand, was the opposite: he took a position of indifference to faith or anything that was metaphysical. Some became what one would call deists, such as Hana, Muadh, and Rakan. Their reasons were subjective, as they did not believe that there is evidence for any position regarding belief in Allah. Rakan said, about Allah, "Those who deny Him and believe in Him are the same," while Muadh went a step further and said, "Those who deny Allah's existence are idiots." For him, his conviction of Allah's presence came through love: "Love is a strange thing . . . life wouldn't continue without love . . . [such] feelings for me were proof of Allah's existence." These positions of belief in Allah cannot be deduced from the factor that prompted the change, nor from the course of the change. They were positions based on individual choices due to individual differences.

Their epistemological conclusions are worth noting: they all seemed to lean toward the idea that we need to accept that there are questions without answers, and none of them considered that it was worthwhile attempting to resolve such questions through serious religious contemplation. Most did not take their disengagement seriously enough to undergo a crisis of

faith; there was no religious crisis, but rather a sense of indifference to religion after they had walked away from it. I started my research thinking
that religious disengagement was serious enough to warrant a tormenting
inner crisis, but discovered that most of them had walked away from religion quietly; no crisis, no drama, and no pain. There was perhaps a sense
of emptiness, as more than one expressed, but it was quickly overcome
and filled with other experiences in life.

Most of the other stories of change here were influenced by exposure to
ideas. But the process whereby this exposure happened depended on the
networks to which these individuals belonged. Thus we see two types: the
individuals who belonged to groups and these who did not. Those who
belonged to a group had to leave the group first, and then some would go
out on their own while others would find another group that better fit their
new ideas. In most cases, we saw that individuals did not leave the group
as a result of tension between themselves and the group but rather due to
unrelated factors, such as graduating from university.

I had assumed that disengagement from Islam as a religion would also
mean disengagement from identifying with Islam. But this was not necessarily the case. Qasim in particular was quite precise about this matter.
He told me:

> I feel more affinity with Muslims . . . , when I take a taxi and he is
> a Muslim I would feel closer to him . . . , the cultural connection
> is more . . . there are commonalities . . . , we have the same holy
> things.

But he insisted that he did not connect to a Muslim in an abstract way; that
is, he did not feel that he belonged to the nation of Muslims. His affinity
was not driven by religious reasons. It was a cultural familiarity, according
to him.

When it came to Allah, I found that all of them had developed various opinions that had little in common except that they were all personal
beliefs and not based on traditional understandings of theology. Lina
desired spiritual experience but did not believe that Allah was the sole
source of this. Her opinion was not based on an intellectual analysis or
philosophical contemplation. Hana had decided to become a deist, also
for subjective reasons. She wanted to be self-empowered and she believed
that suspending her faith in Allah would bring that to her. For Ibrahim,
believing in a god or not had become a factor of need; humans created

the idea of deity because they needed it, and those who still need that idea should continue to retain it.

Belief in hell in the afterlife was one form of faith that I thought all would reject without question. And perhaps here my prediction was somewhat correct. The one thing they had in common was that the idea of being punished in hell for not believing in Allah is insensible. Some, like Lara, still believed that there has to be some form of retribution for evil people, while others thought this was more wishful thinking. Another common trait that I found was that all rejected the idea of hell and heaven in the way the Quran depicts. And all of them were content without giving the matter further thought. The afterlife did not belong to their day-to-day concerns.

4.3. Conclusion

The changes in most of my interlocutors happened in their late teens or early twenties, which is the period when most religious disengagement happens (Regnerus & Uecker, 2006, p. 222). This made me wonder which comes first: disengagement from belief or disengagement from religiosity. Of my interviewees only one, Lara, explicitly stated that she had disengaged from religiosity first and then from belief, while Ahmad and Lina said that they had not been religious at all and then had changed their belief. But in the case of the rest, the disengagement from belief happened first. My sample is small and not statistically representative, so in my cases this may have merely been a coincidence.

There were nine factors that stood out in explaining this shift: a near-death experience; resolving guilt; tension between Islam and sensibility; tension between Islam and Islam; seeking an easier Islam; anger at Allah; the problem of the good *kafir*; surprise from the Saudi *kafir*; and philosophical investigations. These factors were then complemented by new knowledge, whether from books, articles, or videos, that enabled them to connect the dots between doubt and action. None of these factors were unique to my interlocutors, as many other Muslims—Saudis and others— also experience them, yet they do not all move into a process of criticizing religion. The lack of literature on Muslims leaving their religion makes it difficult to be certain about the process. Even studies of non-Muslims leaving religion focus on the correlation between demographic factors and religious exit (Blanes & Oustinova-Stjepanovic, 2015) and are not always helpful in understanding the factors of change at the individual level.

If we look at the narratives in light of the theories on the disengagement of religion that I discussed previously, one finds that Luckmann's theory is highly relevant. Its general argument is on the effect of the estrangement of religion from daily life due to the apparent disconnection between its core message and newly spread values: sensibilities. One also sees Taylor's note quite starkly:

> The religious life or practice that I become part of not only must be my choice, but it must speak to me; it must make sense in terms of my spiritual development, as I understand this. (Taylor, 2011, p. 241)

The other theories that discuss the functional redundancy of religion due to its incapacity to serve a social need or the breakdown of the social foundations that facilitate the continuity of religion are not visible among the narratives of my interlocutors. Perhaps this is because theories related to functional redundancy and the breakdown of memory are too structural to be noticed by an individual. I was surprised that none of my interlocutors pointed to the effect of the erosion of Berger's social plausibility structures, and none of them was consciously aware or consciously raised a statement that took the following form: "Does it make sense that we are right and the whole world is wrong?"

Finally, some very interesting things were absent. On Twitter I saw that frustration with religious authority was quite high, and when I came to this research I was expecting to see that such frustration would also be high among my interlocutors and that it would be one main reason for their disengagement. This was not the case. Not one of them mentioned frustration at Islamic decrees in the process of their disengagement or even after. No one mentioned anger at the Committee or the religious ulama as a source of frustration. Lack of mention does not mean that they were always comfortable with religious decrees or authorities, but it does point to something worth further consideration: the impact of anger in creating disengagement from religion. For all my interlocutors, despite the differences among them, tension between a deeply held value and religious reality motivated personal change. While such tension could have been resolved by apologetic or adaptive techniques used by other Muslims, these individuals broke away from religion.

5

Backlash

MOST OF THE ideas expressed by Saudis that I have discussed in the past chapters are considered heretical according to Saudi orthodoxy. But not all expressions of these ideas elicited a response. As long as they remained within private spaces they were merely the target of general criticism of heresy and were lamented in the complaints of the ulama and other religiously oriented individuals about deviation spreading among Saudis. But once these ideas entered the public space they were transformed from merely heretical ideas to a potential threat to the sanctity of religion. The heretical idea stated in public is no longer personal; instead, it is perceived as an effort to dismantle the faith of others, to normalize deviance, and to actively misguide. This dynamic, in turn, elicits a set of responses from the religious orthodoxy of the country as well as from other Saudis of different levels of religious knowledge and piety. The exact nature of the response varies according to the person expressing the heresy, the timing of the heresy becoming public, and of course the nature of the heresy itself. This chapter explores categories of heresy and orthodoxy as they are understood in Saudi Arabia generally, and examines the ways Saudi ulama responded to heresy prior to and after 2012.

It is first necessary to discuss the use of the term "heresy" and its counterpart "orthodoxy" in the Saudi Muslim context, and more importantly, the applicability of Western-centric theories about heresy and orthodoxy to a Muslim context. Moreover, the terms "orthodoxy" and "heresy" are both adopted from Christianity and, as some scholars would claim, are not indigenous to Islam, yet are widely used today to refer to Muslim religious institutions and practices (Fierro, 2014, p. 158). Heresy, in its original

Christian context, was defined as "a religious error, contrary to the truth as authoritatively defined and promulgated by the Church" (B. Lewis, 1953, p. 57). Islam does not have a church that formally defines right belief, thus, it is claimed, there can be no sense of orthodoxy or heresy within it (Jackson, 2014; Wilson, 2014, pp. 153–155).

There are terms about incorrect forms of belief that are indigenous to Islam, such as *"mulhid," "kafir," "zindiq,"* or *"murtad."* They are not synonymous, and it would be incorrect to use the term "heresy" in place of all of them (Langer & Simon, 2014). *"Mulhid"* is commonly used today to refer to atheists, even though the two words are not exactly equivalent. The original meaning of *mulhid* is "one who deviates," and then it was used for those who deviate from the True path. *"Kafir"* can be used to refer to someone who rejects belief in the fundamental precepts of faith such as belief in the unity of Allah, the afterlife, and the Prophecy; *"zindiq"* can be applied to multiple types of deviants such as atheists and materialists; *"murtad"* refers to the Muslim apostate who renounces Islam, either explicitly by declaring that she or he is no longer a Muslim or implicitly by holding a belief that renders them a *kafir* (Kersten, 2015; B. Lewis, 1953, pp. 52–56). In turn, most cases of apostasy have been of the latter implicit form because very few Muslims explicitly admit nonbelief or denounce Islam (Kersten, 2015). The term *"murtad"* has been widely used in the past and is still frequently used, as we shall see.

Were the purpose of this book to present a theological discussion on heresy according to Muslim theologians, it would be important to be careful about the use of the terms "orthodoxy"/"heresy" in a Muslim context, as their theological connotations would not coincide with the theological connotations of the Arabic terms just mentioned. Instead, my purpose here is to follow a social process of designating people with these labels with the intention of either placing them outside the bounds of Islam or defining them as religiously deviant and punishing them accordingly. From that perspective, I adopt Jackson's position when he says, "The only thing required to establish and sustain orthodoxy is authority, full stop." Such an authority can be formal, stemming from the ulama in religious state institutions or informal, from religious ulama and institutions who have, by virtue of popular support, the power to exert the "threat of stigma, malicious gossip, ostracism, or verbal attack by respected members of the community" (Jackson, 2014, pp. 159–160). This makes social and political practice the main parameters in defining orthodoxy and heresy, rather than questions of theology. Whether it is heresy, orthodoxy, *zandaqa*, or *kufr*, there is an authority in play that draws the lines between those in the tent of Islam and those outside that tent. This authority also makes decisions on how to respond to those who are outside the bounds of legitimate religious thought and practice and to those who are still in this community yet habitually violate its rules.

More importantly, Jackson's view implies that these terms carry different meanings in different sociopolitical settings, even among followers of one religion. That is, if we take a theological perspective, these terms would be defined similarly across one Muslim theological school regardless of time and place; but when placed within distinct sociopolitical processes they would carry different meanings. Thus the meaning of orthodoxy and heresy differs in Indonesia, Saudi Arabia, and Morocco, because the politics of the religious authority are different. Even in the same country, the meaning of these words changes relative to who uses them and the religious authority they follow. Moreover, in situations where religious authority is diffuse, orthodoxy is also diffuse. That is, if a religious authority is divided between different institutions and has multiple ulama leaderships, orthodoxy is also divided according to these institutions and ulama. Looking at the matter in this way opens venues for exploring this religious activity of drawing lines between orthodoxy and heresy. This dimension had been neglected, as the literature on heresy has focused on historical studies, while social studies have tended to neglect or ignore heresy, even though it is a social process and historical studies would benefit greatly from social theorizing (Berlinerblau, 2001, p. 328; Kurtz, 1983, p. 1085). Thus, in what follows I use the term "orthodoxy" to refer to any religious authority; and I use the terms "heresy" and "*kufr*" interchangeably to refer to a creed that an orthodoxy deems to be a deviation worthy of punishment; I use the terms "heretic" and "*kafir*" to refer to a person who is accused of heresy; and I use the term "*takfir*" to mean the act of accusing someone of being a *kafir* or a heretic.

5.1. Orthodoxy and Heresy in Saudi Arabia

Saudi religious orthodoxy is a superordinate compulsory organization composed of an ulama class supported by the Saudi state and other social groups and (1) controls the production and dissemination of religious knowledge in formal contexts and influences that production in informal contexts, (2) articulates correct forms of belief and praxis through the work of rationalizing and consent-generating ulama, (3) identifies incorrect forms of belief and praxis through these same ulama, and (4) institutionally manages deviant individuals and groups through coercive mechanisms. This definition is adapted from Berlinerblau to apply to Saudi Arabia:

> A (religious) orthodoxy (of the purest and hardest type) is a super-ordinate compulsory organisation composed of a leading class in cahoots with other classes and social groups that (1) controls the means of material, intellectual, and symbolic production; (2) articulates "correct" forms of belief and praxis through the work of rationalising and consent-generating intellectuals (and/or priests); (3) identifies "incorrect" forms of belief and praxis through these same intellectuals; (4) institutionally manages deviant individuals and groups through coercive mechanisms. (Berlinerblau, 2001, p. 340)

In Saudi Arabia, as discussed, there is a religious class of ulama that is supported by the Saudi state and also by a wide segment of Saudi society. The Saudi ulama almost fully control the production of religious knowledge that is disseminated by formal religious institutions such as universities and religious schools' textbooks. In addition to this position of power, Saudi Salafi ulama influence religious knowledge produced by informal religious institutions such as sermons in mosques or informal religious lessons, by determining who preaches in public spaces such as mosques, universities, and schools (Prokop, 2003). Although the country is relatively open to nonorthodox versions of religious knowledge, Salafi ulama are able to influence the censoring of many books.

Saudi ulama also articulate and transmit correct forms of belief and praxis and determine what is incorrect. They have the legal capacity to punish and curb deviation, yet the actual performance of this authority has been limited by the Saudi state. Moreover, the Saudi religious institution has the authority—albeit limited—to coerce through the various institutions under its control, such as the Committee and the judiciary.

My definition does not mention the content of orthodoxy but rather its performance, based on power, through institutions and by individuals against other institutions and individuals. While religious scholars may disagree as to what is religiously proper and what is deviant, such positions are only considered orthodoxy once they are promoted by a coercive authority and their competitors are suppressed or ostracized (El-Shamsy, 2014, p. 257). Moreover, since authority is the basic constituent of orthodoxy rather than creed, and since authority is hierarchically distributed in a society, so would be orthodoxy, and since authorities compete with each other, one can envisage a hierarchy of orthodoxies each competing for position in the hierarchy. This competition is critical for understanding accusations of heresy in Saudi Arabia, as such claims are often made for the purpose of retaining ulama authority, while in other times they can be made for the purpose of competition between the various orthodoxies (Kurtz, 1983).

Based on my definition of Saudi orthodoxy, I define "Saudi heresy" as the deviance that a Saudi orthodoxy determines as threatening or that when assaulted can serve the power position of orthodoxy. Accordingly, Saudi heresy is not merely an opinion on creed made by someone that does not match the theological position of Saudi orthodoxy: that is, determinations of heresy are based not on theology but on power. Related to this is the social reality that theological deviation does not become heresy in Saudi Arabia until Saudi orthodoxy concludes that it is heresy. Furthermore, it is necessary to note that only some theological deviations are categorized as heresy, even if all qualify as *kufr* from a theological theological point of view. I have noted many instances of theological deviance by Saudis on Twitter, yet only a handful were the target of the religious orthodoxy of Saudi Arabia. In Saudi Arabia one notices a disproportion between theological deviance and the intensity of a heretical accusation. Finally, it is necessary to note that an accusation of heresy leads to the development of orthodoxy as much as orthodoxy influences definitions of heresy. That is, an opinion that is defined as heretical by orthodoxy becomes more relevant in comparison to other theological issues from that point on, meaning that it becomes relevant in the hierarchy of orthodoxy by virtue of the heresy accusation. The emergence of Saudi orthodoxy is thus not the mere theological opinion as in religious theological text books; instead it is a position that is undergirded by the practice of issuing fatwas to denounce its opponents as heretics, or at least to denounce an action as heretical. Orthodoxy is thus ultimately an inversion of heresy (Berlinerblau, 2001, p. 332). This process is fluid and nonlinear, rendering orthodoxy similarly fluid and changeable. This may narrow the categories of orthodoxy and heresy, but it explains much of the discrepancy in the Saudi way of responding to an alleged heretical opinion.

5.2. Brief History of Heresy Condemnations: *Takfir*

The origins of most types of *takfir* in Islam are found in interpretations of
the Quran and the Hadith. The Quran and canonical Hadith collections contain within them condemnations of various beliefs and actions that serve as
the foundation for much of the *takfir* being practiced by Muslims. There are
other forms of *takfir* that are not directly taken from the Quran and Hadith,
but rather by the implication of the act. An example of the first type of *takfir*,
taken directly from the Quran, is accusing someone of *kufr* due to rejection
of belief in the prophets of Allah; this rejection is an act of *kufr* because the
Quran explicitly says that he who does this is a *kafir* (Quran: al-Nisa', 151).
An example of the second type of *takfir* is accusing someone of *kufr* due to
denying that the Quran as it exists today is the same Quran that existed in
the Prophet's time, that is, a Quran that is free from scriptural falsification or
transmissional errors. Neither the Quran nor the Hadith contain a ruling on
this issue, but Muslims nonetheless consider such a denial to constitute *kufr*,
on the grounds that it implies that Allah was not truthful when he said that
he would preserve and protect the Quran from all corruption (Quran: al-Hijr,
9). This type of *kufr*—*kufr* by implication—is a broad category and includes
the denial of many beliefs and religious edicts.

In Muslim theology there are certain beliefs and actions that are placed
in the category of *ma 'ulima min al-din bi-l-darura*: that is, what is known to
be from religion by necessity (al-Hawali, n.d.-b). I give two examples here,
one of which relates to belief and the other to practice. To claim that those
who do not believe in the Prophecy of Muhammad are *kuffar* and deserve
to go to hell is considered to be a matter of necessity. If someone were
to come and say that unbelievers are not *kuffar* and deserve heaven, his
statement would be considered *kufr*. The example in the domain of practice is the established ruling that fasting only for the month of Ramadan
is compulsory for each Muslim. If a Muslim denies this statement in any
form, such as by saying that fasting is not an obligatory duty, or by sug-
gesting that it is a duty to fast only for part of the month of Ramadan or
longer than Ramadan, this person is considered to be challenging what is
known to be from religion by necessity, and this challenge implies that he/
she is either challenging Allah directly or rejecting Allah's decrees, which
renders their view *kufr*. On the other hand, if the person accepts that fasting during Ramadan is obligatory yet does not fast,[1] he/she is a sinner

---

1. Without a legitimate excuse such as illness.

only (al-Fawzan, 2006; bin Baz, n.d.-d). The difference between these two types of *takfir* is relevant because most *takfir* are of the second type, which renders *takfir* a matter of induction and interpretation. That *takfir* can be a matter of interpretation gives religious orthodoxy more power in determining who is a *kafir*, and thus more social authority.

5.3. Accusations of *Kufr*

Muslims consider *takfir* a serious act due to its consequences. A Muslim who is deemed *kafir* is deprived of many basic rights and the matter can reach a point where his own life is at stake. Yet accusations of heresy among Muslims are as old as the religion itself. The first civil wars between the newly born Muslim community of the seventh century were called the Apostasy Wars. These wars were between the early Companions of the Prophet and some Arab tribes who were accused of being apostates (Shaban, 1976, pp. 16–27). But when the history of *takfir* in Islam is discussed it usually starts with the *Khawarij*. The *Khawarij* were accused of practicing *takfir* freely, starting by accusing Ali bin Abi Talib, the Prophet's cousin and son-in-law and the fourth caliph, of being a *kafir* and subsequently nullifying his rights as a Muslim, including the right to live. After rendering Ali bin Abi Talib a *kafir* they considered it an imperative to fight him and kill him, an ambition that they successfully accomplished in 661 CE (Faramarz Haj et al., 2015).

The *Khawarij* were rebels who used *takfir* to justify violence against their contenders, but the first state-sponsored *takfir* in the history of Islam was the *takfir* of Jaʿd bin Dirham (d. 742) for his opinions on predestination. In 742 CE, during the Umayyad Dynasty (661–750 CE) he was found guilty of *zandaqa* and subsequently executed. This case, however, was an isolated one, and ultimately the Umayyads did not create an institution to track heretics. The Abbasid Dynasty, which overthrew the Umayyads and lasted from 750 to 1258 CE, took a more aggressive approach to heretics. This approach first arose during the reign of its second caliph, al-Mansur (r. 754–775), but took a decisive turn under his successor, al-Mahdi (r. 775–785). On al-Mahdi's orders, an institution was established named *Diwan al-Zanadiqa* (Ministry of Heresies). While most of the new institution's victims were Manichaean (van Oort, 2015), others were also prosecuted. One prominent victim was the poet Bashar bin Burd (d. 784), who was executed for heresy (Enayatollah & Melvin-Koushki, 2015). The motivation for creating such an institution was political, as the Abbasid authorities believed that there was underground opposition to their authority that expressed itself in seditious doctrine (B. Lewis, 1953, pp. 55–56).

The seventh Abbasid caliph, al-Ma'mun (r. 813–833), initiated in 833 CE[2] the second and perhaps the most historically influential inquisition in the history of Islam, known as the *Mihna*, which literally means "the test" (Jad'an, 1989; John, 2015). At that time, there were sharp doctrinal differences between Muslims on various theological issues, and one of these was the metaphysical nature of the Quran as the word of Allah. The crux of the debate was that al-Ma'mun did not believe the word of Allah to be a metaphysical eternal entity that exists outside time and physical space but, instead, that it is a material entity created at a specific time and place. Al-Ma'mun thus sought to interrogate and prosecute those who opposed his opinion. Following al-Ma'mun's death in 833 CE, the caliph's two successors[3] carried on the *Mihna* for 16 years until it was abolished by the 10th Abbasid caliph, al-Mutawakkil (r. 847–861). Religious scholars who openly questioned the doctrine of the creation of the Quran were questioned, and if they resisted complying with the doctrine they were imprisoned and sometimes beaten (Jad'an, 1989). The most prominent religious scholar in this regard was Ahmad bin Hanbal (780–855), eponym of the Hanbali school of jurisprudence and a foundational alem for Salafis. No one was executed during the *Mihna* for their beliefs.

There have been many explanations of al-Ma'mun's decision; the most likely interpretation is that the *Mihna* was an attempt to assert his rule and, more importantly, to assert the role of the caliph as Allah's appointed ruler to whom all must submit (Jad'an, 1989). The main group that rejected such broad authority for caliphs were *Ahl al-Hadith*, the collectors of the Prophet's Hadith, and it also happened that they were the most outspoken group against the doctrine of the creation of the Quran (Nawas, 1994).

The *Mihna* was the last Muslim institution dedicated to tracking heretics, but this did not end their execution and murder. After the *Mihna* ended, the most famous heretic to be executed, quite brutally, was Husayn al-Hallaj (c. 858–922) (Massignon & Mason, 1994). Another case that is less famous, yet was prominent in its time, is the execution of the Andalusian historian, poet, and philosopher Lisan al-Din bin al-Khatib

---

2. It was also the last year of his reign.

3. Al-Mu'tassim and al-Wathiq.

(1313–1374) who was accused of atheism on account of his writings. The authorities imprisoned him, and the ulama issued fatwas that endorsed his death. Some people took it upon themselves to execute the fatwas and infiltrated his prison cell, strangled him, and burned his corpse (Alalwani, 2012). But perhaps the most discussed premodern manifestation of *takfir* was the Wahhabi campaign, which led to the creation of the first Saudi state 300 years ago. Many who did not follow the teachings of Muhammad bin Abdulwahhab were considered to be *kafir* and thus to deserve to be subdued or killed (Firro, 2013).

With the advent of the modern state and the development of modern legal systems, accusations of heresy were enshrined in law in one way or another in many Muslim countries. According to the report "Laws Criminalising Apostasy in Selected Jurisdictions," many countries still have laws on apostasy or blasphemy including Afghanistan, Brunei, Mauritania, Qatar, Saudi Arabia, Sudan, the United Arab Emirates, and Yemen. There are also countries that do not include apostasy in their penal code, including Morocco, Pakistan, Iran, and Jordan, yet individuals are at risk of being prosecuted in religious courts. The report adds a list of countries that "have laws that include broadly-worded provisions on insulting Islam or its Prophet and blasphemy, which could potentially be used to prosecute persons for apostasy" even though they do not have a specific law on apostasy. These countries include Algeria, Bahrain, Indonesia, Iraq, Kuwait, Libya, Oman, and Syria (Goitom, 2014, pp. 1–2). While these countries do not engage in inquisitions to track heretics and bring them before religious courts, the existence of the laws allows people to raise accusations of heresy against individuals.

Although such laws existed on heresy, contemporary accusations leading to execution are very few. One of the very rare cases leading to death after an accusation of "heresy" was that of Mahmoud Taha (1909–1985), a prominent Sudanese intellectual and politician who was convicted of apostasy and executed in Sudan on January 18, 1985. Taha held the view that Muslims are not obligated to implement the Prophet's laws that were revealed to him in Medina, rather only the moral principles revealed in Mecca. This view was considered heretical, as it implied that some of the revealed laws are not obligatory, which in effect means that we are not obliged to apply Shari'a (An-Na'im, 1986). In Saudi Arabia there was also a heresy accusation that ended in execution. The Shiite Sadiq Abdulkarim Malallah (1970–1992) was executed on the grounds of being an apostate (Amnesty International, 1993). Another Saudi was almost executed: Hadi

Said al-Mutif, an Ismaili from Najran south of Saudi Arabia. At 18, while training to become a policeman, he made a joke that implied mockery and lack of respect for the Prophet. He was accused of blasphemy and sentenced to death. At that time King Abdullah was the de facto monarch and stopped the execution, but al-Mutif remained in prison for almost 19 years (Whitaker, 2006). He was released in February 2012, after he announced his repentance (Human Rights Watch, 2012).

5.3.1. Takfir in Saudi Arabia: Before 2012

There is a widespread view that Wahhabis view all Muslims who reject their creed as unbelievers who should be killed without fault (Green, 2010). But this is not exactly accurate, as most Salafi ulama warn of looseness in applying *takfir* to a Muslim, citing many Prophetic Hadiths that warn against it. In Saudi Arabia many lectures and pamphlets criticize the practice of *takfir* without the proper credentials and causes (Abu Luwz, 1998; al-Ghulu Fi-l-Din, 2014; al-Jibrin, n.d.; al-Sayf al-Hashimi, 2011). In Saudi Arabia concern over laxity in *takfir* has been a central issue in religious and political debates, not because Wahhabis are quick to engage in *takfir* but rather because the Wahhabi creed applies the *takfir* judgment to a wide spectrum of actions and beliefs that many Muslims practice, thus potentially rendering them *kuffar*.

While Salafi ulama apply *takfir* to a wide range of issues, they are quite careful—theoretically at least—when it comes to applying it to specific individuals. Saudi ulama, following the tradition of many Muslim scholars in the past, divide the process of *takfir* into two steps: *generalized takfir* and *specific takfir*. The former is the first step of *takfir*, in which an alim deems that a specific action constitutes heresy, apostasy, or blasphemy; this can include cursing the Prophet or visiting the grave of a revered person in the hope of acquiring that person's blessing (al-Saqqaf, n.d.; bin Baz, n.d.-e). But Muslim scholars have been keen to note that it does not follow that a specific person who commits actions that are *kufr* is necessarily a *kafir*: that is, the person who commits heresy is not necessarily a heretic. The mere performance of nonbelief does not make one a disbeliever. It is here that the second step of *takfir* comes in, which is labeled specific *takfir*. In generalized *takfir* the alim bases his argument on interpretation of the Quran and the Hadith. But in specific *takfir* the alim must asses the individual case of a specific person and assess whether or not that act was done willfully, and whether there were extenuating circumstances. After this assessment, the alim either issues a decree of specific *takfir* or decides that the deeds were heretical but the individual is not a heretic (al-Rashid, 2004).

Weber considers it important for the state as an entity to have and maintain a monopoly on the legal use of violence (Weber, 2004, p. 33). In Saudi Arabia the state has been seeking a monopoly on *takfir*. The first step of *takfir* has been considered part of the domain monopolized by the ulama, who want to be the only source that makes such a determination. But the second step is contested by the state and the ulama. The state wants to restrict that step to its court system in order to control the concrete consequences of *takfir*, such as the execution of heretics. The ulama, on the other hand, believe that they have the right to issue specific *takfir* if they have properly explored the issue. The Saudi state, in response to the proliferation of *takfir*, frequently sponsors events to support state monopoly on *takfir*, such as a conference entitled The Phenomenon of Takfir: Causes, Consequences and Solutions, with 120 participants who presented studies on various angles of *takfir*. The conference ended by recommending a strategy for confronting the culture of *takfir* and insisting that specific *takfir* must be solely within the legislation of the ruler or one who represents him (Lafi, 2011; Wakalat, 2011)

Despite the state's efforts to manage *takfir*, there have been many *takfir* fatwas in Saudi Arabia. Some of the targets of these fatwas have been ulama, though most were liberals. In both cases, one can consider *takfir* a tool by which Saudi orthodoxy retains its authority. One of the ulama who was a target of heretical accusations was Salih Ibrahim al-Bilayhi (d. 1989), a very prominent Saudi alim (al-Thuwayni, 2005). In one of his fatwas al-Bilayhi made a remark that was interpreted as impolite to the Prophet (al-Nogaidan, 2003). He was severely criticized, and his faith was questioned. Another alim accused of heresy was ibnʿUthaymin, for a fatwa that concerned Allah's attributes. This prominent Saudi alim was forced to retract and repent of his opinion in the presence of the mufti of the time, ibn Baz (Munasir al-Haramayn, 2013). Both accusations were serious, but neither the state nor society were called on to take action against the ulama with the deviant opinions, as they were still ulama. Instead, such cases were treated as family arguments that were dealt with internally without allowing external interference. Accusations of *takfir* among the ulama were thus a means of asserting the existing hierarchal order.

The more serious *takfir* fatwas have been those directed against liberals in Saudi Arabia, as they were meant to initiate social ostracization and state action. One case is the *takfir* of Mansour al-Nogaidan in 2003. In an interview al-Nogaidan stated—among other things—that truth is relative, that no one religion has a monopoly on it, that no one should be considered a *kafir*, and that his own religion was humanism (al-Nogaidan, 2012). These statements are heretical, as they deny the absolute truth of Islam, reject the explicit Quranic division of people into believers and nonbelievers, and, most seriously, imply rejection of Islam. Despite these claims, however, the reaction to his *kufr* was relatively limited. Al-Nogaidan was harshly attacked on Internet forums, and some ulama issued statements of *takfir* against him in which they listed al-Nogaidan's heresies and quoted the opinions of many ulama who deem these who believe in similar statements to be *kuffar*, thus concluding that he, too, was a *kafir* (al-Ali, 2003). The response to the online *takfir* statement came mainly in the form of articles supporting some of his ideas but also framed the proliferation of *takfir* fatwas as an attempt to deter individuals from independent and critical thinking in matters of religion (al-Ali, 2003; al-Mustafa, 2003). The state however did not take any action against al-Nogaidan, nor against those who had issued the *takfir* statement. It is important to note that the state here played a role in protecting al-Nogaidan rather than supporting efforts to punish him. It had no interest at the time in indulging the *takfir* voices in the country, especially after the events of 9/11, which had placed religion in Saudi Arabia in the international spotlight. On the contrary, the state, according to al-Nogaidan,[4] assigned him police protection for some months. Another thing to note was that despite the theological gravity of al-Nogaidan's statements the *takfir* was somewhat limited, which indicates that his *takfir* was about competition for power and not merely tracking heretics. These who made the *takfir* statements against him were mainly showing their constituencies that they did not tolerate liberals speaking against Islam, and that it was in their power to take action against them and mobilize the state to punish them.

Another serious *takfir* fatwa came in June 2007. This was issued by Salih al-Fawzan, a senior and prominent member of the Council of Senior Ulama. Unlike the *takfir* statement against al-Nogaidan, this was a *takfir* fatwa; that is, it came in response to a question, while the former *takfir* statement was issued without a question. This makes the *takfir* more relevant, due to the symbolic power of fatwa in Muslim communities. The

---

4. In a personal interview February 21, 2015, Dubai, United Arab Emirates.

question that al-Fawzan responded to was formulated in such a way as to avoid mention of names, yet at the same time it was clearly directed toward a particular segment of Saudi society. Such a formulation protects the petitioner (*al-mustafti*) as well as those who answer it (*al-mufti*). As I have mentioned, the state was keen to control specific *takfir*, and a question that does not specify a name yet points to a category of people is still considered an indirect specific *takfir*. Moreover al-Fawzan, as an alim working within the state-controlled Council of Senior Ulama, was obliged to follow state guidelines on such matters. The petitioner, in turn, asked about advocates of liberal thought who do not want to abide by Shari'a, who prefer secular law, and who want people to have freedom unrestrained by Allah's will and wisdom. Al-Fawzan's response was carefully articulated to avoid his being accused of issuing a specific *takfir*; it explained that such a person is a rebel against Allah who wants to corrupt Muslims, and thus this person should not be considered a Muslim, nor does such a person have the right to claim that he is a Muslim (al-Fawzan, n.d.-a).

Although the fatwa did not specify particular people it was understood to have targeted those in Saudi Arabia who define themselves as liberal and promote liberal values. Many Saudis, if asked who the liberals of the country are, can single out a number of writers and journalists (Hijabi, 2010). Even though al-Fawzan did not specify his target, the fatwa sent shockwaves throughout Saudi Arabia. Liberal writers considered it a threat to their lives and a number of leading Saudi conservative ulama such as Muhammad al-Nujaymi (b. 1961) agreed, expressing the fear that the fatwa could lead to the murder of liberals as a consequence of misreading it (al-Muhammad, 2008). What made the fatwa more explosive was that it followed a 3-year wave of terrorism in Saudi Arabia between 2003 and 2006. At the time there were still many terrorists at large and thus liberals were rightfully concerned that they might be targeted. Yet although someone such as al-Nujaymi expressed concern about its consequences, he also defended al-Fawzan by arguing that the fatwa was merely hypothetical. Nonetheless, al-Nujaymi conceded that the fatwa could have material consequences because some of those who heard or read it might identify liberals as its target and want to act on it. At the same time, though, al-Nujaymi sought to clarify that from a purely jurisprudential perspective al-Fawzan's fatwa did not constitute a specific *takfir*.

Following these reactions, al-Fawzan himself realized the gravity of his fatwa and issued a statement a week later, insisting that he understood the gravity of *takfir* while also arguing that this fatwa was not directed toward specific individuals but rather toward particular ideas. He then reiterated that those ideas are heretical, but qualified this designation by giving a detailed exposé in which he stressed that adopting a heretical idea does not automatically make one a heretic, and that only a court can deem someone a heretic (al-Zaydan, 2007). Al-Fawzan's clarification was most likely prompted by the state's frustration that such a fatwa had come from a senior alim. A few weeks later, the mufti of Saudi Arabia himself said that rushing to *takfir* is a mistake, and that many people do not appreciate the consequences of their actions (Alarabiyya, 2008). The mufti's response represented an official criticism of al-Fawzan, and underscored the fact that the state could not tolerate such statements made by the ulama that it employed. As in the case of al-Nogaidan, the ripples of al-Fawzan's fatwa remained confined to intellectual and religious elites and some discussions on the Internet; while society at large was absent from this debate. In the former case of al-Nogaidan, the state did not intervene directly against those who issued the *takfir* statement, while in al-Fawzan's case it did, through the mufti. In neither case did the state take action against the subjects of the fatwa; on the contrary, it protected them.

A few months after al-Fawzan's fatwa, a well-known but informal alim, Abdulrahman al-Barrak (b. 1933), issued a fatwa against two Saudi writers, Abdullah bin Bijad al-ʿUtaybi (b. 1971) and Yusuf Aba-l-Khayl (b. 1962). The fatwa was prompted by two articles. The first article, titled "Islam of Scripture and Islam of Conflict," was written by Abdullah al-ʿUtaybi (al-ʿUtaybi, 2008), and the second, titled "The Other According to Islam," was written by Yusuf Aba-l-Khayl (al-Khayl, 2007). Both articles criticized *takfir*, claiming that such a concept is alien to Islam and that it was only introduced into Islam for the purpose of serving the interests of powerful factions in the early Muslim community, and had thus created social schisms rather than uniting the community. Their criticism of *takfir* was essentially the same as al-Nogaidan's, and was also considered heretical for denying something fundamental to Islam.

Al-Fawzan first commented on the two articles the day after they were published, in a statement titled "Halt Your Animosity Toward Islam" (al-Fawzan, 2008). The content of his response did not implicate the writers directly, nor did it render a particular judgment of them, but the title of the statement nonetheless communicated the notion that these two writers and those like them are enemies of Islam. Most likely al-Fawzan also considered them heretics, but he avoided making this statement after his last episode with issuing a *takfir* fatwa. Al-Barrak, on the other hand, was more direct; he was asked about those who criticize the concept of *takfir* and responded by saying that *takfir* is a fundamental concept in Islam and that whoever doubts it is a *kafir*. This, like al-Fawzan's fatwa, was not a specific *takfir*, but al-Barrak went further than al-Fawzan and said that such a person should be killed unless he repents (Ismail, 2008). While al-Fawzan's statement did not explicitly say that liberals should be killed, al-Barrak engaged in a direct incitement of the lives of the two writers.

Al-Barrak's fatwa had local and international reverberations and two statements were made in response to it. The first was a statement with the title "No to Takfir; Yes to Freedom of Expression," signed by 91 Saudi writers and intellectuals. This statement focused on the negative impact of intimidating those who want to practice free speech, calling on the Saudi state to take action against such fatwas. The statement was neither a defense of liberalism nor a criticism of the religious argumentation that some ulama use to label liberals as heretics; instead, it appealed to the values of freedom of expression, stating that an environment of *takfir* stifles that freedom and leaves all in fear from the threat that ensues from such a fatwa (Diya' al-Salik, 2007; Ismail, 2008). The second statement, "A Campaign Against Takfir," came from 101 intellectuals, activists, and institutions of different Arab countries such as Saudi Arabia, Yemen, Iraq, Egypt, Lebanon, and Morocco (Arab Commission for Human Rights, 2008). This statement was similar to the first, except in that it brought up the story of the fatwa against Faraj Fuda, a secular Egyptian intellectual who opposed the enforcement of the Shari'a. He was murdered by two people who belonged to the *Jama'a Islamiyya* (The Islamic Group) following a debate with prominent Egyptian ulama in which Fuda insisted on his secular position and his rejection of involving religion in politics. After the debate a *takfir* fatwa was issued against him and was widely circulated, leading to his death on June 8, 1992 (Khalil, 2014). The second statement also mentioned the 1995 attempted murder, also as a consequence of a *takfir* fatwa, in Cairo of the Egyptian writer and Nobel Laureate Najib Mahfuz (1911–2006). The statement argued these two violent incidents were a result of such fatwas, and concluded by warning that *takfir* fatwas continue to lead to murder.

All the while, in Saudi Arabia, al-Barrak's fatwa was being supported by a number of Saudi ulama. Twenty of them issued a statement in support of the fatwa in two ways; first they argued that al-Barrak did not issue a specific *takfir* fatwa (al-Jibrin, 2008). Second, they argued that the fatwa itself was correct and reiterated that anyone who doubts *takfir* is indeed a *kafir.* There was no criticism of the fatwa from any formal alim, as there had been in the case of al-Fawzan's fatwa. It is most likely that, since al-Barrak was not a formal alim, the Saudi state did not see the need to issue a formal response to his fatwa, nor did it take action against the two writers. The debate in favor of and against the fatwa remained confined to the ulama and conservatives on the one hand and liberal intellectuals on the others; Saudi society was not mobilized in this conflict.

These cases are important in that they give us a background to understand the significant change that happened in *takfir* after 2012. The fatwas and statements were in one way an expression of the rejection by some religious conservatives in Saudi Arabia of the lifestyle espoused by Saudi liberals. Yet based on the definition of heresy discussed earlier, these *takfir* fatwas should also be seen as a means by which the religious orthodoxy in Saudi Arabia asserted its authority vis-à-vis the state and society. By issuing *takfir* fatwas, the ulama wanted to prove to their constituencies that they were upholders of religion and were standing firm against the enemies of Islam.

In 2011, about 2 years after his former *takfir* fatwa, al-Barrak issued another statement accusing a Saudi columnist of being a *kafir* because of an article that called for the formulation of a new concept of deity which the columnist called "civil deity" (Alarabiyya, 2011; al-Barrak, 2011). The writer, Abdulaziz al-Suwayyid, claimed that Muslims needed to break away from the traditional and superstitious concept of deity prevalent today, and that they should reformulate a new deity on the basis of civil and humane concepts. In this instance, al-Barrak did not issue a fatwa based on a question posed to him; instead, he issued a *takfir* statement citing the article and mentioning the writer by name. The statement started "I read the article of him who goes by the name of Abdulaziz al-Suwayyid," and then launched a theological discussion in which he highlighted the heresy in the article. Al-Barrak then explained that "those who deny Allah's attributes are *kuffar*." Although he mentioned the name of the writer in his statement, al-Barrak did not explicitly categorize al-Suwayyid as a *kafir*; instead, he said that anyone who says things similar to those in the article is a *kafir*. By now, Twitter was widely used by Saudis, and a hashtag, #alsuwayyid, was created to highlight the matter and to attack al-Suwayyid. In response to this fatwa, the Saudi state banned al-Suwayyid from writing in newspapers (Sabq, 2011) and his article was taken off the newspaper's website, although some websites retain a copy of it ('Uqaylan, 2011).

Why did this fatwa occasion such a strong response from the state? One explanation is that al-Suwayyid's article touched on the idea of deity, making it difficult for the state to ignore it; otherwise it would seem that it did not pay attention to defending Islam. But the response can better be explained in reference to the period of the article and fatwa, which came toward the end of 2011 during the Arab Spring. At the time the Saudi state was dependent on its ulama and religious institutions for support as it sought to bolster its own legitimacy and emphasize the illegitimacy of public protests (Lacroix, 2011b; al-Rasheed, 2013b). Moreover, this was also the time when Twitter was becoming a major tool for disseminating opinion; consequently *takfir* was no longer restricted to Internet forum pages, which were less frequented by the average Saudi. Twitter expanded the publicity of *takfir*, thus prompting a stronger response from society and the state. The events of the Arab Spring and the use of Twitter can also help in explaining why *takfir* fatwas would become *takfir* campaigns, how the public was brought in as an active agent of these campaigns, and why the state took more aggressive steps against some of the targets of the campaigns.

5.3.2. Takfir *Campaigns: 2012–2013*

The *takfir* fatwas and statements mentioned thus far are a sample of the type of *takfir* that was initiated by Saudi ulama against Saudi liberals and their ideas. Beginning in 2012, a new form of *takfir* was initiated with three key characteristics that differentiated it from prior forms of *takfir*. The first difference lay in the target of the accusation: while prior fatwas targeted liberal values, this new form of *takfir* was directed against atheism, and particularly its promotion. This is significant in that for the first time in Saudi Arabia ulama acknowledged that atheism had spread in Saudi Arabia and that it was serious enough to warrant their intervention through fatwas, awareness-spreading efforts, and legal procedures directed against the alleged atheists. This acknowledgment happened after the Kashgari case in February 2012, to which I turn later in this chapter. The second difference between this new form of *takfir* and its predecessor lay in the presentation in the form of a petition to the state and the public. While previous *kufr* accusations came in the form of classical fatwas structured as a question with an answer, or in the form of a statement made by an alim, these new claims came as statements signed by public figures in Saudi Arabia demanding that the state intervene against those who spread atheism. At the same time, this new form of *takfir* would speak to the Saudi national community, warning it against the active promotion of atheism and calling on it to be vigilant. The third and perhaps most important difference is that this new form of *takfir* used the Internet to mobilize public support for the fatwa and to condemn the persons in question. Crucially, Twitter was the leading online tool that was used to propagate the campaign and mobilize support for it.

This *takfir* campaign challenged those who sought to use Twitter to criticize religion in Saudi Arabia. One may say that the development of *takfir* campaigns was a natural response to what is perceived as the ultimate sin: atheism and the promotion of atheism. But as serious as these two accusations are, there were two important factors that acted as catalysts for this new form of *takfir*.

The first are steps taken by the Saudi state to limit the authority of informal religious institutions in the country. I mention three such steps here, all of which caused a lot of frustration for many of the religious leaders in Saudi Arabia. One is the decision taken by Prince Khalid al-Faisal, the governor of the Mecca region in the west of Saudi Arabia, to nationalize all teachers at Quran *tahfidh* (memorization) centers in the Mecca region. Most of the Quran teachers at these centers at the time had been foreign nationals, and nationalizing them meant that the 8,500 current teachers had to be laid off (Ba'amer, 2010). Quranic centers were a main tool for the religious indoctrination of young Saudis, and most of the teachers belonged to or were influenced by one religious current or another in Saudi Arabia. The effectiveness of indoctrination depended on the loyalty of these teachers. Firing them all in one decision was a great loss to the influence of religious leaders at these centers and on the students who attended (Jehadnet, 2010). The second step came in March 2011, when al-Faisal closed down the Islamic summer camps, also in the Mecca region, under the pretext that they were being used to train young men to use arms (al-Shihri, 2011). The camps were a main source of authority and recruits for Islamist actors in Saudi Arabia, and closing them was a signal that the state was taking steps to dry up their recruitment pool. The third step was in January 2012, when King Abdullah fired the existing head of the Committee, Abdulaziz al-Humayyin (b. 1964) and assigned a more moderate person in his place (CNN, 2012). While the firing itself caused anger among religious actors (Anha', 2012), the appointment of the replacement was widely interpreted as a step by the state to reform the Committee (al-Shayiʿ, 2012), and for the more conservative Saudis that implied weakening it. The new head was continuously attacked in the conservative media and even accused of being the destroyer of *hisba*[5] (Raʾis al-Hayʾat, 2014; anawin, 2014). This third step happened just 3 weeks before the Kashgari case. These three steps were all interpreted as part of an organized effort by the Saudi state to weaken the grip of religion on Saudi society, and they increased the frustration of the religious community toward the state.

The second factor that catalyzed the development of *takfir* campaigns was the Arab Spring. With its advent and the subsequent demonstrations against Arab rulers, the Saudi state feared that these events would inspire Saudi youth to do the same. It thus needed to curb the enthusiasm of its youth and make sure that popular frustration did not turn into popular political action against the state. To do so it used three tools: the security forces; financial packages for the population, including the creation of hundreds of thousands of new jobs (Aleqtisadiah, 2011); and the legitimacy it could garner from the ulama, who were required to preach against all forms of political action, especially demonstrations and political petitions. In February 2011, the mufti of Saudi Arabia issued a fatwa prohibiting demonstrations, blaming the demonstrations in Egypt and Tunisia for the violence and bloodshed that had happened there, and warning Muslims about plans to divide the countries of the region (al-Suhayl, 2011). A month later the Council of Senior Ulama issued a statement, also stressing the prohibition of all forms of political opposition to the state, demonstrations, and political petitions. It insisted that such means lead to discord and threatened the Islamic character of the Saudi state (al-Sharq al-Awsat, 2011). This last fatwa was issued a few days before a demonstration that was planned to take place on March 11, 2011 (CNN, 2011; RevolutionKSA@ gmail.com, 2011). Despite these fatwas, the anonymous organizers mobilized Saudis online and the state feared that they could shake its control of the country. Accordingly, the state also called on the country's judges— a crucial religious institution—to warn the population of the legal consequences of participating in a demonstration or encouraging others to do so (al-Rifaʿi, 2011). The ulama expected more authority and financial

---

5. *Hisba* is to take one into account for their actions. In Muslim communities it means taking sinners into account and is considered a form of forbidding vice. Here "destroyer of *hisba*" means one who wants to destroy the institution of forbidding vice—that is, the Committee.

support in return for supporting the state, yet they got very little in return. The *takfir* campaigns, in turn, served as a method of putting pressure on the state and asserting ulama authority. Finally, Twitter and social media facilitated the spread of the fatwas and the mass mobilization of Saudis in the country.

5.3.3. Takfir *Petitions*

A key element in this new form of *takfir* campaign was the *takfir* petition. The purpose was to mobilize the Saudi population against the objects of *takfir* and to pressure the state to take action against them. The main two petitions issued after 2012 were prompted by the Hamza Kashgari case, in which Kashgari had disseminated a series of tweets that were deemed by Saudi ulama to be blasphemous. The petition did not target Kashgari per se; instead, it focused on an alleged wave of atheism in which Kashgari was seen as a victim rather than an initiator. The petitions sought to mobilize the public against this alleged activity in the hope that the state would respond and intervene.

The first petition, titled "Statement of the Ulama and Preachers of Jeddah About Incubators of Deviation and the Spread of Scepticism" was issued in March 2012 and signed by 76 well-known ulama, scholars, and preachers from the city of Jeddah. The petition began by asserting the importance of the city of Jeddah as the gate to the two Holy Mosques of Mecca and Medina. It then went on to say that the eternal struggle between Truth and Falsehood—*al-Haq wa-l-Batil*—is part of Allah's plan. Next, it detailed the events that preceded the petition, most notably Kashgari's blasphemous tweets, which it tied to the broader phenomenon of people casting doubt on the existence of Allah. Most serious, however, was the alleged discovery of key sites for the organized dissemination of blasphemy and atheism; that is, social gatherings and café meetings that were active in promoting *kufr*.

After describing the situation as the signatories perceived it, the petition addressed Saudis. It first acknowledged that society was indeed saddened by such un-Islamic activity, but then warned that if society stayed silent about such grave deviations the country would risk Allah's wrath falling on it. Then the petitioners directed their attention to the state. First they complained again about the fact that such organizations existed in Saudi Arabia, the heartland of Islam, and argued that this state of affairs had arisen due to both negligence by the state and its stifling of religious activities. Here they were referring to steps such as the three mentioned previously. They accused those active in these groups of having relationships with foreign embassies, thus adding the specter of a foreign conspiracy. They then indirectly accused the state of playing a balancing game between the religious and the liberals, but such a situation, they said, should not be part of that game. After that they made their demands of the state. They wanted the state to support the inoculation of the youth to protect them from such devious activities. They wanted it to take action against activities that spread atheism and to shut down all cafés and private salons where atheists function. They demanded that the state intensify religious learning in Jeddah and set up more religious institutions there. They also demanded the creation of committees of specialists in ideas, Shari'a, and psychology to advise and guide the victims of heretical ideas who are living in Saudi Arabia or abroad on scholarship programs. Finally they demanded that all deviance be taken seriously and its initiators tried by the religious courts (al-Khamis, 2012). The summation of their demands was more authority for religious actors in Saudi Arabia.

The second petition was written shortly after this and also concerned the alleged wave of atheism that was spreading in the land of the Two Holy Mosques. Signed by 105 religious scholars and ulama in Saudi Arabia, it differed from its predecessor in two ways: first, it petitioned on behalf of the entire country, as atheism, it claimed, had spread beyond Jeddah; and second, it referred to specific individuals who were engaged in heresy. Most notably, it mentioned Turki al-Hamad, the Saudi intellectual and writer mentioned earlier, whose novels have been targeted since the mid-1990s. It also mentioned Raif Badawi (b. 1984), the owner and manager of the Internet forum The Liberal Saudi Network, which was later shut down on the orders of the Saudi state. The third Saudi mentioned was Hamza Kashgari (b. 1989), a young intellectual who, as a teenager, had actively participated in groups of religious activists in the city of Jeddah. The fourth was myself, as I was accused of creating sleeper cells to spread atheism. The fifth was Hissa al-Alshaykh, a female Saudi columnist who frequently criticized the religious establishment and was a target of heresy campaigns because of her tweets. The sixth was Badriyya al-Bishr (b. 1967), a female Saudi novelist accused of being a *kafira* for a statement in one of her novels that "Allah in his harshness would manifest in the face of my mother, who is always angry at us" (al-Hijri, 2012). This statement was seen as constituting heresy, and they demanded that she be held accountable for it.

These two petitions share many characteristics. Both speak to society, demanding that it be more vigilant, and both address their message to ulama, intellectuals, and opinion-makers in Saudi Arabia. Moreover, both call on the various social segments to unite against the spread of atheism, and both emphasize a cosmic view of the eternal fight between Good and Evil, considering the social world a reflection of the cosmic struggle. Finally, both suggest providing support for those who go astray and hunting down the perpetrators of the crime of spreading atheism and taking them to court.

The purpose of such petitions was not only to incite society but also to encourage state intervention. They wanted to bring the case to the state in the hope that it would punish the perpetrators. Fatwas in themselves may lead to state intervention, and may not, as we saw in chapter 2, with the many fatwas against sins in Saudi Arabia that were ignored, and also in some of the *takfir* fatwas discussed earlier in this chapter. In Saudi Arabia, state intervention has taken two main forms. First, when an issue is formally brought to the attention of the state, such as when people petition through *hisba* law,[6] the state intervenes through its judicial system, although the public prosecutor can reject *hisba* petitions. The second form of intervention occurs when the state's legitimacy as protector of the faith is challenged. This second form had become particularly important with the advent of social media, and instigators of *takfir* petitions publicly promoted their case against heresy in order to put pressure on the state to act. *Takfir* petitions thus put the state in a position where it has to show that it is defending the faith.

5.3.4. Perfect Takfir

As noted earlier, the *takfir* campaigns began with the Kashgari case. This case was also the beginning of a witch-hunt for heretics and ended up significantly limiting discussions on Twitter criticizing religion. The Kashgari case should thus be seen as a milestone in the history of *takfir* in Saudi Arabia, as it initiated what could be considered a perfect *takfir*:— that is, a *takfir* with the following elements: (1) it was instigated by formal and informal fatwas or statements; (2) it was associated with a *takfir* campaign; (3) it gained popular support for the campaign; and (4) the state

---

6. Legislation that allows private citizens to raise a legal case against sinners.

acted in support of the *takfir*. In Saudi Arabia such a situation had never existed before except in four cases starting in 2012 with the Kashgari case. I discuss three of these cases of perfect *takfir* whose targets were Hamza Kashgari, Turki al-Hamad, and Raif Badawi. I also discuss a fourth case that contained these three characteristics, but the target had familial relations that led to a limitation of state action.

The first and key case was that of Kashgari. It began with a number of tweets that Kashgari made on the occasion of the birthday of the Prophet, the *Mawlid*, on Saturday, February 4, 2012. His tweets said:

> On your birthday, I say that I have loved the rebel in you, that you have always been a source of inspiration to me, and that I do not like the halos of divinity around you. I shall not pray for you.
>
> On your birthday, I find you wherever I turn. I say that I have loved aspects of you, hated others, and could not understand many more.
>
> On your birthday, I shall not bow to you. I shall not kiss your hand. Rather, I shall shake it as equals do, and smile at you as you smile at me. I shall speak to you as a friend, no more. (Indvik, 2012)

The tweets were emotionally charged, conveying awe and love combined with pride and questioning. Kashgari imagined an audience with the Prophet where both would meet as equals, peers, and friends, rather than as leader and follower or one of lesser status. Yet according to the imagination and theological belief of all Muslims one must only imagine oneself as being of lesser status than the Prophet. In Kashgari's tweets he imagines himself telling the Prophet, "I will not kiss your hands," signaling that he would not approach the Prophet as one of higher status. He also imagines himself telling the Prophet that there were many things he loved about him and things he hated. Through this statement he sought to humanize the Prophet and the relationship with him. He thus explained that rather than seeing a totally perfect human being in the Prophet, he saw a human being whom he respects, but whom he also considered flawed. This in itself was considered blasphemous. The Muslim belief about the Prophet is that he is perfect, that one should love every aspect of him and not question him in any way (al-Saqqaf, n.d.). In this imagined dialogue the Prophet was warning Kashgari of the reactions of his followers. Kashgari thus recognized that what he was saying was not acceptable to the public, but he could not have imagined the public response.

By Sunday afternoon, the day after these tweets were posted, hundreds of tweets had already been posted in response to Kashgari. But one particular response amplified the attention to them, from a well-known extremist alim, Nasir al-ʿUmar, who also hosted a Sunday religious lesson weekly, which he then posted on YouTube (almoslimnet, 2012). That Sunday his whole lesson was dedicated to the Hamza's tweets, and this lesson played a critical role in initiating and magnifying the *takfir* campaign against Kashgari, as al-ʿUmar had more than a million followers on Twitter at the time. I summarize the main points of his sermon as well as explicating its underlying logic, because this particular sermon was the starting point of what amounted to an attempt at an inquisition in Saudi Arabia, and the beginning of a *takfir* campaign that was unprecedented in Saudi Arabian history.

Al-ʿUmar began his lesson by reciting the verse:

And when We intend to destroy a city, We command its affluent but they
     defiantly disobey therein; so the word comes into effect upon it, and
     We destroy it with [complete] destruction. (Quran: al-Israʾ, 16)

As he read the verse he cried for a few seconds and then continued reciting the remainder. The verse is frequently quoted by religious puritans in Saudi Arabia when lamenting the social decadence of their times. Its message is that if the faithful do not take it upon themselves to stop corruption, Allah's wrath will befall everyone, the pious and the corrupt alike. His tears were meant to emphasize his fear of the wrath that was imminently to fall. After he finished reciting this verse he recited another: "Would You destroy us for what the foolish among us have done?" (Quran: al-Aʾraf, 155). This verse is supposed to amplify the emotion of fear of the wrath of Allah, which will surely fall on the society that allows corruption. It was a plea to Allah not to punish the faithful for the actions of the corrupt and the degenerate. Then al-ʿUmar stated that he could not give a lesson that evening when "Allah and his Prophet are being publicly cursed." He began to cry once again and repeated the essential meaning of the verses. The words were measured, and their purpose was to elicit an emotional response from the audience and arouse fear for their well-being. He then went on to speak of the catastrophes that had befallen the countries near Saudi Arabia. This lesson was given on February 5, 2012, at the peak of the events of the Arab Spring, and many Saudis were fearful of the chaotic situation that other Arab countries were enduring. Al-ʿUmar contrasted the security that Saudi Arabia enjoyed with that of their neighbors, and then remarked that this chaos around Saudi was happening at a time when people in Saudi were belittling Allah. If these heretics were not punished, al-ʿUmar warned that all Saudis would be punished by Allah.

Then he started speaking about what Kashgari had said on both his blog and Twitter, and explained that he was merely an example of those liberals who would bring catastrophe to the land. Al-ʿUmar wanted to initiate a campaign against all those whom he considered liberal in Saudi Arabia, and Kashgari was merely the steppingstone toward that campaign. He quoted some excerpts from Kashgari's writings about Allah. In one of these excerpts, Kashgari said that no one can be absolutely sure of Allah's existence unless one has a direct experience of Him; as a result, belief in Allah is not obligatory, because Allah would not make it obligatory to believe in anything without clear evidence. This was considered a challenge to an understanding of a deity who demands absolute belief in Him. Al-ʿUmar went on in his sermon to quote some of Kashgari's tweets about theodicy that cast doubt on Allah's mercy and wisdom, quoting these and asserting that this was clearly and utterly *kufr*. Kashgari's tweets were part of the discussion on Twitter, and al-ʿUmar took advantage of them to unleash a backlash against criticizing religion in Saudi Arabia.

Al-ʿUmar's target was not so much Kashgari as it was the broader liberal trend within Saudi Arabia. So while he did in fact comment on the Kashgari tweets related to the Prophet, and while he did express his anger that Kashgari claimed to be a peer to the Prophet, or that he dared to express hatred of any quality of the Prophet, he only did so briefly. Quickly, he moved on to attack liberals more generally, stressing to his audience that the Kashgari tweets were part of a series of liberal, secular, and atheist activities. His purpose was to transform the anger against Kashgari into anger against all liberals and secularists in Saudi Arabia; his ultimate purpose was to convince his audience that there was organized activity in Saudi Arabia that sought to spread atheism and to destroy Islam. He concluded his sermon by proposing solutions. He first said that his preferred solution was "the sword," meaning he would prefer to see these liberals executed. But he quickly warned his audience not to take action such as personal assaults on Kashgari or those like him without state approval. While he did prefer the execution of liberals, he was careful not to provoke the state and to avoid direct incitement. Instead, he advocated going through legal channels and insisted that his listeners send telegrams to the political and religious leadership of the country such as the king, the mufti, and the crown prince, demanding action. He also advised them to use social media in responding to the heresy of Kashgari and other liberals.

His audience responded to his call, and the social media campaign against Kashgari grew exponentially as thousands called for his arrest, trial, and execution. The tone was brutal and unforgiving. Thousands of faxes and telegrams were sent to the Royal Court, and thousands of people went to court to raise *hisba* cases against Kashgari (al-Rifa'i, 2012). Thousands more on Twitter called for his death. Some went as far as to tweet his home address and details of his car. Surprisingly, the demands for his execution were being expressed by people from all spectrums of society and with various degrees of religiosity. The minister of information, Abdulmaqsud Khuja, expressed extreme grief and anger at what Kashgari had written, issuing a ban on his writing in any Saudi publication (al-Barqawi, 2012c). Kashgari had left the country for Malaysia on the day following al-ʿUmar's sermon, and he posted a letter in which he declared that he had made a mistake in this specific instance and had returned to Islam, thus reaffirming his faith in Allah and the Prophet (al-Barqawi, 2012a). Some thought that this should close the matter, but most considered it irrelevant, based on a fatwa that states that those who curse the Prophet must be punished even if they repent. The Council of Senior Ulama issued a statement that insisted that any criticism of the Prophet, no matter how minor, is considered to be on the same level as cursing him. Such acts are punished by execution, and there is no opportunity for retraction or repentance (al-Salafi, 2012; al-Zahrani, 2012). Kashgari left the country on February 6, and the next day King Abdullah ordered his arrest (Toumi, 2012). He was arrested in Malaysia and extradited to Saudi Arabia, where he was put in prison (Gooch & Goodman, 2012). He was released on October 29, 2013, after nearly 2 years in prison.

As with the *takfir* fatwas mentioned earlier, some more liberally oriented Saudis criticized the campaign against Kashgari. A group of them posted a statement titled "Bayan al-Shabab al-Saʿudy Bikhusus Dhaman al-Huriyyat wa ʾadab al-ʾikhtilaf (The Guarantee of Freedoms and the Manners of Disagreement)," signed by almost 3,000 people. In it they declared that they rejected anyone who sought to cast doubt on one's sincerity to faith; that they rejected efforts to monopolize religious learning and attempts by the ulama to act as guardians of society in the name of protecting it; and that individuals should be allowed to think independently.

The statement also rejected all attempts to suppress others and said that this was a situation that past generations had had to go through and had led to the divergence of cultural and intellectual discourse from important to minor matters. Here they were referring to the changes the country had undergone after the Juhayman incident in 1979, which in their view had resulted in a fundamental shift in Saudi Arabia toward conservativism in the public sphere. They also made references to the modernity battles of the 1980s, which they characterized as a dark episode in Saudi history that should not be repeated. They concluded their statement by warning people not to revert to *takfir* when confronting ideas, and cautioned against inciting the state against *as-hab al-ra'y* (people of opinion). Instead, Saudis who cared about their religion and their country should focus on what unites society rather than on what divides it. But the *takfir* campaign was too intense for such a message to have an effect on either the public or the position of the state (al-Saudi, 2012).

After Kashgari's arrest in Malaysia, Khidir bin Sanad, a scholar of religion and history living in Jeddah, started to question the factors surrounding Kashgari's deviation through a series of Tweets. In them he pointed to me and claimed that I had created sleeper cells in Jeddah to spread atheism (@khader_sanad, 2012; @malturki, 2012). His analysis of the causes behind Kashgari's alleged deviation gained popular support, and he was eventually invited onto a talk show to explain the history of these sleeper cells and the danger that they pose to Saudi's youth (Alcetraz, 2012). The influence of his idea of sleeper cells was strong enough to become a main theme in the petitions mentioned previously. I tried to respond to these accusations and appeared on the Saudi channel al-Arabiya to speak about this topic, to little avail (al-Dakhil, 2012). People called for my arrest and trial and a *hisba* case was filed against me, but the public prosecutor rejected it (Akhbar24, 2012a, 2012b).

The campaign was then extended to anyone tweeting what was deemed heresy. The female columnist mentioned in the second *takfir* petition, Hissa al-Alshaykh, had tweeted about the voice of a singer, comparing it to the voice of Allah:

Oh Glory to He who created the voice of Muhammad [Abduh][7] above other voices, you do not know when approaching it with your ear are you listening to Allah, or Allah is giving you ecstasy.

---

7. An iconic Saudi singer.

Within minutes there was a Twitter campaign against her with thousands of tweets demanding her arrest and trial. She immediately closed her account and denied that it had ever belonged to her (al-Barqawi, 2012b). Yet the campaign continued. Muhammad al-ʿUrayfi, whom she had mocked in one of her columns (H. al-Alshaykh, 2011), mobilized against her with a lecture and some tweets (@MohamadAlarefe, 2012; wa7eed6, 2012). He tweeted:

> More than four thousand individuals raised a case against Hamza Kashgari at court to . . . so which of you will be active in raising a case against Hissa al-Alshaykh.

Al-ʿUrayfi at the time had more than 3 million followers. One alim went on television and cried as he described the horror of reading such blasphemy (Qanat al-Muhtaseb, 2012). Another alim posted a poll stating that what Hissa al-Alshaykh had said was *kufr* and that she deserved to be killed, and asking whether or not pollsters supported her being put on trial and then executed. The results showed that 168,000 individuals participated, 98% of whom demanded that she be tried (@alsaleeh, 2012). It is of course not possible to confirm the results, but considering the intensity of the campaign, the high profile of those leading it, and the reaction of state religious officials, one can at least assume they were quite accurate. A few days later, the head of the Committee issued a statement that they would take action once this was proved (Sabq, 2012). Hissa al-Alshaykh, though, was from the same family as the mufti, which served her well in this case. The mufti issued a statement calling on people to stop accusing others without proof. He did not mention his relative explicitly, but it was understood that he meant Hissa al-Alshaykh (al-Qahtani, 2012). After the mufti's statement the campaign died down, prompting a comparison among some Saudis between the treatment afforded to her and that of Kashgari. Her being a member of the elite family of al-Alshaykh helped her to avoid punishment, while Kashgari did not, simply because he had no one to support him.

The effect of the *takfir* campaign was extended to a café called Jusur in the city of Jeddah. It had opened in 2010 and became a hub for youth activity in Jeddah, where various youth book clubs and other cultural youth groups and visitors from various socioeconomic backgrounds—including Kashgari and myself—gathered. Jusur's café organizers invited speakers of different backgrounds to speak about diverse issues. Its overall environment was liberal and it provoked the conservatives, becoming a target of criticism for some time before the Kashgari case. The advocates of the campaign against Kashgari and myself accused both of us of being involved with the sleeper cells to spread atheism, and claimed that we used Jusur café for some our so called activities. Consequently the Saudi state ordered that Jusur café be shut down (al-Rasheed, 2013b; Safi, 2012).

The campaigns also focused on two people who had been targets of *takfir* for many years before, Raif Badawi and Turki al-Hamad. Badawi is the founder of the liberal website The Liberal Saudi Network and had been on the radar of religious conservatives for some time because of the allegedly heretical content that he published on his website. In March 2012, Badawi attempted to defend himself from accusations of heresy by publicly claiming on a Saudi satellite channel that there were indeed heretical statements posted on his website, but that they were not written by him; he merely provided a space for free and open discussion (al-Abdulmun'im, 2012). Instead of his statement being taken as proof of his innocence, it was taken as a self-indictment. After his statement was aired, al-Barrak was asked about a person who allows heretic content to be published on a website that he owns, and responded by saying that such an act was undoubtedly *kufr*. But the campaign and the fatwa could not bring Badawi to trial. In June 2012, however, he was arrested not on grounds of heresy but rather on the grounds that he was a disobedient son (Sasapost, 2015). This situation was similar to that of Nasr Hamid Abu Zayd (1943–2010). Abu Zayd was an Egyptian scholar of linguistics. He was accused by some Egyptian ulama of promoting heretical views on the Quran. But Egypt had no specific laws to punish heretics, and his accusers could not use his heresy to bring him to court. Thus they reverted to the law of *hisba*, which makes it "incumbent upon every Muslim to promote the good and combat evil." That is the law gives Muslims the right to report to the courts sins being committed by individuals, and the court is obliged to take action. The accusers of Abu Zayd could not try him nor punish him for heresy, but were able raise a case against his marriage using the *hisba* rule. They claimed that he was living with his wife in sin, on grounds that he was a *heretic*, and heretics cannot continue living in marriage with a Muslim wife. The prosecutor had to accept the case, and the court affirmed Abu Zayd's heresy, and while it could not punish him, it nullified his marriage. After Abu Zayd's case, the law in Egypt changed. It restricted those who can initiate a *hisba* case in domestic matters to the prosecutor alone (Sfeir, 1998).

Similarly Badawi's adversaries could not find legal grounds to bring him to court on account of heresy, so they found another way, which was to use a law that punishes disobedient sons. Badawi's father, angry at his son, supported this case. The difference from the Abu Zayd case, however, was that Saudi Arabia has laws that punish heresy. Yet the challenge that Badawi's adversaries faced was in bringing him before a judge, something the public prosecutor would have to accept. The public prosecutor rejected the charge of heresy but accepted that of disobedience. The rejection was because the state was worried that the escalation of heresy accusations could spin out of control. Between February 2012 and the time of his arrest in June 2012, Twitter had become a key arena for *takfir* campaigns and more and more people were being encouraged to raise *hisba* cases against those accused of heresy. These campaigns were being initiated to put pressure on the state so that it would give the religious institutions the increased authority they demanded.

Although it was an accusation of disobedience that brought him to court, the indictment did in fact mention that Badawi had set up an electronic website for Saudi liberals, and that the site had allowed people to mock religious values and insult the ulama. The accusation also pointed to some of Badawi's heretical statements, such as one he had made on Valentines Day: "All people of earth are lucky for Valentines and we are lucky for [having] virtue." This was considered a mockery of virtue, which constitutes heresy. Badawi was finally indicted of setting up a website that threatened public order (Anha', 2013a, 2013b). The indictment was a statement on how the religious authorities view heresy. It was not merely seen as an opinion against Allah but also as potential for social discord and instability. He stayed in prison until December 17, 2012, when he was put on trial, but the judge transferred his case to the General Court and recommended that Badawi be tried for apostasy (Akhbar24, 2012c). Finally, on December 25, 2013, a judge recommended that Badawi should be again referred to the General Court on charges of apostasy (Akhbar24, 2013b). The case of disobedience was merely a means of bringing Badawi before a judge, who would then have the right to try him for heresy.

Saudi reactions on Twitter to Badawi's case were mixed, though most called for his execution. I focus on two different periods, the first during his trial and the second sometime after his sentencing. The tweets present us with instances of Saudi reactions to both Badawi's deeds and to the punishment he was facing. There were more than 5,000 tweets following each step of the trial, from the moment it was set to start to its end. Emotions were mixed, and the most common sentiment was expressed in tweets such as "Let them cut off his head and eradicate his impurity and rid the country of them" (@mn, 2012). Like al-ʿUmar, this tweet sought to indict not only Badawi but also his Saudi liberal allies. Most tweets expressed this very feeling. On the other hand, there were those who were angry at the very idea of him being on trial and at the comments made against him. For example, a tweet read "Forgive us Raif! Those who were opening their hearts to dialogue with the Jew, the Christian, and the Buddhist, their hearts have now closed to dialogue with the enlightened Muslim and they have said kill and imprison him" (@dh, 2012). This tweet points to a Saudi-funded center in Vienna, the King Abdullah bin Abdulaziz International Centre for Interreligious and Intercultural Dialogue (KAICIID, n.d.), set up to promote dialogue between followers of the different religions of the world. Specifically, this tweet expresses anger at the contradiction between calling for dialogue between religions *outside* Saudi Arabia, while at the same punishing people *inside* Saudi Arabia who have different opinions about religion.

Some tweeters were disappointed by the response of Saudi human rights activists, most of whom are of Islamist background and whose popular base is conservative; when Badawi went on trial these activists preferred to stay silent to avoid a backlash from their own constituencies. As one tweet noted, "The silence of Islamic rights activists proves that the real Saudi rights activists are few, and the rest are defenders of their own parties and their own extremists" (@Yz, 2012). Others pointed to the contrast between the way the state treated terrorists and the way it treated liberals. Saudi Arabia had initiated a special program to rehabilitate terrorists during which terrorists were well treated (Braude, 2014). So some people wondered why such a contrast existed between the treatment of a man with an opinion and that of a man who had committed violent crimes. One tweeter expressed shock, saying:

I cannot understand how one who accuses a whole country of being *kafir* and who desires to kill everyone without exception is rehabilitated and at the same time someone is tried for his ideas. (@Mu, 2012)

The same sentiments were expressed 2 years later, when on September 14, 2014, *al-Hayat* newspaper reported that preparations were under way to whip someone who had set up a website that threatened public order (al-Hilali, 2014). It was understood that the person was Badawi, and a hashtag titled "the whipping of Raif Badawi next month" was immediately created. One tweeter mocked the liberals who participated in the hashtag, saying:

> a hashtag that is crowded with the lowest members of society and some psychos from the liberal foreigners, this is the best solution to stop their belittlement [of religion]. (@Ta, 2014)

Describing liberals as foreigners was a way to imply that they did not belong in Saudi Arabia and were intruders who should leave the country.[8] Although the sentiments in this hashtag were the same as those in the previous one, the intensity was much less. The mood of the Arab Spring was over, and the ulama were not as able as they had been a year earlier to mobilize mass support in the same way.

The third person to be arrested after Kashgari was Turki al-Hamad, a Saudi intellectual and a former university professor. In the 1990s, al-Hamad had published a trilogy that contained various statements in fictional contexts. In the novels, his characters question Islam through various statements about religion, deity, and good and evil. But the one statement that was most quoted was *"Allah wa al-Shaytan wajhan li-ʿumlah wahidah"* (Allah and the Devil are two sides of one coin), (al-Hamad, 2002, pp. 50, 62 78, 137). The Saudi ulama considered the mere making of such statements heretical, even in a fictional work. These words spurred *kufr* accusations that went on for many years (al-Badr, 2008; Buraydah, 2002; al-Shuʾaybi, 1999; al-Zahrani, 2010). The *takfir* started during the first phase of *takfir* in Saudi Arabia—that is before 2012—but continued into the second phase, and thus we can clearly see a difference in the means of *takfir* and its outcome.

When his *takfir* case started in the mid-1990s, al-Hamad was asked to clarify his position in an semiformal setting headed by the minister of interior. He was acquitted on the basis that his statements were made in the context of a creative work and should not be taken literally, nor should

---

8. Liberals are sometimes called *bani liberal*, which literally means "the clan of liberals." It was as if the clearest way to speak of them as a group was to imagine them as a tribe. They are also referred to as *al-jaliyyah*, which means "the foreign community."

they be considered statements from the author.[9] One of the first who issued a fatwa against him was Hamud al-ʿUqla (1927–2010), a prominent informal alim. His fatwa, like the ones before, came in the form of a question and answer. The question was "What is your opinion of someone who says . . . ," and the fatwa mentioned a number of quotes from al-Hamad's novels. Then it asked the follow-up question: "And what is your opinion of those who protect the likes of these?" The purpose of such framing was, as mentioned previously, to avoid specific *takfir* and to restrict the matter to generalized *takfir*. Al-ʿUqla's answer started with a long introduction, explaining the jurisprudential logic behind his fatwa, and then said:

> The ruler of the country that this person belongs to must implement upon him Allah's decree which is to kill him without giving him the chance of repentance.

And then he said "Whoever defends the likes of this or protects him then he is also an apostate and must be killed." Yet, despite this detailed fatwa and a subsequent continuous stream of criticism targeting al-Hamad, he was never arrested and no legal case was ever brought against him on the grounds of what he had written in his novels. Unlike in the period that followed, al-Hamad had only faced *kufr* accusations rather than a *takfir* campaign strengthened by social networks. When al-Hamad was later targeted for something he had said during the *takfir* campaign phase he was imprisoned, even though the statements attributed to him during the *takfir* campaign phase were far less heretical than those in his novels.

On December 22, 2012, at the height of the Arab spring, Turki al-Hamad tweeted:

> Just as our beloved Prophet once came to rectify the faith of Abraham, the time has now come in which we need someone to rectify the faith of Muhammad. (Saleh, 2013)

What he meant was that Muslims needed to rectify the way Muslim's understood Islam—the faith of Muhammad—in the same way that

---

9. In a personal communication November 11, 2015. Abu Dhabi, UAE.

Muhammad the Prophet had rectified what the Arabs had understood to be the faith of the Patriarch Abraham. But some people on Twitter claimed that al-Hamad was casting doubt on the integrity of the faith of the Prophet, and a massive media campaign was launched against him through both Twitter and satellite channels. There were calls for his arrest and execution.

People were asked to go and raise a *hisba* case against him, but this time they were given a specific template to sign and deliver to the public prosecutor. This was a serious development in the *takfir* campaigns, indicating a higher level of organization. The template first referred to the Royal Decree on *hisba* law. It then stated that Turki al-Hamad had openly and explicitly cursed Allah and His Prophet, and that there were witnesses able and willing to testify to this. It continued that the punishment for cursing Allah and the Prophet is execution, citing various scholarly opinions to that effect. The petition then requested that the public prosecutor investigate al-Hamad and raise a criminal case against him for the sake of Allah and His Prophet (al-Madani, 2012). Al-Hamad was arrested and remained in prison for 6 months. Many of the country's intellectuals and social activists petitioned then–Crown Prince Salman bin Abulaziz (b. 1935), without effect (al-Weeam, 2012). Al-Hamad was released in June 2013 (McDowall, 2013), and that was the last *perfect takfir* campaign in Saudi Arabia until the end of 2018. Not that the *takfir* campaigns stopped: they continued on Twitter, but without the effect they had had between 2012 and 2014.

5.4. Conclusion

Takfir in Saudi Arabia thus went through two phases. The first was the *takfir fatwa* and *takfir* statement, and the second was the *takfir campaign*. The social backlash against those critiquing religion came in the second phase, which made it effective. But as we have seen, the impact of the backlash was selective. Among the many who had made heretical statements, only a few were targeted with campaigns effective in inciting the public and spurring state action. The three main sectors responding to *takfir* campaigns were the ulama, the public, and the state, but the motivations for their responses varied.

It is understandable that the state takes action against those who challenge the existing social order, even if that challenge comes in the form of ideas. As I noted earlier, Durkheim observed that the state's "first and foremost function is to ensure respect for beliefs, tradition and collective practices" (Durkheim, 1984, p. 66), and the Saudi state is no different in this regard. But while the Saudi state ensures respect for Islam, it does not persecute heretics unless their heresy becomes a matter of public interest. This is where the *takfir* campaigns and petitions come in, as they placed the Saudi state in a position in which it felt compelled to act or risk forfeiting its image as a protector of Islam. Compelling the state can happen in two ways; the first is by persuading the mufti or another member in the Council of Senior Ulama to champion the case for *takfir* and to formally bring the case to the state's attention. The second is by propelling the *takfir* case into the public sphere in a way that placed pressure on the state to take action. In the latter case, the response of the state depended on the nature of the heresy and the timing. So when understanding the backlash it is important to know why the public was incited, and why the ulama saw it as their responsibility to lead the public against heretics, and what was the context of the state's intervention.

5.4.1. The Public and Takfir

Unraveling the reaction of the public is more complex, especially in a country where most people practice various forms of sin and are ambivalently religious. Given this, why would the public support *takfir* campaigns? For a better understanding of their reaction, it is helpful to look at the worldview that is propagated to Saudis in sermons, short readable treatises, and most importantly in their 12 years of school education.[10] Saudis are taught that worshiping Allah happens in the Kingdom of Allah, which is the Cosmos. The metaphor used to imagine this kingdom is that of a Divine Court resembling the royal courts of kings (almaxicy hasan, 2010). In this world, the devil has vowed eternal animosity to human beings and is on a quest to tempt humans away from Allah and lead them to hell. This theme is common in sermons (Bramjna, 2012; Mosad, 2012). There is even a modern dramatization on YouTube of the ways of the devil that shows how he tricks humans into committing sin (Yahia, 2010). A popular short treatise to explain the philosophy of history states that neither Marx's economic theory nor Huntington's clash of civilizations theory explains the course of history: instead, history is driven by the fight

---

10. I see the content of these sources as heuristical rather than evidential, because being propagated does not necessarily mean that Saudis actually adopt it.

between good, embodied in the faithful, and evil, embodied in those who lead people astray (IslamWeb, n.d.). The success of those who worship Allah depends on the fulfillment of duties prescribed to them as Muslims, including prayer, performing jihad, and supporting the faithful.

First, in this worldview, if one is pious he/she is an ally or soldier of Allah, and if one is a sinner he/she is an ally and soldier of the devil (bin Taymiyya, 1982; Haris, 2011). Preachers frequently warn their audiences against becoming soldiers of the devil (Abdullah5588, 2010). Being a soldier of the devil is not seen as a metaphor; instead, it is a description of a real state of affairs, and accusing someone of being a soldier of the devil is taken seriously and could be considered defamation (al-Dani, 2010). Even sinners cautiously avoid becoming soldiers of the devil and are keen to support the soldiers of Allah, the pious. By being support-ers of the soldiers of Allah, sinners can partially redeem themselves. I mentioned earlier that one of the key mindsets that explains the way Saudis practice religion is "I love the pious but I am not one of them" (al-Suwaylim, 2013). This desire to be with the pious by those who are not pious is transformed into intense and sincere support for the pious when they rally against Satan's soldiers. The support that the *takfir* campaigns gained can be partially understood in reference to such a worldview.

Second, the heretic is considered an enemy of the existing social order, and of the way of life to which the public is attached. A heretic is consid-ered not only an enemy of Allah but also an enemy of every member in the community, because the heretic threatens to change the order of things. One common way to defame liberals who support women's rights is to claim that they do not want liberty for women; rather they want freedom in sexual relations. Prince Nayif bin Abdulaziz, when minister of interior, himself said, *"Inna Allathin Yunadun Bi-Huriyyat al-Mar'ah La Yuridun Hurriyyataha Bal Yuridun Hurriyat al-Wusul 'Ilayha"* (those advocating for woman's freedom do not want her freedom, rather they want free ac-cess to her) (@Badr_bin_, 2013). Fatwas against certain liberal behavior such as gender mixing cite social consequences and not merely religious ones. I mentioned earlier the way that al-'Umar framed his case against Kashgari and liberals. He was painting them as enemies of society rather than merely enemies of Allah. They were people who would bring de-struction on the whole society and country if action was not taken against them. This way of depicting heretics is not peculiar to Saudi Arabia; Muhammad al-Ghazali (1917–1996), a religious reformer and one of the most prominent Muslim ulama of the late 20th century, said in his defense of the murderers of Faraj Fudah (1945–1992):

> The presence of an apostate in society is tantamount to a germ that spreads its poison by encouraging people to leave Islam, thus the governor must kill him, and if he does not then it is the duty of individual people. (al-Qardawi, 2000, pp. 284–285)

Al-Ghazali was painting the heretic, like al-ʿUmar, as a threat and a danger to society, and not merely as a person with a wrong opinion or a sinner for whom judgment is reserved to Allah.

Third, the heretic is publicly targeted because he is understood to be a person who wants to challenge group unity. In Saudi Arabia, religion is considered the backbone of unity, and the mass condemnation mobilized against the heretic can be considered a punishment against him/her because he/she committed a crime against the unity of the group (Berlinerblau, 2001; Simmel, 1905, p. 344). The crime against the group is considered so dangerous that in Saudi law atheism was recently considered an act of terrorism (WAS, 2014; Withnall, 2014). The state's position on this matter came as part of new law declaring various groups, actions, and affiliations tantamount to terrorism. Some of the actions mentioned are breaking allegiance to the rulers of the country and giving allegiance to foreign parties, organizations, or states. Here the state is referring to the Muslim Brotherhood, who are accused of giving their allegiance to the leader of the group in Egypt; it is also referring to Shiʿa radicals, who are frequently accused of giving their allegiance to Iran or to Shiʿa ulama outside Saudi Arabia. Also mentioned in the law is participation in or incitement to fighting in foreign countries and support for, affiliation to, or belonging to foreign parties and organizations. The law also stated says that those who try to shake the social fabric of the Saudi society would also be considered terrorists. The social fabric includes religion, and this shows the seriousness of the Saudi state in its duty to protect the social fabric of the country. It also shows that the state considers heresy a threat to the social fabric. The law's specific reference to atheism is brief and general: anyone found "preaching atheist thought in any form or [found] doubting the foundations of Islamic religion on which this country was based" would be considered a terrorist. There is no explanation or definition of atheism, nor is there clarification on what the foundations of Islam are. In placing atheism with other violent crimes and affiliation to violent groups that atheism is not merely considered an intellectual position but rather a threat to the security of the country.

Belief in Islam is not only tied to salvation in the afterlife; there is also a strong subconscious link between faith in Islam and "the interests and life-styles of these who are choosing them" (Kurtz, 1983, p. 1095). The masses may like to think that they are targeting the heretic solely because he has committed a violation against Islam, but there is the possibility that there are such unconscious social motives at play (Simmel, 1905, pp. 344, 345). Finally, the heretic's statement leads to anxiety because heresy "places the true believer in a state of cognitive dissonance, imbalance or incongruity" (Zito, 1983, p. 128). The way to be relieved of this cognitive dissonance is by silencing the heretic. Collectively, these factors may explain why the public reacted the way they did, even though many of them sin themselves.

5.4.2. The Ulama and Takfir

Understanding the motives of the ulama is easier, especially according to the definition of orthodoxy stated previously. Heresy for the ulama is an attack on the narrative they present to their followers. That narrative gives the ulama authority, and heresy threatens their authority by exposing its weakness and incoherence (Zito, 1983, pp. 125, 129). Accordingly, the response of the Saudi ulama to heresy is not peculiar to them, but rather common to all authorities that depend on a specific narrative. Moreover, the ulama may attack heretics to strengthen their own authority, as suppressing heretics is one way to assert such authority (Kurtz, 1983, p. 1087). Attacks on heretics emphasize the role of ulama authority as the main protector of the faith and also provide the ulama with a tool to distract their flock from the many problems that the ulama themselves face in Saudi Arabia. The campaigns against Kashgari, al-Hamad, al-Alshaykh, Badawi, and others all came at a time when the state was intensively working to limit the institutional power of the ulama and when public criticism of the religious institutions was growing. The ulama were not only responding to perceived transgressions of the sanctity of Allah and Islam but also attempting to deflect attention from their own faults, to convince the state that they still had popular support, and ultimately to retain their authority by reasserting their role as protectors of the faith.

The state, the public, and the ulama had different reasons for targeting heresy, and perfect *takfir* was an instance when these reasons happened all at once against the same people. The weight of the *takfir* campaigns between 2012 and 2014 effectively limited the degree of openness in the discussions that were happening on Twitter. They also eliminated discussions that were taking place in physical spaces such as cafés and open salons.

6

Evolution of Saudi Religion

IN THIS BOOK I tackled the emergence of contemporary groups in Saudi Arabia that criticize religion. Over the course of the previous chapters I have confirmed the existence of such groups, yet this confirmation is insufficient to show the various ways nor the actual extent to which such criticism manifests. Accordingly, I have explored some of the probable reasons behind this emergence. I have shown some of the varieties of criticism that are emerging; there is criticism that can still be considered legitimate from an Islamic point of view; criticism that borders on nonbelief; and finally, criticism that is considered nonbelief altogether. I have also shown that almost all aspects of religion, major and minor, are now being questioned and sometimes ridiculed by thousands of Saudis. Indeed, a significant number of challenges to religion come not from intellectuals or philosophers or scholars of religion, but rather from laymen and laywomen. The degree of their knowledge is reflected in the way they question religion and ridicule it.

In order to probe the depths of this issue, I needed to situate it in its context of Saudi Arabian religiosity. Previous studies of Saudi Arabia, which have mainly focused on manifestations of religiosity in both state and society, have given the impression that Saudi Arabian society is very religious. I have noted previously that it is not difficult to reach such a conclusion in a country where upholding religion is considered a basic duty of the state and public space is supposed to be charged with sacred meanings. In this research I have shown that this is not the case, and that Saudi Arabia cannot be considered religious nor nonreligious but rather should be understood as "ambivalently religious." The Saudi state pronounces itself religious, even as it institutionalizes many acts that are considered sinful under Salafi Islamic law. Although Saudi ulama denounce such sins they have also found ways to incorporate some of them into their daily practice, such as the sin of using a satellite dish, which was soon normalized by the Saudi ulama. Saudi society, on the other hand, is diverse in its religiosity, but even those who describe themselves as religious consistently engage in multiple categories of sin such as listening to music or traveling to the countries of disbelievers.

Describing the ambivalent nature of Saudi religiosity is important because it influences the way one considers the issue of the emergence of individuals who criticize religion. To speak of the emergence of such criticism in a religious country is to speak of an exceptional situation that is somewhat isolated from the rest of society, while to speak of it in an ambivalently religious society is to normalize it, or at least to consider it as one shade in the spectrum of ambivalent religiosity. Criticizing religion in Saudi Arabia is an understudied phenomenon that is only surprising or exceptional if one considers Saudi Arabian society to be exceptionally religious.

While not all religious, Saudis have responded violently to the public emergence of the criticism of religion by either campaigning against people accused of skepticism and nonbelief or lobbying the state to incarcerate them. There are many probable reasons for this kind of violent response, one of which is that the nonreligious Saudi still wanted to be considered in Allah's camp even if he/she is not practicing His commandments. In this context, he/she may consider a violent response to these skeptics a means of redemption. Another probable reason is that they consider the skeptic an enemy of the existing social order, the way of life to which the public is attached. Accordingly, such individuals are enemies of every member of the community because the heretic threatens to change the order of things. Another factor that possibly influenced the violent response of the public was the Arab Spring. It was fundamental in the widespread use of Twitter in Saudi Arabia, and it also influenced the spread of the *takfir* fatwas and their successful transformation to *takfir* campaigns, where the public was involved with intense emotions and mobilized to take action against those accused of *kufr*. After the Arab Spring the *takfir* campaigns were less successful and fewer of the public were involved.

Through the interviews I conducted with Saudis I have been able to cast light on some of the factors driving the criticism of religion. I found nine reasons: (1) a near-death experience whereby the individual reaches the conclusion that life is too short to be constrained by religious thinking and religious demands; (2) the resolution of guilt, where one cannot live with the guilt of sin, and instead of leaving the sin decides to leave the religion that judges his/her behavior as sinful; (3) tension between Islam and sensibility, whereby one's inner values are in direct contradiction to Islamic decrees of beliefs; (4) tension between Islam and Islam, where contradictions within Islam lead one to discredit the religion all together and move away from it; (5) frustration with some of the rigid Islamic commandments and thus an effort to seek a less demanding religious interpretation, which leads to leaving Islam altogether; (6) anger at Allah because of human suffering and because of some of the commandments are considered to be unjust; (7) the problem of the good *kafir*, which creates an inner tension between one's belief that Allah sends all *kuffar* to hell and the sense of immorality in doing that; (8) surprise from the Saudi *kafir*, which leads one to lose confidence in the absolute integrity of the evidence on which Islam is based; and finally, (9) philosophical investigations, whereby one challenges Islam through methodical analysis of Islamic foundational beliefs. Highlighting these reasons is important in order to understand the motivation behind the process of criticizing religion, and is also important in showing how complex understanding this emergence in Saudi Arabia is and why it was important to use a qualitative method instead of a quantitative one.

The central thesis of book is based on observations on Twitter, interviews with a small number of Saudis, and various texts that describe and reflect the religious situation in Saudi Arabia. I acknowledge that my sources had limitations in their capacity to make generalizations. Nonetheless, my sources and method were effective in achieving what I sought at the outset of this research, namely to demonstrate the presence of Saudis who seek to criticize religion. It is not, of course, possible to speculate as to the social reach of this trend: important as it is, this is not the purpose of this book. Moreover a representative study is only possible after a qualitative understanding of this phenomena that defines the parameters of the survey.

The tweets that I have analyzed have shown the variety of issues that the criticism of religion covers. There are those who are merely critical of some of the ways in which religious decrees such as the prohibition of music are practiced, while others question the obligations of Islam such as women donning hijab or the prohibition of alcohol consumption. A third group of tweets takes this criticism further, taking aim at theological issues such as the monopoly of heaven by Muslims. These are different attitudes to issues of different degrees of importance, and while they can be all lumped under the category of the criticism of religion, they say different things about the relation to religion. Moreover, the tweets have shown that it is not possible to make generalizations with regard to one's relationship to religion. Specifically, one may exhibit a critical attitude toward one or more religious foundation while at the same holding firmly to others. A woman may support the decree of the hijab and at the same time be critical of the permissibility of slavery. In addition, we find Saudis critical of a foundational belief in Islam such as the belief in Muslims' monopoly of heaven even as they adhere firmly to the Islamic prohibition of alcohol consumption. Relationship to religion is not imagined as a relationship with a complete system of faith, but rather with separate units or sets of beliefs and commandments.

This research challenged many of my initial assumptions. I had thought at first that criticizing religion was restricted to intellectuals or highly educated Saudis. But I discovered that there are many critics of religion whose knowledge of Islam or philosophy is minimal. I had also thought that the main motivation behind the various forms of criticizing religion was frustration at the imposition of the religious institution on the lives of Saudis or the strictness of the Wahhabi version of Islam. What I discovered, however, was that this is not necessarily the case. All of the Saudis I interviewed were critical of Saudi religious institutions, did not approve their broad authority, and did not appreciate Wahhabi religious decrees; but the frustration I had assumed to be a motivator was largely absent in their narratives about turning away from religion. My interviewees are not representative of Saudi society, so there is the likelihood that there are many Saudis motivated by frustration. But the mere discovery that my assumption about the effect of frustration was wrong has been revealing for me, and could be for others who assume that it is the main reason for Saudis to move away from religion.

The most important assumption that I started with was that belief is an intellectual process; that people believe or disbelieve because of the availability of evidence or the absence thereof. This assumption persisted even after I had read some of the theories of religious transformation that consider belief to be largely a social process. I still thought that these theories might explain disengagement from religion, but that to understand the criticism of religion one still needed to consider it an intellectual process founded on thoughtful analysis and logical refutation of religious claims. I observed Saudis whose writings exhibited lay religious or philosophical knowledge as well as Saudis who exhibited a strong understanding of these two disciplines. This research, however, has revealed that the criticism of religion in Saudi Arabia is not an intellectual process. Instead I have found statements challenging religion or rejecting religious theological tenets and religious commandments to be based on the person's simple knowledge or belief in how things ought to be, and not on an understanding of philosophical refutations or on religiously based evidence. People were not rejecting Muslims' monopoly of heaven because they had concluded from a good understanding of the Quran and Hadith that indeed non-Muslims can go to heaven. They were simply saying that it does not make sense. Using common sense as a standard for interpreting the Quran or rejecting certain prevalent creeds has precedence in Islamic history among the Mu'tazila school of thought, but they had developed a whole epistemological theory about how sensibility is acquired and what kind of sensibility should be used and what should not be used when it comes to religion. This is in contrast to the Saudis whom I observed, who intuitively and sometimes inconsistently used their personal sensibilities and exhibited little theoretical sophistication as they articulated their criticism of religion.

At the outset of this research, I read about various theories that explain disengagement from religion in Western societies. These theories include a structural dimension, in that they explain changes in religious belief and practice with reference to shifts in social and cultural structures, institutionalization, and the spread of the media. The theories discuss the functional redundancy of religion due to its incapacity to serve a social need and the estrangement of religion from daily life due to the apparent disconnect between its core message and newly spread values, and finally the breakdown of the social foundations that facilitate the continuity of religion. For Durkheim, religion serves the solidarity of a society; for Luckmann, religion loses significance when the meaning for life that it provides is too different from the meanings that people have acquired; and Berger and Hervieu-Léger argue that when the social networks that sustain confidence in faith or sustain the transmission of faith erode, one can also expect a transformation of religiosity. One of my surprises was that the contradiction between science and religion was not highlighted as a reason for disengaging from religion. In my interviews with people who turned away from religion, this contradiction was not highlighted and when mentioned, it was as a sort of afternote. Even on Twitter, reference to science was promoting respect for scientists and challenging ulama authority more than it was being used to discredit religion per se.

In addition to exploring the emergence of disengagement and some of the personal and individual reasons for shifts in religious belief and practice, I examined which of these factors is present in Saudi Arabia and shapes Saudis' relation to religion. My research revealed three key findings, the first of which is that traces of these social factors were indeed present in the tweets that I analyzed and in the narratives of my interlocutors. This is something I had already assumed based on the fact that Saudis have undergone changes similar in kind—although not in degree—to the changes that other societies have undergone. And the research has validated my assumption to a degree. The second thing I discovered is that the most relevant theory is Luckmann's theory, which centers on the apparent disconnect between religion's core message and newly spread values, and how this dynamic leads to the estrangement of religion from daily life and its growing irrelevance. Many of the statements of my interlocutors and the tweets expressed a degree of that disconnect. Those critiquing religion were doing it based on the new values they had acquired. The third key finding of this book is that there seem to be two main stages for these who leave religion. The first is the disengagement phase, and the second is the process that follows disengagement.

There are very few studies on belief and nonbelief among Muslims, and none that I know of among Saudis. Accordingly I hope that this book will open the door to further studies. The media had already highlighted the existence of atheism in Saudi Arabia, but I wanted to go deeper and discuss it as a multidimensional emerging process. I also wanted to explore its contours and motivations. Specifically, I hoped to trace the criticism of religion by examining it holistically in the context of religious life in Saudi Arabia. I believe this study and further studies on the criticism of religion will be important for understanding Islam in modernity. Most of the studies on "Islam and modernity" center on a prism of authenticity and identity and have not paid enough attention to the spiritual and doctrinal dilemmas faced by the average Muslim and how they affect his or her personal life. On the other hand, most—if not all—of the studies on the weakening relationship between Muslims and their religion have focused on disbelief and atheism. My approach in this book has been to consider disengagement from religion as a phenomenon in its own right, regardless of whether it leads to disbelief or atheism. Disengagement from religion, I argue, is due to the tension between changing sensibilities and religious understanding rather than intellectual reasoning, and manifests in indifference to religion rather than in outright rejections of doctrine. This phenomenon of disengagement seems to be more widespread, yet little attention has been paid to it—it is less visible, as it does not necessarily manifest itself in the more visible aspect of an outright rejection of religion or atheism.

Focusing on atheists, disbelievers, and their motivations is important, and it is welcome that more attention is being paid to it. A relatively new book by Brian Whitaker (2014), *Arabs Without Deity*, includes a number of interviews with a number of self-identified atheists and provides insights to understanding disengagement from religion. The book focuses on individuals whose main reasons for becoming atheists were doctrinal issues such as the existence of hell, or social injustices committed by Muslims and sanctioned by Shariʿa, such as the treatment of women. Similar material—mostly articles—has been coming out recently discussing the rise in the number of atheists in Arab and Muslim countries; the challenges they face and the reasons behind their atheism (Benchemsi, 2015; Khalife, 2017; Nabeel, 2017, Oduah, 2018); the ways they use technologies to develop their ideas and anonymize and express themselves online (Noman, 2015); or the motivations behind their disbelief (Schielke, 2012).

That being said, I think it would be useful to study atheism and disbelief as part of a larger phenomenon of disengagement from religion due to the tension between sensibilities and religious understanding. Moreover, we may need to theorize two main phases of that disengagement. The first includes the causes of the disengagement from religion and the second includes the sets of choices made as a result of that disengagement. The causes of the first phase could be tension between personal sensibilities and religion, something people of many different faiths experience. The choices made in the second phase are more complex, as the process after disengagement from religion is not always leaving the faith. Some may hold on to it even more fanatically as an identity or a source of inner stability in a fast and chaotic world, others may find ways to accommodate the tension between their sensibility and religion, others make take a position of indifference, and others may decide to leave in different ways, atheism being one of them.

I have mentioned above that the most important conclusion that I have come out with is that those expressing various forms of religious criticism were not founding their criticism on intellectual or religious argumentation. Criticism was based on personal sensibility. The changed sensibilities that influenced the criticism of religion also have other implications for social and political life. For example, there were Saudis rejecting religious authority based on an increased sense of individuality. This raises questions about the impact of that sensibility on other institutions in Saudi Arabia. Religion is the most difficult barrier to cross, and if individuality has the power to push a person away from basic religious commandments or creeds, does it also have the power to erode other social structures in the country? To answer this question, one needs to understand the nature of this sensibility and how it varies between critics and their sources. Such an understanding can be helpful in understanding social and political changes in Saudi Arabia and can open the door for further research on understanding Islam in modern Saudi Arabia and Islam in modernity in general.

The social response to the emergence of the criticism of religion is also indicative of important social processes in Saudi Arabia. While it is violent and passionate, its sources are not always people of a religious inclination. I have mentioned that one probable explanation is that the critic of religion is considered a rebel against the existing social solidarity. Saudis were not angry at the heretic because he disobeyed Allah but because they still believe that their unity is based on Islam. In Saudi Arabia religion has replaced national identity, creating what is called "religious nationalism." In this context, many Saudis consider critiquing religion a form of treason and not just disobedience to Allah. I mentioned in the discussion on the ambivalence of religion that Saudis live with major sins that they practice and that are institutionalized by the state. A stark example is interest-based banks. Saudis tolerate the public presence of these banks because they are sinful, but they do not tolerate the public presence of a heretical idea in the same way because that betrays the foundation of their unity.

The process of the criticism of religion and the response to it shows that Saudis are developing certain sensibilities that are challenging religious authority and its understanding of Islam's most fundamental tenets. The extent of this challenge is likely to grow, due to the direction the country has taken. Beginning in April 2016, Saudi Arabia embarked on a comprehensive transformational strategy that touched on all aspects of public and private life. The most visible expression of that transformation was Vision 2030, which was introduced by Prince Muhammad bin Salman soon after the succession of his father King Salman bin Abdulaziz to the throne. This was primarily driven by the state's intent to transform the Saudi economy and decrease its dependence on oil, yet Vision 2030 also included cultural initiatives that challenge religious authority and that can potentially have a fundamental impact on the sensibilities of Saudis. One key cultural component of the vision was the development of an entertainment industry for the country. By the end of 2018 almost 10,000 entertainment events were organized across the country and cinemas in Saudi Arabia were allowed to operate after a near 30-year ban.

The step that will fundamentally change the Saudi religious landscape is the Saudi state's decision to totally break it ties with all forms of political Islam and religious extremism while also proposing a new narrative for the relationship between religion and society, which can summarized as: "before 1979 the country was religiously moderate, but after the 1979 revolution in Iran many of the country's religious actors were inspired by what the revolution achieved and sought to emulate it in Saudi Arabia. Now it was time to go back to that moment and reverse the process generated by religious extremists." This new narrative does not depict the state affairs before 1979, as many historians and individuals living in that period have attested to. The support for the political Islamists (i.e., Muslim Brotherhood) had started well before the Iranian revolution during King Faisal's reign as a strategy to confront the spread of socialism in Arab and Muslim countries. And religious extremism had always been present throughout the country's history. Historical accuracy is beside the point for our purposes here. The point is that a new narrative is being constructed, one that calls for a new relationship with religion, and more importantly a narrative that many in Saudi Arabia have decided to adopt, even those who know of its historical inaccuracy. For those Saudis, this was a narrative to shape the future regardless of how the past actually was.

The changes Saudi Arabia is undergoing do not, at least until end of 2018, include expanding freedoms of expression in public spaces, and Twitter itself has lost much of its vigor as an alternative public space due to the rise of a wave of populism on the Saudi Twitter sphere. Hashtag debates became controlled by the populists and many tweeters preferred to avoid controversy as tweeters were frequently ostracized and attacked for even benignly dissenting opinions. Thus it is difficult to predict the effect of all of those changes taken together on the criticism of religion and religious disengagement. However, the future of religion in Saudi Arabia lies at the intersection of evolving sensibilities among Saudis, ambivalent religiosity, religious nationalism, and religious indignation in a context of deep social and cultural changes.

Twitter Hashtag Sources

Ziyarat al-mashayikh Li-Bayan Khatar al-ʾIbtiʿath: https://twitter.com/sear
ch?q=%23زيارة_المشايخ_لبيان_خطر_الابتعاث&src=typd

Al-Din   al-Saudi: https://twitter.com/search?f=tweets&q=%23الدين_السع
ودي&src=typd

Suʾal   Mantiqi   la   ʾAhad   Yikaffirni: https://twitter.com/hashtag/
سؤال_منطقي_لحد_يكفرني

Al-Din al-Saudi vs. Al-Islam: https://twitter.com/search?q=%23الإسلام_vs_
الدين_السعودي&src=typd

Al-Mafhum   al-Saudi   Li-l-Tadayyun: https://twitter.com/search?q=%23
المفهوم_السعودي_للتدين&src=typd

Taʿalamtu   min   al-Wahhabiyya: https://twitter.com/search?q=%23
تعلمت_من_الوهابية&src=typd

Matha Qaddamt al-Wahhabiyya Li-l-ʿArab Wa-l-Muslimin: https://twitter.
com/search?q=%23ماذا_قدمت_الوهابية_للعرب_والمسلمين&src=typd

Kan Haram wa Sar Halal: https://twitter.com/hashtag/كان_حرام_وصار_حلال
?src=hash

Fatawi Mudhhika: https://twitter.com/hashtag/فتاوى_مضحكة?src=hash

Al-Kumidya al-Muqaddasa: https://twitter.com/hashtag/الكوميديا_المقدسة?
src=hash

Matha Haramani al-hijab: https://twitter.com/hashtag/ماذا_حرمني_الحجاب
?src=hash

ʾIsqat Wisayat Rijal al-Din: https://twitter.com/hashtag/إسقاط_وصاية_رجال
الدين?src=hash

Limatha Yatrukun al-ʾIslam: https://twitter.com/hashtag/لماذا_يتركون_الإسلام
?src=hash

Risala ʾila Mulhid: https://twitter.com/search?q=%23رسالة_الى_ملحد&src=
    typd

Risala   ʾila   Allah: https://twitter.com/search?q=%23رسالة_الى_الله&src=t
    ypd

Al-Saudiyya   al-Mulhida: https://twitter.com/hashtag/السعودية_الُملحدة?src
    =hash

References

Abdel-Latif, O. (2009). Trends in Salafism. In M. Emerson, K. Kausch, R. Youngs, & O. Abdel-Latif (Eds.), *Islamist Radicalisation: The Challenge for Euro-Mediterranean Relations* (pp. 69–86). Brussels and Madrid: The Centre for European Policy Studies and FRIDE. doi: http://fride.org/descarga/Book_islamist_radicalisation_ENG_may09.pdf

Abdullah5588. (Producer). (2010). Junud 'Iblis D. Muhammad al-ʿUrayfi. Retrieved June 2, 2016, from https://www.youtube.com/watch?v=iTStfrBp0DE

Abdulmunʿim, M al-. (2012). Hiwar Ibrahim al-Skaran wa Mufti maʾ Raiʾf Badawi. February 21, 2012. Retrieved November 2, 2015, from https://www.youtube.com/watch?v=AL03ZF57yVM

Abu Luwz, A. b. H. (1998). *Fitnat al-Takfir* (2nd ed.). al-Riyadh, KSA: Dar Ibn Khuzaymah.

Abu-Rabiʿ, I. (1996). *Intellectual Origins of Islamic Resurgence in the Modern Arab World.* Albany: SUNY.

Abu Zahr, A. a.-I. (2008, April 28). Hukm al-Taswir Li-l-Shaykh al-ʾAlbani. Retrieved November 2, 2015, from http://www.sahab.net/forums/index.php?showtopic=90573

Ahmad, A. (1960). Sayyid Ahmad Khan, Jamal al-din al-Afghani and Muslim India *Studia Islamica, 13,* 55–78. http://www.jstor.org/stable/1595240

Ahmad, W. al-. (2012, September 5). al-Tarbiyah' Tuʿid Siyaghat Dars ʾalʾIbtiʿath. *Al-Hayat.* Retrieved June 15, 2016, from http://alhayat.com/Details/432239

Ahmed, L. (2011). *A Quiet Revolution: The Veil's Resurgence, from the Middle East to America.* New Haven, CT: Yale University Press.

Akhbar24. (2012a, February 17). al-Shaykh Abdulaziz al-Fawzan Yutalib Bi-Muhakamat ʿAbdullah Hamid al-Din' wa Yasifahu Bi-Shaykh Hamza Kashgari. Retrieved November 2, 2015, from http://akhbaar24.argaam.com/article/detail/50583

Akhbar24. (2012b, February 21). al-Tahqiq wa al-ʾIdiʿaʾ al-ʿAm Tarfudh Daʿawi Hisba Dhud Turki al-Hamad wa Hamid al-Din. Retrieved

November   2,   2015,   from   http://akhbaar24.argaam.com/article/
التحقيق-والادعاء-العام-ترفض-دعاوى-حسبة-ضد-تركي-الحمد-وحميد-الدين/detail/52476

Akhbar24. (2012c, December 17). ʾIhalat Raif Badawi Li-l-Mahkama al-ʿAmmah Bi-Jiddah Bi-Tuhmat al-Riddah. Retrieved November 2, 2015, from http://akh-baar24.argaam.com/article/detail/120401

Akhbar24. (2013a, December 25). al-Juzʾiyya Tuhil Raif Badawi Li-l-Mahkama al-ʿAmah Li-Tatbiq Had al-Ridda. Retrieved November 2, 2015, from http://akh-baar24.argaam.com/article/detail/159664

Akhbar24. (2013b, July 19). Bi-l-Video. Yusuf al-Ahmad Yunasih al-Qaʾimin ʿala Majmuʿat Rotana ʿabr Qanat La-Hum. Retrieved September 29, 2013, from http://akhbaar24.argaam.com/article/
بالفيديو-يوسف-الأحمد-يناصح-القائمين-على-مجموعة-روتانا-عبر-قناة-لهم/detail/142916

Alalwani, T. J. (2012). *Apostasy in Islam: A Historical and Scriptural Analysis*. Herndon, VA: International Institute of Islamic Thought (IIIT).

Alarabiyya. (2008, July 14). Mufti al-Suʿudiyya Yuhathir min Takfir Kuttab al-Raʾy wa al-Maqalat al-Sahaafiyyah. Retrieved June 15, 2015, from http://www.alarabiya.net/articles/2008/07/14/53066.html

Alarabiyya. (2011, September 18). al-Shaykh Abdulrahman al-Barrak Yadʿu Li-Muhakamat Katib Suʿudi wa Yasifahu Bi-l-Dhal. Retrieved November 2, 2015, from http://www.alarabiya.net/articles/2011/09/18/167494.html

Alarabiyya. (2012, January 28). Mufti al-Suʿudiyyah Yuhathir min ʾAkathib wa Fitan "Twitter." Retrieved November 2, 2015, from http://www.alarabiya.net/articles/2012/01/28/191001.html

Alawi, A. (Producer). (2010). Al-Kalbani Yujiz al-Ghenaʾ bi-Shurut. Retrieved June 15, 2016, from https://www.youtube.com/watch?v=yeoXkbW2vhI

albader16. (Producer). (2013). Wujub Taʿat Wally al-ʾAmr. Retrieved June 15, 2016, from https://www.youtube.com/watch?v=LyFkKHPb_uc

Albilad. (2008September 17). Al-Fawzan la Yujiz Alʾhtifalat fi Alshawariʿ wa Altajamoʿat ʾitifalan BilYawn Alwatani. *Albilad*. Retrieved June 15, 2016, from http://www.albiladdaily.com/news.php?action=show&id=6737

Albleahy, I. (Producer). (2012). Idaʾat Ibrahim Albleahy. Retrieved June 15, 2016, from https://www.youtube.com/watch?v=YCF1_ab8MDo

Alcetraz. (Producer). (2012). Fur Shabab maʿ Khidr bin Sanad wa Zandaqat Hamid al-Din. Retrieved June 15, 2016, from https://www.youtube.com/watch?v=V5bSdyV7eO8

Aleqtisadiah. (2011). al-Malik Yaʾmur Bi-sarf Ratibayan. *Aleqtisadiah*. Retrieved June 15, 2016, from http://www.aleqt.com/2011/03/18/article_516127.html

Ali, W. al-. (2003). Bayan fi Riddat Mansour al-Nogaidan.. Retrieved November 2, 2015, from http://www.buraydahcity.net/vb/archive/index.php/t-20881.html

Almaxicy, H. (Producer). (2010). ʿAalam al-Malaʾika - Nabil al-ʿAwadhi - Mashahid. Retrieved June 15, 2016, from http://www.youtube.com/watch?v=LzyZWE5_6z8

Almoslim. (2010a). Ba'd Hamlat al-Muqata'ah. Masadir Sahafiyyah "Hyper Banda" Tuwqif Tawzif al-Khashirat. Retrieved October 6, 2014, from http://www.almoslim.net/node/133205

Almoslim. (2010b). D. al-'Umar: Tawzif Nisa' "Kashirat" 'ahad 'awjuh al-Mashru' al-Taghribi. Retrieved October 6, 2014, from http://almoslim.net/node/133154

Almoslimnet. (Producer). (2012). Inna Allathin Yu'zun Allah wa Rasulahu La'anahumu Allah. Retrieved June 15, 2016, from https://www.youtube.com/watch?v=5MXN11EKeMk

almuslim1994, Q. (Producer). (2010). Ayn Rahmata Allah fi 'idkhal al-Kuffar al-Nar. Retrieved June 15, 2016, from https://www.youtube.com/watch?v=8wAbLjhpB_E

AlnaserLedinAllah. (Producer). (2012). Al-Shaykh Saleh al-Maghamsi - al-Yawm al-Watani wa al-'ayad Ta'sil Fiqhi. Retrieved June 15, 2016, from http://www.youtube.com/watch?v=9g9-9iXKoUo

Al Omran, A. (2013, February 9). Saudi Cleric Warns Against "Sinful" Hashtags on Https://twitter. Retrieved February 15, 2013, from http://riyadhbureau.com/blog/2013/2/saudi-sinful-hashtags

Alshamsi, M. (2011). *Islam and Political Reform in Saudi Arabia: The Quest for Political Change and Reform.* Oxon, UK: Routledge.

Alshaykh, A. al-. (2011). Yanbaghi 'an Yakun al-Yawm al-Watani Yawm Shukr Li-Allah wa la Bud min al-Sam' wa al-Ta'ah Li-Wulat al-'amr, *Okaz.* Retrieved June 15, 2016, from http://www.okaz.com.sa/new/Issues/20110923/Con20110923446567.htm

Alshaykh, H. al-. (2011, April 16). Man Huwa al-'Urayfi?! *Al-Watan.* Retrieved June 15, 2016, from http://www.alwatan.com.sa/Articles/Detail.aspx?ArticleId=5259

Alshaykh, M. al-. (1979a). *Fatawi wa Rasa'il Samahat Alshaykh Muhammad bin Ibrahim bin Abdullatif Al-alshaykh* (Vol. 2). Makkah Almukarramah: Matba'at al-Hukuma.

Alshaykh, M. al-. (1979b). *Fatawi wa Rasa'il Samahat Alshaykh Muhammad bin Ibrahim bin Abdullatif Al-alshaykh* (Vol. 8). Makkah Almukarramah: Matba'at al-Hukuma.

Alshaykh, M. al-. (1979c). *Fatawi wa Rasa'il Samahat Alshaykh Muhammad bin Ibrahim bin Abdullatif Al-alshaykh* (Vol. 10). Makkah Almukarramah: Matba'at al-Hukuma.

Alvesson, M., & Skoldberg, K. (2000). *Reflexive Methodology: New Vistas for Qualitative Research.* London, UK: Sage.

Alwan, A. (2004). *Nitham al-Riq fi al-'Islam.* Cairo, Egypt: Dar al-Salam.

Amnesty International. (1993, May 15). Saudi Arabia: An Upsurge in Public Executions. Retrieved October 6, 2015, from https://goo.gl/dTLCso

anawin. (2014). Khalid bin Talal Yasif Al-alshaykh bi "Mudammir al-Hay'ah wa Muharib al-Hisba." Retrieved March 1, 2015, from http://www.anaween.com/?p=26211

Anha'. (2012, January 13). al-Barrak Yastankir 'Iqalat al-Humayn. Retrieved March 5, 2015, from http://akhbaar24.argaam.com/article/detail/34745

Anha². (2013a, April 25). Zawjat Raif Badawi Tuzawwid ²Anha Bi-sura Min La²ihat al-²ittiham al-Muwwajjaha Dhid Zawjaha wa Tutalib Bi-²itlaq Sarahihi. Retrieved November 2, 2015, from http://www.an7a.com/102662/

Anha². (2013b, June 29). al-Sijn 7 Sanawat wa 600 Jalda Limu²assis al-Shabaka al-Libraliyya wa ²isqat Had al-Ridda ʿAnhu Li-ʿadam Thubutih. Retrieved November 2, 2015, from http://www.an7a.com/114258/

Annahar. (2010, March 26). Qanat "Bidaya" Tabarra²at min al-Shaykh al-Ahmad. *Jaridat Annahar al-Kuwaytiyya*. Retrieved June 15, 2016, from http://www.anna-harkw.com/annahar/ArticlePrint.aspx?id=201966

An-Naʾim, A. A. (1986). The Islamic Law of Apostasy and Its Modern Applicability. *Religion, 16*(3), 197–224. doi: 10.1016/0048-721X(86)90033-3

Ansari, M al-. (2005,November 1). Mufaj²ah: al-Malik Abdulaziz Qarrar ²ijazat "al-Yawm al-Watani" Qabl 57 ʿaman ʿUlama² al-Suʿudiyyah Yunhun ʿuqudan min Tahrim al-²ihtifal Bi-l-Munasaba. Retrieved September 30, 2013, from http://www.alarabiya.net/articles/2005/09/23/17052.html

Arab Commission for Human Rights. (2008). Hamla Dhud al-Takfir Mi²at Muthaqaf ʿArabi Dhud al-Takfir. Retrieved November 2, 2015, from http://www.achr.eu/art323.htm

Arkoun, M. (2004). *Tarikhiyyat al-Fikr al-²Islami. al-Dar al-Baida²*. Morroco: al-Markaz al-Thaqafi al-ʿarabi.

Asad, T. (1993). *Genealogies of Religion: Discipline and Reasons of Power in Christianity and Islam*. Baltimore, MD: Johns Hopkins University Press.

Asad, T. (1999). Religion, Nation-State, Secularism. In P. van der Veer & H. Lehmann (Eds.), *Nation and Religion: Perspectives on Europe and Asia* (pp. 178–196). Princeton, NJ: Princeton University Press.

Asbar Center. (n.d.). *Tadayyun Alsuʿudyyin: Dirasah 'Istiqra'iah*. Vol. 1.

Atawneh, M. al-. (2009). Is Saudi Arabia a Theocracy? Religion and Governance in Contemporary Saudi Arabia. *Middle Eastern Studies, 45*(5), 721–737. doi: 10.1080/00263200802586105

Awadhi, M. al-. (Producer). (2012). Munaqashat al-²ilhad. Retrieved June 15, 2016, from https://www.youtube.com/watch?v=wu04Nd2R1NY

azazi911 (Producer). (2008). al-Libraliyyin al-Shaykh Saʿd al-Birayk Yuwaddih Khatar al-Libraliyyin. Retrieved June 15, 2016, from http://www.youtube.com/watch?v=aHbcPsoCTCw

Azmeh, A. al-. (1993). *Islams and Modernities*. London, UK: Verso.

Aydin, C. (2017). *The Idea of the Muslim World: A Global Intellectual History*. Cambridge, MA: Harvard University Press.

Baʿamer, Y. (2010). al-Saʿudiyya Tughliq Marakiz al-Quran Bi-l-Mamlaka. Retrieved December 25, 2015, from www.aljazeera.net/news/arabic/2010/10/28/السعودة-تغلق-مراكز-القرآن-بالمملكة-

Baddah, A. al-. (2011). al-²ibtiʿath: Tarikhuhu wa ²atharuhu. Retrieved June 15, 2016, from http://ia600609.us.archive.org/16/items/bbre88/bbre88.pdf

Badr, A. al-. (2008). al-Mustahiq Li-l-muhakamah Huwa Turki al-Hamad. Retrieved November 2, 2015, from https://sites.google.com/site/oalbadr/1turki

Bailey, B. (2010). Evidence of the Moon Having Been Split in Two. Retrieved December 15, 2014, from http://sservi.nasa.gov/?question=evidence-moon-having-been-split-two

Bakshy, E., Hofman, J. M., Mason, W. A., & Watts, D. J. (2011). *Everyone's an Influencer: Quantifying Influence on Twitter.* Paper presented at the Proceedings of the Fourth ACM International Conference on Web Search and Data Mining (WSDM '11), Hong Kong, China. Retrieved from http://misc.si.umich.edu/media/papers/wsdm333w-bakshy.pdf

Barker, E. (2005). Crossing the Boundary: New Challenges to Religious Authority and Control as a Consequence of Access to the Internet. In M. Hojsgaard & M. Warburg (Eds.), *Religion and Cyberspace* (pp. 67–85). New York, NY: Routledge.

Barker, J. (2012). The Ethnographic Interview in an Age of Globalisation. In R. Fardon, O. Harris, T. H. J. Marchand, M. Nuttall, C. Shore, V. Strang, & R. A. Wilson (Eds.), *The Sage Handbook of Social Anthropology* (pp. 54–69). London, UK: Sage.

Barlas, A. (2002). *Believing Women in Islam: Unreading Patriarchal Interpretations of the Qur'an.* Austin: University of Texas Press.

Barqawi, A. al-. (2012a, February 6). Khujah Y⁽ulin ʾiqaf al-Katib "Kashgari" li-Tatwil-ihi ⁽ala al-That al-ʾilahiyyah wa al-Rasul al-Karim. Retrieved August 15, 2015, from http://sabq.org/Lrcfde

Barqawi, A. al-. (2012b, February 7). al-Katib Kashgari Yataraja⁽ wa Yu⁽lin al-Taw-bah: Kitabati Natija ⁽an Halat Nafsiyyah. Retrieved November 2, 2015, from http://sabq.org/7tcfde

Barqawi, A. al-. (2012c, May 11). al-Katiba Hissa Al al-Shaykh Tuwaddih Li-Sabaq: Hisab Twitter Muntahil Li-Shakhsiyyati. Retrieved November 2, 2015, from http://sabq.org/Uuhfde

Barrak, A. al-. (2011). Abdulaziz Suwayyid Hafid al-Jahmiyya. Retrieved August 15, 2015, from ar.islamway.net/article/9715/عبد-العزيز-السويد-حفيد-الجهمية

Bayat, A. (2007). *Making Islam Democratic: Social Movements and the Post-Islamist Turn.* Stanford, CA: Stanford University Press

Beckford, J. A. (2003). *Social Theory and Religion.* Cambridge, UK: Cambridge University Press.

Belson, W. A. (1967). Tape Recording: Its Effect on Accuracy of Response in Survey Interviews. *Journal of Marketing Research, 4*(3), 253–260. doi:10.2307/3149457

Benchemsi, A. (2015, April 24). Invisible Atheists: The Spread of Disbelief in the Arab World. Retrieved March 21, 2019, from https://newrepublic.com/article/121559/rise-arab-atheists

Bendix, R. (1967). Tradition and Modernity Reconsidered. *Comparative Studies in Society and History, 9*(3), 292–346. http://www.jstor.org/stable/177869

Beranek, O. (2009). Divided We Survive: A Landscape of Fragmentation in Saudi Arabia. *Crown Center for Middle East Studies,* (33). http://www.brandeis.edu/crown/publications/meb/MEB33.pdf

Berger, P. L. (1967). *The Sacred Canopy: Elements of a Sociological Theory of Religion.* New York, NY: Anchor Doubleday.

Berger, P. L. (1999). *The Desecularisation of the World: The Resurgence of Religion in World Politics.* Washington, DC: Eerdmans.

Berghammer, C., & Fliegenschnee, K. (2014). Developing a Concept of Muslim Religiosity: An Analysis of Everyday Lived Religion Among Female Migrants in Austria. *Journal of Contemporary Religion, 29*(1), 89–104. doi:10.1080/13537903.2014.864810

Bergunder, M. (2014). What Is Religion? *Method and Theory in the Study of Religion, 26*(3), 246–286. doi: 10.1163/15700682-12341320

Berlinerblau, J. (2001). Toward a Sociology of Heresy, Orthodoxy, and Doxa. *History of Religions,* 40(4), 327–351. http://www.jstor.org/stable/3176370?seq=1#page_scan_tab_contents

Bilayhi, I. al-. (2010). *Husun al-Takhalluf.* Beirut, Lebanon: Manshurat al-Jamal.

bin Baz, A. (n.d.-a). Hukm Mushahadat al-Talafizyun. Retrieved October 6, 2014, from http://www.alifta.net/Fatawa/FatawaChapters.aspx?View=Page&PageID=1315&PageNo=1&BookID=4

bin Baz, A. (n.d.-b). ʾistiʿmal al-Dish Munkar Kabir. Retrieved October 6, 2014, from http://www.binbaz.org.sa/mat/8383

bin Baz, A. (n.d.-c). *Kitab Majmuʿ Fatawi wa Maqalat Mutanawwiʿah* (M. b. S. d. Al-Shuwayʿir, Ed.). Retrieved June 15, 2016, from http://www.ibnbaz.org.sa/book/m009.pdf

bin Baz, A. (n.d.-d). al-Rad ʿala man Yaʿtabir al-ʾahkam al-Sharʿiyyah Ghayr Mutanasiba Maʿ al-ʿasr al-Hadhir. Retrieved November 6, 2015, from http://www.binbaz.org.sa/node/135

bin Baz, A. (n.d.-e). Hukm al-Tawassul Wa-l-ʾistiʿana Bi-l-Salihin. Retrieved November 6, 2015, from http://www.ibnbaz.org.sa/node/9799

bin Baz, A. (n.d.-f). Hukm Halq al-Lihya. Retrieved November 6, 2015, from http://www.binbaz.org.sa/node/4287

bin Baz, A. (n.d.-g). Hukm man Lam Yukkafir al-Kafir. Retrieved November 6, 2015, from http://www.binbaz.org.sa/node/18159

bin Baz, A. (n.d.-h). Rad ʾala al-Muftarin ʿala al-ʿulamaʾ. Retrieved November 6, 2015, from http://www.binbaz.org.sa/node/8640

bin Sunaytan, M. (2004). *al-Nukhab al-Suʿudiya: Dirasah Fi-l-Tahawwulaat Wa-l-Ikhfaqat.* Beirut, Lebanon: Markaz Dirasat al-Wahdah al-ʿArabiyyah.

bin Taymiyya, S. a.-I. (1982). *Al-Farq Bayn ʾawlyaʾ alRahman wa ʾawlyaʾ Alshaytan* Retrieved June 15, 2016, from http://goo.gl/xXoKp9

bin ʿUthaymin, M. (1996). Man Mat wa Khallaf fi Baytihi (Aldish) Faqad Gash Raʿiyyatahu. Retrieved December 25, 2015, from http://www3.ozzo.com/2011/07/30/07/247115152.jpg

Blanes, R. L., & Oustinova-Stjepanovic, G. (2015). Introduction: Godless People, Doubt, and Atheism. *Social Analysis, 59*(2). http://www.ingentaconnect.com/content/berghahn/socan/2015/00000059/00000002/art00001

Boshoff, L. L. (1986). Saudi Arabia: Arbitration vs. Litigation. *Arab Law Quarterly, 1*(3), 299–311. http://www.jstor.org/stable/3381751 doi:10.2307/3381751

Boucek, C. (2010). Saudi Fatwa Restrictions and the State-Clerical Relationship. http://carnegieendowment.org/2010/10/27/saudi-fatwa-restrictions-and-state-clerical-relationship/6b81

Bramjna. (Producer). (2012). Hamsa - Harb Alshyatan Li-shaykh Ya'qub. Retrieved June 15, 2016, from http://www.youtube.com/watch?v=ZGU21fPH1VE

Braude, J. (2014, April 3). Saudi Reforms Rising Quietly from Within. Retrieved December 25, 2015, from http://www.the-american-interest.com/2014/04/03/saudi-reforms-rising-quietly-from-within/

Brotherrachid. (Producer). (n.d.). DaringQuestions. Retrieved June 15, 2016, from https://www.youtube.com/channel/UCfVwBTHtG_Qk6hXAd6wHu5A

Bruce, S. (1996). *Religion in the Modern World: From Cathedrals to Cults.* New York, NY: Oxford University Press.

Bruce, S. (2013). *Secularization: In Defence of an Unfashionable Theory.* Oxford, UK: Oxford University Press.

Bucher, R., Fritz, C. E., & Quarantelli, E. L. (1956). Tape Recorded Interviews in Social Research. *American Sociological Review, 21*(3), 359–364. http://www.jstor.org/stable/2089294

Bunt, G. R. (2000). *Virtually Islamic: Computer-Mediated Communication and Cyber Islamic Environments.* Cardiff, UK: University of Wales Press.

Bunt, G. R. (2009). *iMuslims: Rewiring the House of Islam.* London, UK: Hurst.

Buraydah, M. S. (2002). Fatwa al-Shaykh Ali al-Khudayr. Retrieved November 2, 2015, from http://www.buraydahcity.net/vb/showthread.php?t=5695

Campanini, M. (2012). The Mu'tazila in Islamic History and Thought. *Religion Compass, 6*(1), 41–50. http://dx.doi.org/10.1111/j.1749-8171.2011.00273.x

Campbell, H. (2006). Religion and the Internet. *Communication Research Trends, 25*(1). http://cscc.scu.edu/trends/v25/v25_1.pdf

Campbell, H. (2007). Who's Got the Power? Religious Authority and the Internet. *Journal of Computer-Mediated Communication, 12*(3), 1043–1062. doi:10.1111/j.1083-6101.2007.00362.x

Campbell, H. (Ed.). (2013). *Digital Religion: Understanding Religious Practice in New Media Worlds.* London, UK: Routledge.

Campbell, H. A. (2013). Introduction: The Rise of the Study of Digital Religion. In H. A. Campbell (Ed.), *Digital Religion: Understanding Religious Practice in New Media Worlds* (pp. 1–21). London, UK: Routledge.

Cary, L. J. (1999). Unexpected Stories: Life History and The Limits of Representation. *Qualitative Inquiry, 5*(3), 411–427. doi:10.1177/107780049900500307

Casanova, J. (1994). *Public Religions in the Modern World.* Chicago, IL: University of Chicago Press.

Casanova, J. (2008). Public Religions Revisited. In H. D. Vries (Ed.), *Religion: Beyond a Concept* (pp. 101–119). New York, NY: Fordham University Press.

Center for Religious Freedom. (2006). Saudi Arabia's Curriculum of Intolerance. http://www.freedomhouse.org/sites/default/files/CurriculumOfIntolerance.pdf

Ch905 (Producer). (2010a). Al-Shaykh al-Sudays Yutaleb Bi al-Hajr ʿala Ashab al-Fatawa al-Shazzah. Retrieved June 15, 2016, from https://www.youtube.com/watch?v=zvmCdTBR8XA

ch905 (Producer). (2010b). Al-Shaykh Nasir al-ʿUmar Yadʿu ʾila Muqataʿt Aswaq Hyper Panda. Retrieved June 15, 2016, from http://www.youtube.com/watch?v=ikoSiHkeJlM

ch905 (Producer). (2010c). Al-Shaykh Yusuf al-Ahmad fi Khaymat Zid Rasidak ʿala Qanat Bidaya. Retrieved June 15, 2016, from http://www.youtube.com/watch?v=M25KUblFZUI

ch905 (Producer). (2010d). Al-Shaykh Yusuf al-Ahmad wa ʾijabat ʿan Kurat al-Qadam. Retrieved June 15, 2016, from http://www.youtube.com/watch?v=ZEB8hfP_pvo

ch905 (Producer). (2010e). Al-Shaykh Yusuf al-Ahmad Yadʿu ʾila Muqataʿat Aswaq Hyper Panda. Retrieved June 15, 2016, from http://www.youtube.com/watch?v=2uNh9GgMsEQ

Chapra, M. U. (2006). The Nature of *Riba* in Islam. *Journal of Islamic Economics and Finance*, 2(1), 7–25. http://ierc.sbu.ac.ir/File/Article/THE%20NATURE%20OF%20RIBA%20IN%20ISLAM_94669.pdf

Choudhury, M. A. (2015). Usury. *Encyclopaedia of the Qurʾān*. Retrieved from http://referenceworks.brillonline.com/entries/encyclopaedia-of-the-quran/usury-EQSIM_00438

Clarence-Smith, W. G. (2006). *Islam and the Abolition of Slavery*. New York, NY: Oxford University Press.

CNN. (2011). al-Facebook al-ʾArabi: Ayyam Ghadhab min al-Muhit ʿIla al-Khalij. Retrieved November 2, 2015, from http://archive.arabic.cnn.com/2011/facebook/3/1/arab.youth_angry/

CNN. (2012). Shaykh Ajaz al-ʾIkhtilaj Yarʾas Hayʾat al-ʾAmr Bi-l-Maʾruf. Retrieved November 2, 2015, from http://archive.arabic.cnn.com/2012/middle_east/1/13/saudi.newhead/

Coleman, I. (2013). Women, Religion, and Security: Islamic Feminism on the Frontlines of Change. In C. Seiple, D. R. Hoover, & P. Otis (Eds.), *The Routledge Handbook of Religion and Security* (pp. 148–159). New York, NY: Routledge.

Collins, R. (1988). The Durkheimian Tradition in Conflict Sociology. In J. C. Alexander (Ed.), *Durkheimian Sociology* (pp. 107–128). Cambridge, UK: Cambridge University Press.

Cook, M. (2000). *Commanding Right and Forbidding Wrong in Islamic Thought*. Cambridge, UK: Cambridge University Press.

Cook, M. (2015). Virtues and Vices, Commanding and Forbidding. *Encyclopaedia of the Qurʾān*. Retrieved March, 21, 2019, from http://

referenceworks.brillonline.com/entries/encyclopaedia-of-the-quran/
virtues-and-vices-commanding-and-forbidding-EQCOM_00212

Cooper, J., Nettler, R. L., & Mahmoud, M. (1998). *Islam and Modernity: Muslim Intellectuals Respond*. London, UK: I.B. Tauris.

Council, S. (1992). The Basic Law of Government. Retrieved October 6, 2014, from http://www.shura.gov.sa/wps/wcm/connect/shuraen/internet/Laws+and+Regulations/The+Basic+Law+Of+Government/

Cowan, D. E. (2007). Religion on the Internet. In J. A. Beckford & J. Demerath (Eds.), *The SAGE Handbook of the Sociology of Religion* (pp. 357–376). London, UK: SAGE.

Dahab, W. (Producer). (2013). Tahrim Zahab al-'Awa'l Li-l-Janadiriyyah - al-Shaykh Saleh al-Fawzan. Retrieved June 15, 2016, from https://www.youtube.com/watch?v=3TBYJINxuhI

Dakhil, T. al-. (Producer). (2010). ʾidaʾat Abdullah Hamid al-Din. Retrieved June 15, 2016, from https://www.youtube.com/watch?v=jAPmoP-LlRE

Dani, A. al-. (2010, July 15). Wasf al-Sahafiyyeen bi 'Jund al-Shaytan' Qazf wa ʾitiham Jaʾir, *Okaz*. Retrieved June 15, 2016, from http://www.okaz.com.sa/new/Issues/20100715/Con20100715361660.htm

Davie, G. (1994). *Religion in Britain Since 1945: Believing Without Belonging*. Oxford, UK: Blackwell.

Davies, C. A. (2008). *Reflexive Ethnography: A Guide to Researching Selves and Others* (2nd ed.). London, UK: Routledge.

Dawson, L. L. (2005). The Mediation of Religious Experience in Cyber Space. In M. Hojsgaard & M. Warburg (Eds.), *In Religion and Cyberspace* (pp. 22–44). New York, NY: Routledge.

Dearden, L. (2015, February 18). Saudi Muslim Cleric Claims the Earth Is "Stationary" and the Sun Rotates Around It. *The Independent*. Retrieved June 15, 2016, from http://www.independent.co.uk/news/world/middle-east/saudi-muslim-cleric-claims-the-earth-is-stationary-and-the-sun-rotates-around-it-10053516.html

Deeb, L. (2006). *An Enchanted Modern: Gender and Public Piety in Shiʿi Lebanon*. Princeton, NJ: Princeton University Press.

Dekmejian, R. (1994). The Rise of Political Islamism in Saudi Arabia. *Middle East Journal*, 48(4), 627-643, http://www.jstor.org/stable/4328744

Dekmejian, R. (2003). The Liberal Impulse in Saudi Arabia. *Middle East Journal*, 57(3), 400–413. http://www.jstor.org/stable/4329911

Diya' al-Salik. (2007). 'La Li-l-Takfir . . . Naʿam Li-Huryyat al-Taʿbir' Bayan Li ʾakthar min Tisʿin Libraly bi-Manʿ al-Takfir. Retrieved November 2, 2014, from http://majles.alukah.net/t14146/

Doumato, E. A. (2003). Manning the Barricades: Islam According to Saudi Arabia's School Texts. *Middle East Journal*, 57(2), 230–247. http://www.jstor.org/stable/4329879

Dunford, F. W., & Kunz, P. R. (1973). The Neutralization of Religious Dissonance. *Review of Religious Research, 15*(1), 2–9. doi:10.2307/3510291

Durkheim, E. (1912 / 1995). *The Elementary Forms of Religious Life* (K. E. Fields, Trans.). New York, NY: Free Press.

Durkheim, E. (1933 /1984). *The Division of Labour in Society* (W. D. Halls, Trans.). Basingstoke, UK: Macmillan.

Duwayhi, A. al-. (2007). Qaʾidah al-ʾAsl Fi al-ʾashyaʾ al-ʾibahah. Retrieved June 15, 2016, from https://archive.org/stream/kaidat_al_assel#page/n37/mode/2up

Eickelman, D., & Anderson, J. (2003). Redefining Muslim Publics. In D. Eickelman & J. Anderson (Eds.), *New Media in the Muslim World: The Emerging Public Sphere* (pp. 1–18) (2nd ed.). Bloomington, IN: Indiana University Press.

Eisenstadt, S. N. (2000). Multiple Modernities. *Daedalus, 129*(1), 1–29. http://www.jstor.org/stable/20027613

Elvin, M. (1986). A Working Definition of "Modernity"? *Past and Present,* (113), 209–213. http://www.jstor.org/stable/650986

Fatehi-nezhad, E., & Melvin-Koushki, M. (2015). Bashshār b. Burd. In W. Madelung & F. Daftary (Eds.), *Encyclopaedia Islamica* (p. 4:492b). Brill Online: Brill. Retrieved June 15, 2016, from http://referenceworks.brillonline.com/entries/encyclopaedia-islamica/bashshar-b-burd-COM_00000092.

Ende, W. (1997). The Nakhawila, a Shiʿte Community in Medina Past and Present. *Die Welt des Islams, 37*(3), 263–348. http://www.jstor.org/stable/1570656

Esack, F. (1997). *Qur'an Liberation and Pluralism: An Islamic Perspective of Interreligious Solidarity Against Oppression.* Oxford, UK: Oneworld Publications.

Esposito, J. L., & Voll, J. O. (2001). *Makers of Contemporary Islam.* New York, NY: Oxford University Press.

Faisal, T. al- (2002, 20 January, 2002). al-Wulat Hum al-Hukkam wa Taʿatuhum Wajibah ʾamma al-ʿulama fa-Hum Mustasharun. *al-Sharq al-Awsat.* Retrieved June 15, 2016, from http://archive.aawsat.com/details.asp?section=17&article=83764&issueno=8454#.VoPAIkp97Dc

Fandy, M. (1999a). CyberResistance: Saudi Opposition Between Globalization and Localization. *Comparative Studies in Society and History, 41*(1), 124–147. http://www.jstor.org/stable/179251

Fandy, M. (1999b). *Saudi Arabia and the Politics of Dissent.* London, UK: Macmillan.

Fanjari, M. al-. (2006). *al-Mazhab al-ʾiqtisadi fi al-ʾislam.* Cario, Egypt: al-Hayʾa al-Misriyya al-'Ammah Li-l-Kitab.

Faubion, J. D. (1995). *Modern Greek Lessons: A Primer in Historical Constructivism.* Princeton, NJ: Princeton University Press.

Fawzan, A. al-. (n.d.). Hukm al-Yawm al-Watani. Retrieved February 18, 2013, from http://www.saaid.net/fatwa/f65.htm

Fawzan, S. al-. (2006). al-Maqsud Bi-l-Maʿlum min al-Din Bi-l-Dharura. Retrieved November 6, 2015, from www.ar.islamway.net/fatwa/8440/المقصود-بالمعلوم-من-الدين-بالضرورة

Fawzan, S. al-. (n.d.-a). Fatwa al-Libraliyya. Retrieved November 2, 2015, from http://www.alfawzan.af.org.sa/node/2350

Fazwan, S al-. (n.d.-b). Hukm al-Safar Li-l-siyaha. Retrieved September 10, 2013, from http://www.islam-qa.com/ar/52845

Fawzan, S. al-. (n.d.-c). Ta'allum al-Falsafa. Retrieved November 6, 2015, from http://www.alfawzan.af.org.sa/node/3729

Fawzan, S. al-. (n.d.-d). Wajubuna Tijah Wulat al-ʾamr wa al-ʿulama. Retrieved November 2, 2015, from http://www.alfawzan.af.org.sa/node/2018

Fawzan, S. al- (n.d.-e). *al-Tawhid*: n/a.

Fawzan, S. al-. (2008). Kuffu ʿudwanukum ʿala al-ʾislam. Retrieved July 21, 2015, from http://www.alfawzan.af.org.sa/node/2311

Fierro, M. (2014). Introduction. In M. Fierro (Ed.), *Orthodoxy and Heresy in Islam*. Oxon, UK: Routledge.

Firro, T. K. (2013). The Political Context of Early Wahhabi Discourse of Takfir. *Middle Eastern Studies, 49*(5), 770–789. http://dx.doi.org/10.1080/00263206.2013.811648

Fitzgerald, T. (2000). *The Ideology of Religious Studies*. New York, NY: Oxford University Press.

Flood, G. (2006). Reflections on Tradition and Inquiry in the Study of Religions. *Journal of the American Academy of Religion, 74*(1), 47–58. doi:10.1093/jaarel/lfj012

Fluehr-Lobban, C. (Ed.). (1998). *Against Islamic Extremism: The Writings of Muhammad Saʿid al-ʿAshmawy*. Gainesville: University Press of Florida.

Flyvbjerg, B. (2006). Five Misunderstandings About Case-Study Research. *Qualitative Inquiry, 12*(2), 219–245. doi: 10.1177/1077800405284363

Frank, J. (1990). You Call That a Rhetorical Question? *Journal of Pragmatics, 14*(5), 723–738. doi: http://dx.doi.org/10.1016/0378-2166(90)90003-V

Frolov, D. V. (2015). Stoning. In J. D. McAuliffe (Ed.), *Encyclopaedia of the Qurʾān*. Brill Online. Retrieved June 15, 2016, from http://referenceworks.brillonline.com/entries/encyclopaedia-of-the-quran/stoning-EQSIM_00404.

Gallie, W. B. (1955). Essentially Contested Concepts. *Proceedings of the Aristotelian Society, 56*. doi: 10.2307/4544562

Gane, N. (2002). *Max Weber and Postmodern Theory: Rationalization Versus Re-enchantment*. New York, NY: Palgrave Macmillan.

Geaves, R. (2009). Forget Transmitted Memory: The De-traditionalised "Religion" of Prem Rawat. *Journal of Contemporary Religion, 24*(1), 19–33. doi: 10.1080/13537900802630471

Ghadyan, A. al-. (1998). The Judiciary in Saudi Arabia. *Arab Law Quarterly, 13*(3), 235–251. http://www.jstor.org/stable/3382009

Ghays, K. al-. (2008). al-Wataniyya wa Hub al-Watan. Retrieved September 29 2013, 2013, from http://www.almoslim.net/node/96796

Ghuluww Fi-l-Din al-. (Producer). (2014). al-Tahthir min al-Takfir. Retrieved June 15, 2016, from https://www.youtube.com/watch?v=GA7jxMjQ4iQ

Giddens, A. (1986). *Durkheim*. London, UK: Fontana Press.

Gilani, I. S., Shahid, R., & Zuettel, I. (2012). Global Index of Religiosity and Atheism. http://www.wingia.com/web/files/news/14/file/14.pdf

Goitom, H. (2014). Laws Criminalizing Apostasy in Selected Jurisdictions. http://www.loc.gov/law/help/apostasy/apostasy.pdf

Goldman, R., Hunt, M. K., Allen, J. D., Hauser, S., Emmons, K., Maeda, M., & Sorensen, G. (2003). The Life History Interview Method: Applications to Intervention Development. *Health Education and Behavior, 30*(5), 564–581. doi:10.1177/1090198103254393

Gole, N. (2003). Contemporary Islamist Movements and New Sources for Religious Tolerance. *Journal of Human Rights, 2*(1), 17–30. doi: 10.1080/1475483032000054941

Gooch, L., & Goodman, J. D. (2012, February 10). Malaysia Detains Saudi over Twitter Posts on Prophet. *New York Times*. Retrieved June 15, 2016, from http://www.nytimes.com/2012/02/11/world/asia/malaysia-detains-saudi-over-https://twitter-posts-on-prophet.html?_r=0

Green, C. A. (2010). *The Khawaari J and the Creed of Takfeer: Declaring a Muslim to Be an Apostate and Its Effects upon Modern Day Islaamic Movements*. Boca Raton, FL: Dissertation.com.

Griffel, F. (2015). What Do We Mean by "Salafī"? Connecting Muḥammad ʿAbduh with Egypt's Nūr Party in Islam's Contemporary Intellectual History. *Die Welt des Islams, 55*(2), 186–220. doi:10.1163/15700607-00552p02

Gruzd, A., Wellman, B., & Takhteyev, Y. (2011). Imagining Twitter as an Imagined Community. *American Behavioral Scientist, 55*(10), 1294–1318. doi: 10.1177/0002764211409378

Habermas, J. (2003). *The Future of Human Nature*. Cambridge, UK: Polity Press.

Habib, T. al-. (Producer). (2012). al-ʾilhad min Ruʾya Nafsiyya. Retrieved June 15, 2016, from http://www.youtube.com/watch?v=uYZ9BwTT-wc

Hackett, R. I. J. (2006). Religion and the Internet. *Diogenes, 53*(3), 67–76. doi:10.1177/0392192106069015

Haddad, Y. (1991). The Revivalist Literature and the Literature on Revival: An Introduction. In Y. Y. Haddad, J. O. Voll, & J. L. Esposito (Eds.), *The Contemporary Islamic Revival: A Critical Survey and Bibliography* (pp. 3–22). Westport, CT: Greenwood.

Haj, S. (2009). *Reconfiguring Islamic Tradition: Reform, Rationality, and Modernity*. Stanford, CA: Stanford University Press.

Halim, F. A. (2015). Reformulating the in Cyberspace: Legal Authority, Doctrines, and Ijtihad Among Contemporary Shafi'i Ulama. *Islamic Law and Society, 22*(4), 413–435. doi:10.1163/15685195-00224p04

Hamad, T. al-. (2002). *al-Karadib*. Beirut, Lebanon: Dar al-Saqi.

Hamdan, A. (2005). Women and Education in Saudi Arabia: Challenges and Achievements. *International Education Journal, 6*(1), 42–64. http://ehlt.flinders.edu.au/education/iej/articles/v6n1/hamdan/paper.pdf

Hamidaddin, A. (2016). Harmonious Being: A Space for an Alternative Way of Exploring Religion. In S. Olsson & C. Kersten (Eds.), *Alternative Islamic Discourses and Religious Authority* (pp. 133–150). New York, NY: Routledge.

Hanson, S. (1997). The Secularisation Thesis: Talking at Cross Purposes. *Journal of Contemporary Religion, 12*(2), 159–179. doi:10.1080/13537909708580797

Harithi, F. al-. (2010). al-Tajriba al-Hiwariyya al-Akthar Buruzan fi al-ʿaqd al-Hali. Retrieved November 2, 2015, from http://www.yaam1.com/vb/showthread.php?t=12186

Hariz, M. (Producer). (2011). Saʿid bin Musfir Alqahtani - Jund al-Rahman wa Jund al-Shaytan. Retrieved June 15, 2016, from https://www.youtube.com/watch?v=yecNF6dPxeU

Hassan, R. (2015). Islamic Reformist and Discourse in South Asia. In S. Hunter (Ed.), *Reformist Voices of Islam: Mediating Islam and Modernity* (pp. 159–186). New York, NY: Routledge.

Hawali, S al-. (2000). *Sharh Tahkim al-Qawanin.* Jeddah, KSA: Maktabat Dar al-Sahabah.

Hawali, S. al-. (n.d.-a). al-ʿitiradh ʿala ʾamr Allah al-Sharʿi. Retrieved November 6, 2015, from http://www.alhawali.com/popups/print_window.aspx?article_no=5483&type=3&expand=1

Hawali, S. al-. (n.d.-b). Man Ankar Maʿluman min al-Din Bi-l-darura Fa-huwa Kafir Bi-l-ʾijmaʿ. Retrieved October 6, 2015, from http://www.alhawali.com/popups/print_window.aspx?article_no=2183&type=3&expand=1

Hayat TV al-. (Producer). (2013). Suʾal Jariʾ 285 Muqaranah Bayn Miʿraj Muhammad wa Miʿraj Akhnokh. Retrieved June 15, 2016, from https://www.youtube.com/watch?v=5FBuV7xj570

Heelas, P., & Woodhead, L. (2005). *The Spiritual Revolution: Why Religion Is Giving Way to Spirituality.* Oxford, UK: Blackwell.

Hegghammer, T. (2010). *Jihad in Saudi Arabia: Violence and Pan-Islamism Since 1979.* New York, NY: Cambridge University Press.

Hegghammer, T., & Lacroix, S. (2007). Rejectionist Islamism in Saudi Arabia: The Story of Juhayman al-ʿUtaybi Revisited. *International Journal of Middle East Studies, 39*(01), 103–122. doi: 10.1017.S0020743806391064

Helland, C. (2013). Ritual. In H. Campbell (Ed.), *Digital Religion: Understanding Religious Practice in New Media Worlds* (pp. 25–40). London, UK: Routledge.

Hervieu-Léger, D. (2000). *Religion as a Chain of Memory* New Brunswick, NJ: Rutgers University Press.

Hijabi, I. (2010). Man Hum Rumuz al-Libraliyya fi al-Saʿudiyya? Retrieved November 2, 2015, from http://www.alagidah.com/vb/showthread.php?t=6936

Hijri, S. al-. d. (2012). Bayan fi Mawjat al-ʾilhad fi Bilad al-Haramyan. Retrieved November 2, 2015, from http://www.almoslim.net/node/166284

Hilali, A. al-. (2014, September 14). Jihat Mukhtassa Tashraʿ fi Jald Muʾassis Mawqiʿ ʾiliktruni Mas al-Nitham al-ʿam. *al-Hayat.* Retrieved June 15, 2016, from http://alhayat.com/Articles/4590799

Hirschkind, C. (2006). *The Ethical Soundscape: Cassette Sermons and Islamic Counterpublics.* New York, NY: Columbia University Press.

Hjarvard, S. (2016). Mediatization and the Changing Authority of Religion. *Media Culture, and Society, 38*(1), 8–17. doi:10.1177/0163443715615412

Hoebink, M. (1999). Thinking About Renewal in Islam: Towards a History of Islamic Ideas on Modernization and Secularization. *Arabica, 46,* 29–62. http://www.jstor.org/stable/4057249

Hoffman, L. (2012). An Existential-Phenomenological Approach to the Psychology of Religion. *Pastoral Psychology, 61*(5), 783–795. doi: 10.1007/s11089-011-0393-0

Hookway, N. (2012). "Entering the Blogosphere": Some Strategies for Using Blogs in Social Research: Papers Addressing the "Mundane Embeddedness" of CMC in Daily Life. In B. Dicks (Ed.), *Digital Qualitative Research Methods* (Vol. 1, pp. 153–175). Los Angeles, CA: Sage. doi:10.3167/sa.2015.590201

Hubert, S. (2015). *The Impact of Religiosity on Fertility.* doi:10.1007/978-3-658-07008-3_3

Human Rights Watch. (2012). Saudi Arabia: Writer Faces Apostasy Trial. Retrieved October 6, 2015, from https://www.hrw.org/news/2012/02/13/saudi-arabia-writer-faces-apostasy-trial

Humphreys, M. (2005). Getting Personal: Reflexivity and Autoethnographic Vignettes. *Qualitative Inquiry, 11*(6), 840–860. doi:10.1177/1077800404269425

Ibrahim, M. (2013, March 17). ʾistiʿradh Fatawi Tahrim Tahawallat ʿala al-ʾibaha fi al-Suʿudiyyah. Retrieved 30 May, 2014, from www.alarabiya.net/ar/saudi-today/2013/03/17/مراجعة-نصف-قرن-من-فتاوى-التحريم-والتراجع-عنها-عبر-تويتر.html

Indvik, L. (2012). Saudi Journalist Arrested After Tweeting About Prophet Muhammad. Retrieved July 20, 2015, from http://mashable.com/2012/02/10/saudi-journalist-arrested-tweets-prophet-muhammad/

IslamicoVideos (Producer). (2012). Hukm Tʿallum ʾilm al-Mantiq Dhimn al-ʿulum al-Sharʿiyyah. Retrieved June 15, 2016, from https://www.youtube.com/watch?v=ynA-gJFZf7w

Islammemo. (2010, November 5). al-Mutlaq: Fatwa al-Kashirat Kharajat Bi ʾijmaʿ al-Lajna al-Daʾima. Retrieved October 6, 2014, from http://www.islammemo.cc/akhbar/arab/2010/11/05/110409.html

IslamWeb. (2009). La Tahtaj Lisuʾal ahl al-ʿilm Liʾanna Allah Wahabaha ʿaqlan. Retrieved November 2, 2015, from http://fatwa.islamweb.net/fatwa/index.php?page=showfatwa&Option=FatwaId&lang=A&Id=123196

IslamWeb. (2011). Al-Tahlil wa al-Tahrim Haq Khalis li Allah Taʿala. Retrieved September 8, 2014, from http://fatwa.islamweb.net/fatwa/index.php?page=showfatwa&Option=FatwaId&Id=165007

IslamWeb. (n.d). Al-Quran wa Siraʿ al-Haq wa al-Batil. Retrieved 5 July, 2014, from http://articles.islamweb.net/media/index.php?id=160812&lang=A&page=article

Ismail, F. (2008). Muthaqafun ʿarab wa Muʾssasat Huquqiyya Yadinun Takfir Katibayn Saʿudiyyin. Retrieved November 2, 2015, from http://www.alarabiya.net/articles/2008/03/31/47683.html

Jabiri, M. al-. (2014). *Takwin al-ʿaql al-ʿarabi* (12th ed.). Beirut, Lebanon: Markaz Derasat al-Wihdah al-Arabiyyah.

Jackson, S. A. (2014). On the Boundaries of Theological Tolerance in Islam: Abū Ḥāmid al-Ghazālīʾs Fayṣal al-Tafriqa Bayna al-Islām wa al-Zandaqa. In M. Fierro (Ed.), *Orthodoxy and Heresy in Islam* (Vol. 2, pp. 84–112). Oxon, UK: Routledge.

Jadʾan, F. (1989). *al-Mihna: Bahth fi Jadalliyat al-Dini wal-Siyasi fi al-Islam*. Amman, Jordan: Dar al-Shuruq.

Jameson, F. (2002). *A Singular Modernity: Essay on the Ontology of the Present*. London, UK: Verso.

Jarbou, A. al-. (2007). The Role of Traditionalists and Modernists on the Development of the Saudi Legal System. *Arab Law Quarterly, 21*(3), 191–229. http://www.jstor.org/stable/27650587

Jarid, I. al-. (n.d.). Madaris Tahfith al-Quran fi al-Mamlaka al-ʿArabiyya al-Suʿudiyyah Retrieved June 15, 2016, from http://goo.gl/MWnB9B

Jawziyyah, H. al-. (1991). *Iʾlam al-Muqiʾin ʾAn Rab al-ʾAlamin* (M. Ibrahim, Ed.). Beirut, Lebanon: Dar al-Kutub al-ʾIlmiyyah.

Jazirah, al-. (2001, March 25). "Al-Pokemon" Muharram Shiraʾuʾhu wa bayʿuhu wa ʿala al-Muslimin al-Hathar minhu. *al-Jazirah*. Retrieved June 15, 2016, from http://www.al-jazirah.com/2001/20010325/ln14.htm

Jehadnet. (2010). Jihad Dur Tahfith al-Quran al-Karim Bi-Mintiqat Makkah al-Mukkaramah. Retrieved July 7, 2014, from http://www.dd-sunnah.net/forum/archive/index.php/t-110801.html

Jibrin, A. al-. (2008). Bayan Fi Munasarat Fatwa al-ʿAllamah Abdulrahman al-Barrak. Retrieved August 15, 2014, from http://www.islamlight.net/index.php?option=content&task=view&id=8699

Jibrin, A. al-. (n.d.). Sharh al-ʿAqidah al-Tahawiyyah: Li-l-Shaykh Abdullah bin Abdulrahman al-Jibrin. Retrieved October 6, 2015, from http://audio.islamweb.net/audio/Fulltxt.php?audioid=149242

John, P. T. (2015). Aḥmad b. Abi Duʾad. In *Encyclopaedia of Islam*. Brill. Retrieved June 15, 2016, from http://referenceworks.brillonline.com/entries/encyclopaedia-of-islam-3/ahmad-b-abi-duad-SIM_0064.

Johnson-Miller, B. (2005). Visiting the Labyrinth of Religious Transformation. *Journal of Beliefs and Values, 26*(1), 1–15. doi:10.1080/13617670500046576

Joinson, A. N. (2001). Self-Disclosure in Computer-Mediated Communication: The Role of Self-Awareness and Visual Anonymity. *European Journal of Social Psychology, 31*(2), 177–192. doi:10.1002/ejsp.36

Jones, J. (2014). Switching in Https://twitter's Hashtagged Exchanges. *Journal of Business and Technical Communication, 28*(1), 83–108. http://jbt.sagepub.com/content/28/1/83.abstract doi:10.1177/1050651913502358

Jones, T. C. (2006). Rebellion on the Saudi Periphery: Modernity, Marginalization, and the Shiʿa Uprising of 1979. *International Journal of Middle East Studies, 32*(2), 213–233. http://www.jstor.org/stable/3879971

KAICIID. (n.d.) King Abdullah bin Abdulaziz International Centre for Interreligious and Intercultural Dialogue. Retrieved July 7, 2014, from http://www.kaiciid.org/

Karner, C., & Aldridge, A. (2004). Theorizing Religion in a Globalizing World. *International Journal of Politics, Culture, and Society, 18*(1–2), 5–32. doi:10.1023/B:IJPS.0000048105.59395.do

Karpov, V. (2010). Desecularization: A Conceptual Framework. *Journal of Church and State, 52*(2), 232–270. doi: 10.1093/jcs/csq058

Kechichian, J. (1990). Islamic Revivalism and Change in Saudi Arabia: Juhayman al-ʿUtaybi's "letters" to the Saudi People. *The Muslim World, 80*(1), 1–16. doi:10.1111/j.1478-1913.1990.tb03478.x

Kechichian, J. A. (1986). The Role of the Ulama in the Politics of an Islamic State: The Case of Saudi Arabia. *International Journal of Middle East Studies, 18*(1), 53–71. http://www.jstor.org/stable/162860

Kechichian, J. A. (2001). *Succession in Saudi Arabia.* New York, NY: Palgrave.

Keddie, N. R. (1983). *An Islamic Response to Imperialism: Political and Religious Writings of Sayyid Jamal ad-Din al-Afghani.* Berkeley: University of California Press.

Kersten, C. (2011). *Cosmoplitans and Heretics: New Muslim Intellectuals and the Study of Islam.* London, UK: Hurst.

Kersten, C. (2015). Atheism (modern). In K. Fleet, G. Krämer, D. Matringe, J. Nawas, & E. Rowson (Eds.), *Encyclopaedia of Islam, Three.* Brill Online: Brill. Retrieved June 15, 2016, from http://referenceworks.brillonline.com/entries/encyclopaedia-of-islam-3/atheism-modern-COM_25009.

Khalife, L. (2017, July 31). We Talked to "Muslim atheists" About Why They Don't Believe. Retrieved March 21, 2019, from https://stepfeed.com/we-talked-to-muslim-atheists-about-why-they-don-t-believe-9650

Khalijyyah. (Producer). (2012). Fi al-Samim - al-Halaqa al-Thaminah maʿ Turki al-Hamad. Retrieved June 15, 2016, from https://www.youtube.com/watch?v=9RVEZHJ1S50

Khalijyyah. (Producer). (2013). al-ʾIlhad fi al-Suʿudyyah. Retrieved June 15, 2016, from https://www.youtube.com/watch?v=_Q8JmoWlBk4

Khalil, M. (2014). al-Shabaka al-Jahannamiyya allati Qatalat Faraj Fudah. Retrieved March 21, 2019, from http://middle-east-online.com/?id=171640

Khamis, I. al-. (2012). Bayan ulama wa Duʿat Jidda ʿAn Mahadin al-ʾInhiraf wa al-Tashkik. Retrieved November 2, 2015, from http://www.saaid.net/fatwa/f101.htm

Khannous, T. (2011). Virtual Gender: Moroccan and Saudi Women's Cyberspace. *Journal of Women of the Middle East and the Islamic World, 8,* 358–387. doi:http://dx.doi.org/10.1163/156920811X599121

Khayl, Y. al-. (2007, December 16). al-ʾAkhar fi Mizan al-Islam. *al-Riyadh.* Retrieved June 15, 2016, from http://www.alriyadh.com/301993

Khidr, A. al-. (2010, May 6). Muhammad ʿAbid al-Jabiry .. wa al-Mashhad al-Thaqafi al-Saʿudy. *al-Riyadh.* Retrieved June 15, 2016, from http://www.alriyadh.com/523105

Khidr, A. al-. (2011). *Al-Suʿudiyya: Sirat Dawla wa Mujtamaʿ: Qira'ah fi Tajribat Thulth Qarn min al-Tahawwulat al-Fikriyya Wa-l-Siyasiyya Wa-l-Tanmawiyya* (2nd ed.). Beirut, Lebanon: Al-Shabakah al-ʿArabīyah Li-l-Abhath wa-al-Nashr.

Khoei, Y. al-. (2001). Marja and the Survival of a Community: The Shiʿa of Medina. In L. S. Walbridge (Ed.), *The Most Learned of the Shi'a: The Institution of the Marja' Taqlid* (pp. 263–348). New York, NY: Oxford University Press.

Khraim, H. (2010). Measuring Religiosity in Consumer Research from an Islamic Perspective. *Journal of Economic and Administrative Sciences, 26*(1), 52–78. doi: 10.1108/10264116201000003

Khulayfi, A. al-. (2011). Kalam al-Shaykhayn Muhammad Bin Ibrahim al-Alshaykh wa Hamud al-Tuwayjiri fi Kurat al-Qadam. Retrieved October 6, 2014, from http://www.sahab.net/forums/index.php?showtopic=125016

Khuzaym, Y. al-. (2012). Hasad Al-Taghrib fi Bilad Al-Haramayn. Retrieved September 23, 2013, from http://www.almokhtsar.com/node/54310

King, N., & Horrocks, C. (2010). *Interviews in Qualitative Research*. London, UK: SAGE Publications.

Kinninmont, J. (2013). To What Extent Is Twitter Changing Gulf Societies? Retrieved March 21, 2019, from http://www.chathamhouse.org/sites/default/files/public/Research/Middle%20East/0213kinninmont.pdf

Knowles, S. (2013). Rapture Ready and the World Wide Web: Religious Authority on the Internet. *Journal of Media and Religion, 12*(3), 128–143. doi:10.1080/15348423.2013.820527

Kostiner, J. (1985). On Instruments and Their Designers: The Ikhwan of Najd and the Emergence of the Saudi State. *Middle Eastern Studies, 21*(3), 298–323. http://www.jstor.org/stable/4283073

Kozinets, R. V. (2010). *Netnography: Doing Ethnographic Research Online*. Los Angeles, CA: Sage.

Kozlarek, O. (Ed.). (2014). *Multiple Experiences of Modernity: Toward a Humanist Critique of Modernity*. Goettingen, Germany: V & R University Press.

Kraidy, M. (2012). The Saudi Modernity Wars According to Abdullah Al-Ghathami: A Template for the Study of Arab Culture and Media. In T. Sabry (Ed.), *Arab Cultural Studies: Mapping the Field* (pp. 234–254). London, UK: I.B. Tauris.

Krötke, W., Hock, K., Grund, A., Metzner, R., Holze, H., Abraham, M., . . . Zchomelidse, N. (2015). Sin, Guilt, and ForgivenessReligion Past and Present. Brill Online. Retrieved June 15, 2016, from http://referenceworks.brillonline.com/entries/religion-past-and-present/sin-guilt-and-forgiveness-COM_025015.

krt455 (Producer). (2008). al-ʾAmir Nayif Yardaʾ al-Haqid al-Sahafi Ahmad al-Yusuf. Retrieved June 15, 2016, from https://www.youtube.com/watch?v=RB4JnaK-LZY

Kurtz, L. R. (1983). The Politics of Heresy. *American Journal of Sociology, 88*(6), 1085–1115. http://www.jstor.org/stable/2778965 doi:10.2307/2778965

Lacroix, S. (2004). Between Islamists and Liberals: Saudi Arabia's New "Islamo-Liberal" Reform. *Middle East Journal, 58*(3), 345–365. http://www.jstor.org/stable/4330029

Lacroix, S. (2011a). *Awakening Islam* (G. Holoch, Trans.). Cambridge, MA: Harvard University Press.

Lacroix, S. (2011b). Is Saudi Arabia Immune? *Journal of Democracy, 22*(4), 48–59. doi:10.1353/jod.2011.0055

Lacroix, S. (2014). Saudi Islamists and the Arab Spring. Retrieved March 21, 2019, from   http://eprints.lse.ac.uk/56725/1/Lacroix_Saudi-Islamists-and-theArab-Spring_2014.pdf

Lafi, M. (2011). Mawjat al-Takfir Ghayr al-Mundhabit Bi-Muʾtamar al-Madina al-ʿAlami. Retrieved November 6, 2015, from http://almoslim.net/node/153346

Lambert, Y. (1999). Religion in Modernity as a New Axial Age: Secularization or New Religious Forms? *Sociology of Religion, 60*(3), 303–333. http://www.jstor.org/stable/3711939

Langer, R., & Simon, U. (2014). The Dynamics of Orthodoxy and Heterodoxy. Dealing with Divergence in Muslim Discourses and Islamic Studies. In M. Fierro (Ed.), *Orthodoxy and Heresy in Islam* (Vol. 1, pp. 201–212). Oxon, UK: Routledge.

Larsson, A. O., & Moe, H. (2012). Studying Political Microblogging: Twitter users in the 2010 Swedish Election Campaign. *New Media Society, 14*(5), 729–747. doi:http://dx.doi.org/10.1177/1461444811422894

Lauzière, H. (2010). The Construction of Salafiyya: Reconsidering Salafism from the Perspective of Conceptual History. *International Journal of Middle East Studies, 42*(3), 369–389. doi:10.1017/S0020743810000401.

Lauzière, H. (2016). What We Mean Versus What They Meant by "Salafi": A Reply to Frank Griffel. *Die Welt des Islams, 56*, 89–96. doi:10.1163/15700607-00561p06

Lawrence, B. B. (1998). Transformation. In M. C. Taylor (Ed.), *Critical Terms for Religious Studies* (pp. 334–348). Chicago, IL: University of Chicago Press.

Layth, I. al-. (Producer). (2014). al-ʾIlhad min Ruʾya Nafsya. Retrieved June 15, 2016, from https://www.youtube.com/watch?v=DyKrmkz_-io

Lee, D. E. (1942). The Origins of Pan-Islamism. *American Historical Review, 47*(2), 278–287. http://www.jstor.org/stable/1841668

Lee, R. D. (1997). *Overcoming Tradition and Modernity: The Search for Islamic Authenticity*. Boulder, CO: Westview Press.

Lewis, B. (1953). Some Observations on the Significance of Heresy in the History of Islam. *Studia Islamica*, (1), 43–63. http://www.jstor.org/stable/1595009

Lewis, B. (1992). *Race and Slavery in the Middle East: An Historical Enquiry*. New York, NY: Oxford University Press.

Lewis, D. (2008). Using Life Histories in Social Policy Research: The Case of Third Sector/Public Sector Boundary Crossing. *Journal of Social Policy, 37*(4), 559–578. doi: 10.1017/S0047279408002213

Luckmann, T. (1967). *The Invisible Religion: The Problem of Religion in Modern Society*. New York, NY: Macmillan.

m3zad (Producer). (2011). Al-Shaykh Nasir al-ʾUmar Yantaqidu Tawwajuh wa Siyasat Wazir al-Taʿlim. Retrieved June 15, 2016, from http://www.youtube.com/watch?v=GGAR46YY1jo

Macdonald, D. B. (2015). Bid'a. In M. T. Houtsma, T. W. Arnold, R. Basset, & R. Hartmann (Eds.), *Encyclopaedia of Islam, First Edition (1913–1936)* (pp. I:1199a). Brill Online. Retrieved June 15, 2016, from http://referenceworks.brillonline. com/entries/encyclopaedia-of-islam-2/bida-SIM_1393.

MacFarquhar, N. (2004, April 21). Police Building in Saudi Capital Is Wrecked by Car Bomb. *New York Times*. Retrieved June 15, 2016, from http://www.nytimes. com/2004/04/21/international/middleeast/21CND-SAUD.html

MacFarquhar, N. (2011, June 15). Social Media Help Keep the Door Open to Sustained Dissent Inside Saudi Arabia. *New York Times*. Retrieved June 15, 2016, from http://www.nytimes.com/2011/06/16/world/middleeast/16saudi. html?pagewanted=all&_r=0

Madani, A. Z. a.-. (2012). Sighat Da'wa Dhud al-Safil Turki al-Hamad Yuqaddam fi Jami' Manatiq al-Mamlaka Fa-htasibu. Retrieved November 2, 2015, from http:// www.ahlalhdeeth.com/vb/showthread.php?t=241072

Madelung, W. (2015). Zaydiyya. In P. Bearman, T. Bianquis, C. E. Bosworth, E. v. Donzel, & W. P. Heinrichs (Eds.), *Encyclopaedia of Islam* (2nd ed.). Brill Online. Retrieved June 15, 2016, from http://referenceworks.brillonline.com/entries/ encyclopaedia-of-islam-2/zaydiyya-COM_1385.

Mahaffy, K. A. (1996). Cognitive Dissonance and Its Resolution: A Study of Lesbian Christians. *Journal for the Scientific Study of Religion, 35*(4), 392–402. http://www. jstor.org/stable/1386414

Maliki, H. al-. (2000a). *Qira'ah Fi Kitab al-Tawhid.* Beirut, Lebanon: Markaz al-Dirasat al-Tarikhiyyah.

Maliki, H. al-. (2000b). *Qira'at Fi Kutub al-'Aqa'id: al-Mathhab al-Hanbaly Namuthajan.* Beirut, Lebanon: Markaz al-Dirasat al-Tarikhiyyah.

Manhaj, S. (2014). Did Modern Salafi Scholars Invent the Notion of "Istihlal"? A Critique of Yasir Qadhi's Theory. Retrieved September 8, 2014, from http:// download.salafimanhaj.com/pdf/SalafiManhaj_YasirQadhi.pdf

Manouchehri, F. H., Melvin-Koushki, M., Shah-Kazemi, R., Bahrahmian, A., Pakatchi, A., Waley, M. I., Poor, D., Mohammad, T. M., Brown, K., Jozi, M. R. et al. (2015). 'Alī b. Abī Ṭālib. In W. Madelung & F. Daftary (Eds.), *Encyclopaedia Islamica*. Brill Online. Retrieved June 15, 2016, from http://referenceworks.bril-lonline.com/entries/encyclopaedia-islamica/ali-b-abi-talib-COM_0252.

Maruna, S., & Copes, H. (2005). What Have We Learned from Five Decades of Neutralization Research? *Crime and Justice, 32*, 221–320. http://www.jstor.org/ stable/3488361

Massignon, L., & Mason, H. (1994). *Hallaj: Mystic and Martyr* (Abridged ed.). Princeton, NJ: Princeton University Press.

Masud, M. K., Salvatore, A., & Bruinessen, M. v. (2009). *Islam and Modernity: Key Issues and Debates.* Edinburgh, UK: Edinburgh University Press.

Matthee, R. (1989). Jamal al-Din al-Afghani and the Egyptian National Debate. *International Journal of Middle East Studies, 21*(2), 151–169. http://www.jstor.org/ stable/163072

Matthiesen, T. (2009). Diwaniyyas, Intellectual Salons, and the Limits of Civil Society. Retrieved October 4, 2014, from http://www.mei.edu/content/diwaniyyas-intellectual-salons-and-limits-civil-society

Matthiesen, T. (2010). Hizbullah al-Hijaz: A History of the Most Radical Saudi Shiʿa Opposition Group. *Middle East Journal, 64*(2), 179–197. doi:10.1353/mej.0.0154

Matthiesen, T. (2012). A "Saudi Spring"? The Shiʿa Protest Movement in the Eastern Province 2011–2012. *Middle East Journal, 66*(4), 628–659. http://muse.jhu.edu/journals/mej/summary/vo66/66.4.matthiesen.html

Matthiesen, T. (2014). Migration, Minorities, and Radical Networks: Labour Movements and Opposition Groups in Saudi Arabia, 1950–1975. *International Review of Social History, 59*(3), 473–504. doi:10.1017/S0020859014000455

Matthiesen, T. (2015). *The Other Saudis: Shiism, Dissent and Sectarianism*. Cambridge, UK: Cambridge University Press.

MCB.net. (2014). Thahirat ʾInshiqaq al-Qamar Tuthbit Li "NASA" ʾIʿjaz al-Quran. Retrieved August 29, 2014, from www.mbc.net/ar/programs/sabah-al-khair/articles/ناس--في-العلماء-حيرة-يثير-القمر-انشقاق--صور-.html

McDowall, A. (2013). Saudis Release Writer Jailed for Tweets Against Islamism. Retrieved June 2, 2015, from http://www.reuters.com/article/2013/06/05/us-saudi-writer-idUSBRE95410520130605

McGinty, A. M. (2007). Formation of Alternative Femininities Through Islam: Feminist Approaches Among Muslim Converts in Sweden. *Women's Studies International Forum, 30*(6), 474–485. doi: 10.1016/j.wsif.2007.09.004

mdawy11 (Producer). (2008). Al-Taghrib fi al-Suʿudiyya. Retrieved June 15, 2016, from http://www.youtube.com/watch?v=rpmmliEOJEo

Meijer, R. (2009). *Global Salafism: Islam's New Religious Movement*. New York, NY: Columbia University Press.

Meijer, R. (2010). Reform in Saudi Arabia: The Gender Segregation (ikhtilat) Debate in Saudi Arabia: Reform and the Clash Between ʿUlamaʾ and Liberals. *Journal for Islamic Studies, 30*, 2–32. doi:10.1111/j.1475-4967.2010.00464.x

Menouar, Y. el- (2014). The Five Dimensions of Muslim Religiosity: Result of Empirical Study. *Methods, Data, and Analysis, 8*(1), 53–78. doi:10.12758/mda.2014.003

Meyer, B., & Moors, A. (2006). *Religion, Media, and the Public Sphere*. Bloomington: Indiana University Press.

Mitchell, B. (1984). How Is the Concept of Sin Related to the Concept of Moral Wrongdoing? *Religious Studies, 20*(2), 165–173. http://www.jstor.org/stable/20006041

Moaddel, M. (2006). The Saudi Public Speaks: Religion, Gender, and Politics. *International Journal of Middle East Studies, 38*(1), 79–108. http://www.jstor.org/stable/3879795

Moaddel, M., & Azadarmaki, T. (2002). The Worldviews of Islamic Publics: The Cases of Egypt, Iran, and Jordan. *Comparative Sociology, 1*(3-4), 299–319. doi: 10.1163/156913302100418619

Moaddel, M., & Talattof, K. (Eds.). (2000). *Contemporary Debates in Islam: An Anthology of Modernist and Fundamentalist Thought*. New York, NY: Palgrave Macmillan.

Mosad, K. (Producer). (2012). Alharb ma' Alshaytan. Retrieved June 15, 2016, from http://www.youtube.com/watch?v=yTvnEYHUJrE

Muhammad, A. al-. (2004, March 11). al-Salunat al-Nisa'iyya Juhud Fardiyya Li-'Iithra' al-Thaqafa al-Sa'udiyya. *al-Sharq al-Awsat*. Retrieved June 15, 2016, from http://archive.aawsat.com/details.asp?article=222497&issueno=9235#.ViOyMX4rLDc

Muhammad, A. al-. (2008, June 19). Fatwa Li-l-Fawzan Hawl Takfir al-Libraliyyin Tuthir Jadalan Fi 'Awsat Su'udiyya. Retrieved November 2, 2015, from http://www.alarabiya.net/articles/2007/06/19/35653.html

Muhayni, M. al-. (2007, January 25, 2007). Abdullah al-Qasimi Ya'udu min Jadid. *al-Riyadh*. Retrieved June 15, 2016, from http://www.alriyadh.com/219466

Mulin, M. N. (2011). *'Ulama' al-Islam: Tarikh wa-Binyat Al-Mu'assasah Al-Diniya fi Al-Sa'udiya Bayna Al-Qarnayn Al-Thamin 'Ashar wa-al-hadi wa-al-'ishrin* (M. Salim & A. A. Allah, Trans.). Beirut, Lebanon: al-Shabakah al-'Arabiyah lil-Abhath wa-al-Nashr.

Multaqa al-Khutaba'. (Producer). (2013). (Multaqa al-Khutaba') Asbab al-'Amn wa Qat' al-Fitan. Retrieved June 15, 2016, from http://www.youtube.com/watch?v=Ias4fxDsrIA

Munasir al-Haramayn, M. (Producer). (2013). Qussat 'istitabat al-Shaykh bin 'Uthaymin. Retrieved June 15, 2016, from https://www.youtube.com/watch?v=91_3IXQLD_Y

Murphy, C. (2014, June 10). The Rise of Atheism in Saudi Arabia, Where Talking About Atheism is Illegal. Retrieved March 21, 2019, from https://www.pri.org/stories/2014-06-10/rise-atheism-saudi-arabia-where-talking-about-atheism-illegal

Mushawwah, K. al-. (2012). *Al-Tayyarat Al-Diniyya fi al-Su'udiyya: min al-Salafiya 'ila Jihadiyyat al-Qa'idah wa-ma Baynahuma min Tayyarat* (2nd ed.). Beirut, Lebanon: Mu'assat al-Iintishar al-'Arabi.

Mustafa, H. al-. (2003, February 28). Waqfah Ma' Ba'dh Afkar Mansour al-Nogaidan. Retrieved November 2, 2015, from http://www.alwasatnews.com/175/news/read/198072/1.html

Nabeel, G. (2017, August 1). Atheists in Muslim World: Silent, Resentful and Growing in Number. *Washington Times*. Retrieved November 28, 2018, from www.washingtontimes.com/news/2017/aug/1/atheists-in-muslim-world-growing-silent-minority/.

Nafjan, E. al-. (2012). Teaching Intolerance. *Foreign Policy*, May/June. http://www.foreignpolicy.com/articles/2012/04/23/teaching_intolerance

Najjar, Z. al-. (2006). *Haqa'iq 'Ilmiyyah fi al-Quran al-Karim*. Beirut, Lebanon: Dar al-Ma'rifah.

Nasr, S. V. R. (1996). *Mawdudi and the Making of Islamic Revivalism*. New York, NY: Oxford University Press.

National, The. (2012, August 19). Is Gulf Youth Increasingly Drawn to Atheism? *The National*. Retrieved June 15, 2016, from http://www.thenational.ae/thenationalconversation/comment/is-gulf-youth-increasingly-drawn-to-atheism

Nawas, J. A. (1994). A Reexamination of Three Current Explanations for al-Ma'mun's Introduction of the Mina. *International Journal of Middle East Studies, 26*(04), 615–629. doi: 10.1017/S0020743800061134

Nevo, J. (1998). Religion and National Identity in Saudi Arabia. *Middle Eastern Studies, 34*(3), 34–53. doi: 10.1080/00263209808701231

Nogaidan, M. al-. (2003, August 14). Nadi al-Takfir Bidhʿ atakum Ruddat 'Ilaykum. *al-Riyadh*. Retrieved June 15, 2016, from http://www.alriyadh.com/19989

Nogaidan, M. al-. (2003, November 28). Telling the Truth, Facing the Whip. *New York Times*. Retrieved June 15, 2016, from http://www.nytimes.com/2003/11/28/opinion/telling-the-truth-facing-the-whip.html

Nogaidan, M. al-. (2012). *Al-Muluk Al-Mutasibun: Al'amr bi Alma'ruf wa al-Nahy 'an al-Munkar fi al-Su'diyyah (1927–2007)*. Dubai, UAE: al-Mesbar Studies and Research Center.

Noman, H. (2015). Arab Religious Skeptics Online: Anonymity, Autonomy, and Discourse in a Hostile Environment. *Berkman Center Research*. http://dx.doi.org/10.2139/ssrn.2560491

Norris, P., & Inglehart, R. (2004). *Sacred and Secular: Religion and Politics Worldwide*. Cambridge, UK: Cambridge University Press.

Norton, A. R. (2002). Activism and Reform in Islam. *Current History, 101*, 377–381. http://people.bu.edu/arn/101_658_377.pdf

Oduah, C. (2018, September 18). Nigeria's Undercover Atheists: In Their Words. *Al Jazeera*. Retrieved November 28, 2018, from www.aljazeera.com/indepth/features/nigeria-undercover-atheists-words-180917212711132.html.

OmarHater. (Producer). (2012). Mufti al-Suʿ udiyya: Laʾ Alayk.. al-Shams Hiya Allati Tadur Hawl al-'Ardh. Retrieved June 15, 2016, from https://www.youtube.com/watch?v=-I2ZYodJT1s

OpenNet Initiative. (n.d.). Internet Filtering in Saudi Arabia in 2004. Retrieved January 1, 2015, from https://opennet.net/studies/saudi

Otterbeck, J. (2012). Wahhabi Ideology of Social Control Versus a New Publicness in Saudi Arabia. *Contemporary Islam, 6*, 341–353. doi:10.1007/s11562-012-0223-x

Otterbeck, J. (2014). What Is Islamic Arts? And What Makes Art Islamic? The Example of the Islamic Discourse on Music. *CILE Journal, 1*(1), 7–29.

Parray, T. A. (2011). Islamic Modernist and Reformist Thought: A Study of the Contribution of Sir Sayyid and Muhammad Iqbal. *World Journal of Islamic History and Civilization, 1*(2), 79–93. http://www.idosi.org/wjihc/wjihc1(2)11/2.pdf

PCSRF (2010). (al-Lajnah al-Daʾimah Li-l-Buhuth al-Ilmiyyah wa al-ʾIftaʾ, [Permanent Committee for Scholarly Research and Fatwa]). Fatwa Al Lajnah Al Daʾimah ʿan

Al Kashirat. Retrieved October 6, 2014, from http://www.alfawzan.af.org.sa/node/13111

PCSRF (n.d.-a). Comparison Between Celebrating the Mawlid and Performing Daʿwah Programmmes for Weeks and the National Day. Retrieved October 5, 2014, from http://goo.gl/IMz8Mu

PCSRF. (n.d.-b). Hukm man Yuʾaddi Baʿdh Arkan al-ʾIslam wa Yatruk al-Baʿdh al-ʾAkhar. Retrieved November 6, 2015, from http://www.alifta.net/fatawa/fatawaDetails.aspx?View=Page&PageID=438&PageNo=1&BookID=5

PCSRF. (n.d.-c). al-Safar Li-l-dirasa wa al-Sakan maʿ al-Kuffar. Retrieved December 25, 2015, from http://www.alifta.net/Fatawa/FatawaDetails.aspx?lang=ar&Index ItemID=175&SecItemHitID=182&ind=13&Type=Index&View=Page&PageID=4 381&PageNo=1&BookID=3&Title=DisplayIndexAlpha.aspx

PCSRF. (n.d.-d). Shubuhat Hawl al-Taswir al-Futughrafy. Retrieved December 25, 2015, from http://www.alifta.net/Fatawa/fatawaDetails.aspx?BookID=3&View= Page&PageNo=1&PageID=369&languagename=

PCSRF. (n.d.-e). Tajahul al-Nusus al-Sharʿiyya wa al-ʾAkhth Bi-l-Raʾy wa al-Zawq wa al-ʾIjtihadat al-ʾAqliyya al-Qasira. Retrieved November 6, 2015, from http://www.alifta.net/fatawa/fatawasubjects.aspx?languagename=ar&Vie w=Page&HajjEntryID=0&HajjEntryName=&RamadanEntryID=0&Ramad anEntryName=&NodeID=9418&PageID=13872&SectionID=2&SubjectPag eTitlesID=111203&MarkIndex=5&0

Priego, E. (2014). Twitter as Public Evidence and the Ethics of Twitter Research. Retrieved June 25, 2016, from https://epriego.wordpress.com/2014/05/27/ twitter-as-public-evidence-and-the-ethics-of-twitter-research/

Prokop, M. (2003). Saudi Arabia: the Politics of Education. *International Affairs*, 79(1), 77–89. doi: 10.1080/0026320050119241

Qahtani, A. al-. (2012). al-Mufti: al-Muslim al-Ghayur la Yardha Bi-kalimat Waqiha Tatatawal ʿAla Allah wa Rasuluhu. Retrieved November 2, 2015, from http:// sabq.org/i5hfde#.T7DF1-vTznQ.https://twitter

Qahtani, M. al-. (1992). *Al-Walaʾ wa al-Baraʾ fi al-'Islam*. al-Riyadh, Saudi Arabia: Dar Taybah.

Qanat Abu ʿUmar al-Daʿ awiyyah, Q. A. U. (Producer). (2013). Alshaykh Saʿad Albrayk Yuhhathir min Khatar Alrafida wa Alʾalmaniyya fi al-Suʿudyya. Retrieved June 15, 2016, from https://www.youtube.com/watch?v=LcliV7FQ2Fs

Qanat al-Muhtaseb. (Producer). (2012). Bukaʾ al-Shaykh al-Fawzan min Katiba Tatawalat ʿala Allah. Retrieved June 15, 2016, from https://www.youtube.com/ watch?v=nukDyS5VoYE

Qanat al-Rasmiyyah Li-l-shaykh Nasir al-Qitami al-. (Producer). (2014). Twitter man Yantiq Biʾsmak?! Retrieved June 15, 2016, from https://www.youtube.com/ watch?v=IF1zh-iLh2I#t=14

Qanat tellmeooo. (Producer). (2012). Al-Shaykh Salih al-Luhaydan Yufti Yuharrim Zyarat al-ʿAwaʾil Li-l-Jjanadiriyyah. Retrieved June 15, 2016, from https://www.youtube.com/watch?v=-ZmdbFJunxA

Qardawi, Y. al- (1980). *al-Halal wa al-Haram Fi al-Islam*. Beirut, Lebanon: al-Maktab al-ʾIslami.

Qardawi, Y. al-. (2000). *al-Shaykh al-Ghazali Kama ʿAraftuhu*. Cairo, Egypt: Dar al-Shuruk.

Qasim, A. (2009, February 19). Turki al-Hamad Muʾtarifan. *Okaz*. Retrieved from http://www.okaz.com.sa/okaz/osf/20090219/Con20090219259618.htm

Qunayʾir, H. al-. (2011, September 18). Khatar alʾIbtiʾath. *al-Riyadh*. Retrieved June 15, 2016, from http://www.alriyadh.com/2011/09/18/article668040.html

Quran (2016). *Sahih International Translation*. Retrieved from www.Quran.com

Quwayfili, I. al-. (2002a, August 17). ʿAlam Hawwaʾ al-Mawjud. al-Kaʾin . . . wa al-Mutah (4–4), *al-Sharq al-Awsat*. Retrieved June 15, 2016, from http://archive.aawsat.com/details.asp?issueno=8435&article=118705

Quwayfili, I. al-. (2002b, August 14). Harb al-Muntadayat . . . Guernica al-Elektronyya (1–4). *al-Sharq al-Awsat*. Retrieved June 15, 2016, from http://archive.aawsat.com/details.asp?article=118184&issueno=8660#.ViKbEH4rLDc

Quwayfili, I. al-. (2002c, August 15). Muntada al-Saha al-ʿArabiyyah . . . Mutaqaddim Yanfaridu Bi ʾUturuhatihi (2–4). *al-Sharq al-Awsat*. Retrieved June 15, 2016, from http://archive.aawsat.com/details.asp?issueno=8435&article=118369#.ViKbkH4rLDc

Quwayfili, I. al-. (2002d, August 16). Sahat al-ʾIqlaʿ . . . Fadaʾ Li-l-Tahliq Bihanin Fawq al-Madʾin (3–4). *al-Sharq al-Awsat*. Retrieved June 15, 2016, from http://archive.aawsat.com/details.asp?article=118524&issueno=8662#.ViKccn4rLDc

Raʾis al-Hayʾat. (Producer). (2014). Raʾis al-Hayʾat ʿAbdullatif Al al-Shaykh Matiyyat al-Taghrib. Retrieved June 15, 2016, from https://www.youtube.com/watch?v=iOpreiPqqsM

Rachid, B. (n.d.). Al Hayat Ministries. Retrieved March 21, 2019, from http://alhayat.org/en-us/ouroutreach/speakers/brotherrachid.aspx

Rahman, F. (1984). *Islam and Modernity: Transformation of an Intellectual Tradition*. Chicago, IL: University of Chicago Press.

Ramadan, T. (2009). *Islam, the West and the Challenges of Modernity* (S. Amghar, Trans.). Leicester, UK: Islamic Foundation.

Raphaeli, N. (2005). Demands for Reforms in Saudi Arabia. *Middle Eastern Studies*, 41(4), 517–532. doi: 10.1080/00263200500119241

Rasheed, M. al-. (1996). God, the King and the Nation: Political Rhetoric in Saudi Arabia in the 1990s. *Middle East Journal*, 50(3), 359–371. http://www.jstor.org/stable/4328956

Rasheed, M. al-. (1998). The Shiʿa of Saudi Arabia: A Minority in Search of Cultural Authenticity. *British Journal of Middle Eastern Studies*, 25(1), 121–138. doi: 10.1080/13530199808705657

Rasheed, M. al-. (2007). *Contesting the Saudi State: Islamic Voices from a New Generation.* New York, NY: Cambridge University Press.

Rasheed, M al-. (2010). *A History of Saudi Arabia.* Cambridge, UK: Cambridge University Press.

Rasheed, M. al-. (2011). Sectarianism as Counter-Revolution: Saudi Responses to the Arab Spring. *Studies in Ethnicity and Nationalism, 11*(3), 513–526. doi:10.1111/j.1754-9469.2011.01129.x

Rasheed, M. al-. (2013a). *A Most Masculine State: Gender, Politics and Religion in Saudi Arabia.* New York, NY: Cambridge University Press.

Rasheed, M. al-. (2013b). Saudi Arabia: Local and Regional Challenges. *Contemporary Arab Affairs, 6*(1), 28–40. doi:10.1080/17550912.2012.753797

Rasheed, M. al-. (2014, January 28). New Saudi Writers Offer Form of Islamic Liberation Theology. Retrieved November 6, 2015, from http://www.al-monitor.com/pulse/originals/2014/01/saudi-writers-offer-islamic-liberation-theology.html#

Rashid, A. al-. (2004). *Dhawabit Takfir al-Muʿayyan ʿInd Shaykhi al-Islam ibn Taymiyya wa ibn Abdulwahhab wa ulama al-Dawla al-ʾIslahiyya.* al-Riyadh, KSA: Makatabat al-Rushd.

Rawaf, H. al-, & Simmons, C. (1991). The Education of Women in Saudi Arabia. *Comparative Education, 27*(3), 287–295. doi: 10.1080/0305006910270304

Regnerus, M. D., & Uecker, J. E. (2006). Finding Faith, Losing Faith: The Prevalence and Context of Religious Transformations During Adolescence. *Review of Religious Research, 47*(3), 217–237. doi: 10.2307/3512355

RevolutionKSA@gmail.com. (2011). Thawrat Hunayn 11 Mars al-Suʿudyyah. Retrieved November 2, 2015, from https://www.facebook.com/ThorahKSA

Rifaʿi, H. al-. (2011, March 12). al-Sijn wa al-Jald Taʿziran ʿUqubata Duʿat al-Tajjamuʿat wa al-Muthaharat. *al-Madinah.* Retrieved June 15, 2016, from http://www.al-madina.com/node/292929

Rifaʿi, H. al-. (2012, February 7). 4000 Muhtasib Yatawafadun ʿala al-Mahakim Mutalibin Bimuhakamat al-Mutatawil ʿala Sayyid al-Khalq. *Okaz.* Retrieved June 15, 2016, from http://www.al-madina.com/node/356605

Ross, C., Terras, M., Warwick, C., & Welsh, A. (2011). Enabled Backchannel: Conference Twitter Use by Digital Humanists. *Journal of Documentation, 67*(2), 214–237. http://www.emeraldinsight.com/doi/abs/10.1108/00220411111109449 doi:10.1108/00220411111109449

Roy, O. (2006). *Globalized Islam: The Search for a New Ummah.* New York, NY: Columbia University Press.

Rubin, E. (2004, March 7). The Jihadi Who Kept Asking Why. *New York Times* Retrieved June 15, 2016, from http://www.nytimes.com/2004/03/07/magazine/the-jihadi-who-kept-asking-why.html?pagewanted=all&src=pm

Rugh, W. A. (2002). Education in Saudi Arabia: Choices and Constraints. *Middle East Policy, 9*(2), 40–55. doi: 10.1111/1475-4967.00056

Sabil, A. al-. (n.d.). al-Dharurat Tubih al-Mahthurat. Retrieved November 8, 2015, from www.uqu.edu.sa/page/ar/10613

Sabq. (2011). al-Malik Ya'mur Bil'iqaf al-Fawri Li-Ra'is Tahrir Al-Madina wa al-Katib al-Suwayyid. Retrieved November 2, 2015, from http://sabq.org/A1Zede

Sabq. (2012). al-Ra'is al-ʿAm Li-l-Hay'ah: Sa-Natakhithu Mawqifan Sharʿiyan ʿAjilan Tijah al-Kalam al-Mansub Li "Hissa al-Alshaykh." Retrieved November 2, 2015, from http://sabq.org/Wwhfde

Safi, A. (2012). Difaʿan ʿAn Maqha Jusur. Retrieved November 2, 2015, from   https://groups.google.com/forum/#!msg/azizkasem2/ Z1C6TPMXzQU/3f1fhG8nBGQJ

Safi, L. M. (1994). *The Challenge of Modernity: The Quest for Authenticity in the Arab World.* Lanham, MD: University Press of America.

Safi, O. (Ed.). (2003). *Progressive Muslims: On Justice, Gender and Pluralism.* Oxford, UK: Oneworld Publications.

Saggaf, Y. al-. (2012, June 18–20). *Social Media and Political Participation in Saudi Arabia: The Case of the 2009 Floods in Jeddah.* In M. Strano, H. Hrachovec, F. Sudweeks, & C. Ess (Eds.), *Proceedings of the Eighth International Conference on Cultural Attitudes towards Technology and Communication* (pp. 1–15). Aarhus, Denmark.

Said-Moorhouse, L. (2016, April 15). Saudi Arabia Curbs Its Religious Police. *CNN*, Cable News Network. Retrieved November 28, 2018 from edition.cnn. com/2016/04/14/middleeast/saudi-arabia-religious-police-powers/index.html.

Sakran, I. al-., & al-Qasim, A. (2002). 'Ayn al-Khalal: Qira'ah fi Figh al-Taʿamul maʿ al-'Akhar wa-Alwaqiʿ fi Al-Muqarrat. Retrieved March 21, 2019, from https:// alferssan.wordpress.com/2010/03/09/almoqarrarataddirassiya/

Salafi, A. al-. (2012). al-Lajnah al-Da'imah Lil'ifta': Muhakamat Kashgari Wajiba wa al-'Istihza' Bi-Allah wa al-Rasul Kufr wa Ridda. Retrieved November 2, 2015, from http://www.dd-sunnah.net/forum/showthread.php?t=144641

Saleh, F. (2013). The Arrest of Saudi Intellectual Turki al-Hamad. Retrieved December 25, 2015, from https://en.qantara.de/content/the-arrest-of-saudi-intellectual-turki-al-hamad-one-step-forward-and-two-steps-back

Salem, F. (2017). *The Arab Social Media Report 2017: Social Media and the Internet of Things: Towards Data-Driven Policymaking in the Arab World* (Vol. 7). Dubai: MBR School of Government.

Saler, M. (2006). Modernity and Enchantment: A Historiographic Review. *American Historical Review, 111*(3), 692–716. doi:10.1086/ahr.111.3.692

SAMA. (n.d.). Historical Preview. Retrieved September 29, 2013, from http://www. sama-ksa.org/sites/SAMAEN/AboutSAMA/Pages/SAMAHistory.aspx

Sanabary, N. el- (1994). Female Education in Saudi Arabia and the Reproduction of Gender Division. *Gender and Education, 6*(2), 141–150. doi: 10.1080/0954025940060204

Saqqaf, A. al-. (n.d.). Wujub Tawqiruhu wa Ta'athimuhu Sallah Allah 'Alayhi wa Sallam Wa-l-'Adilla 'ala Thalika. Retrieved November 6, 2015, from http://www. dorar.net/enc/aqadia/379

Sasapost. (2015, January 20). Raif Badawi al-Qissa al-Kamila. November 6, 2015, from http://www.sasapost.com/raef-badawi/

Saudi, al-. (2012). Bayan al-Shabab al-Sa'udy Bikhusus Dhaman al-Huriyyat wa 'adab al-'ikhtilaf. Retrieved November 2, 2015, from https://youthpetition.wordpress. com/

Sayed, H. el-, Greenhill, A., & Westrup, C. (2015). "I Download My Prayer Schedule": Exploring the Technological Mediation of Islamic Religious Practice at Work. *Culture and Religion, 16*(1), 35–50. doi:10.1080/14755610.2015.1023815

Sayf al-Hashimi al-. (Producer). (2011). Muhammad bin Hadi - al-Tahthir al-Mubin. Retrieved June 15, 2016, from https://www.youtube.com/watch?v=lk1XJH-qRAk

Sayf, T. al-. (2013a). 'Alaqat Al-Din bi al-Dawla fi al-Su'udiyya, wa Dawr al-Mu'ssasa al-Wahhabiyya fi al-Hukm. *al-Mustaqbal al-'Arabi,* (407), 32–59. http://www.caus. org.lb/PDF/EmagazineArticles/tawfic%20sayef%2032-59.pdf

Sayf, T. al-. (2013b). An Takun Shi'i fi al-Sa'udiyya. Retrieved June 15, 2016, from http://talsaif.blogspot.co.uk/2012/12/view-to-be-shia-in-saudi-arabia-on_25. html

Schielke, S. (2012). Being a Nonbeliever in a Time of Islamic Revival: Trajectories of Doubt and Certainty in Contemporary Egypt. *International Journal of Middle East Studies, 44*(2), 301–320. doi:10.1017/S0020743812000062

Schmidt, V. H. (2006). Multiple Modernities or Varieties of Modernity? *Current Sociology, 54*(1), 77–97. doi:10.1177/0011392106058835

Sedgwick, M. J. R. (1997). Saudi Sufis: Compromise in the Hijaz, 1925–40. *Die Welt des Islams, 37*(3), 349–368. http://www.jstor.org/stable/1570657

Seidman, S. (2013). *Contested Knowledge: Social Theory Today* (5th ed.). West Sussex, UK: Wiley-Blackwell.

Sfeir, G. N. (1998). Basic Freedoms in a Fractured Legal Culture: Egypt and the Case of Nasr Hamid Abu Zayd. *Middle East Journal, 52*(3), 402–414. doi: 10.2307/4329220

Shaban, M. A. (1976). *Islamic History: A New Interpretation.* Cambridge, MA: Cambridge University Press.

shaikhAdnanIbrahim. (Producer). (2013). La Rajm fi al-Islam. Retrieved June 15, 2016, from https://www.youtube.com/watch?v=hxUXmuct28k

Shamsy, A. el- (2014). The Social Construction of Orthodoxy. In M. Fierro (Ed.), *Orthodoxy and Heresy in Islam* (Vol. 1, pp. 257–274). Oxon, UK: Routledge.

Sharidah, B. al-. (2014, May 5). Badalan min al-Mu'arrifin wa al-Shuhud. "al-Basmah" Li-'Ithbat Hawiyya al-Sa'udiyyat fi al-Mahakim. *al-Sharq al-Awsat.* Retrieved June 15, 2016, from http://archive.aawsat.com/details.asp?section=43&article=77085 2&issueno=12942#.ViKwt34rLDc

Sharq al-Awsat al-. (2011, March 7). Haʾyat Kibar al-ʿUlama fi al-Suʿudiyya Tuharrim al-Muthaharat Fi-l-Bilad wa Tuhathir min al-ʾIrtibatat al-Fikriyya W-l-Hizbiyya al-Munharifa. *al-Sharq al-Awsat*. Retrieved June 15, 2016, from http://ar-chive.aawsat.com/details.asp?section=4&issueno=11787&article=611299#. VbY-qPlViko

Shaty, A. al-. (Producer). (2012). Hukm Fath al-Hisab fi al-Bank al-Rabawi - ibn ʿUthaymin. Retrieved June 15, 2016, from http://www.youtube.com/ watch?v=UDc10PXIy4Q

Shavit, U. (2014). Can Muslims Befriend Non-Muslims? Debating al-walāʾ wa-al-barāʾ (Loyalty and Disavowal) in Theory and Practice. *Islam and Christian–Muslim Relations, 25*(1), 67–88. http://dx.doi.org/10.1080/09596410.2013.851329 doi:10.1080/09596410.2013.851329

Shayiʿ, K. al-. (2012). Muraqibun wa ʾIʿlamiyyun Yuʾakiddun Suʿubat Muhimmat Al al-Shaykh fi ʾIslah al-Hayʾa. Retrieved November 2, 2015, from http://www.alarabiya.net/articles/2012/01/14/188208.html

Shihri, F. al-. (2011, March 22). al-Mukhayyamat al-Daʿawiyyah Tudarrib al-Shabab ʿAla al-Silah. *An7a*. Retrieved June 15, 2016, from http://www.an7a.com/49544/

Shuʾaybi, H. al-. (1999). Fatwa Humud binʿUqla al-Shuʿaybi Fi Turki al-Hamad. Retrieved November 2, 2015, from http://alhmad.8m.com/ftua.htm

Simmel, G. (1905). A Contribution to the Sociology of Religion. *American Journal of Sociology, 11*(3), 359–376. http://www.jstor.org/stable/2762794 doi:10.2307/2762794

Small, M. L. (2009). "How Many Cases Do I Need?": On Science and the Logic of Case Selection in Field-Based Research. *Ethnography, 10*(1), 5–38. doi:10.1177/1466138108099586

Soroush, A. (2009). *The Expansion of Prophetic Experience: Essays on Historicity, Contingency and Plurality in Religion.* Leiden, Holland: Brill.

Speck, S. (2012). Ulrich Beck's "Reflecting Faith": Individualization, Religion and the Desecularization of Reflexive Modernity. *Sociology, 47*(1), 157–172. doi: 10.1177/0038038512448564

Stoeckl, K., & Rosati, M. (Eds.). (2016). *Multiple Modernities and Postsecular Societies.* London, UK: Taylor & Francis.

Stringer, M. D. (2011). *Contemporary Western Ethnography and the Definition of Religion.* London, UK: Continuum.

Sudays, A. al-. (n.d.). Al-Maʿasi wa Atharuha al-Sayyiʾ. Retrieved October 6, 2014, from http://audio.islamweb.net/audio/index.php?page=FullContent&audioid=28229#28616

Suhayl, T. al-. (2011, February 5). Mufti al-SaʿudiyyahYuhathir min Taqsim al-Mintaqa ʾila "Duwal Mutakhallifa." *al-Sharq al-Awsat*. Retrieved June 15, 2016, from http://archive.aawsat.com/details.asp?section=4&article=606976&issueno=11757#.VbY7EPlViko

Suwaylim, L. al-. (2013). Thahira Su'udiyya . . . "'Uhibbu al-Salihin wa Lastu Minhum!" Retrieved December 25, 2015, from http://www.majalla.com/arb/2013/04/article55244553

Taylor, C. (2004). *Modern Social Imaginaries*. Durham, NC: Duke University Press.

Taylor, C. (2007). *A Secular Age*. Cambridge, MA: Cambridge Univesity Press.

Taylor, C. (2011). *Dilemmas and Connections: Selected Essays*: Harvard University Press.

Technology. *The Qualitative Report*, 10(4), 771–794. http://www.nova.edu/ssss/QR/QR10-4/angers.pdf

Teitelbaum, J. (2002). Dueling for "Da' wa": State vs. Society on the Saudi Internet. *Middle East Journal, 56*(2), 222–239. http://www.jstor.org/stable/4329752

Tezcur, G., & Azadarmaki, T. (2008). Religiosity and Islamic Rule in Iran. *Journal for the Scientific Study of Religion, 47*(2), 211–224. doi: 10.1111/j.1468-5906.2008.00403.x

TheFhad555. (Producer). (2012). Hal Kul al-'Ajanib al-Kuffar fi al-Nar. Retrieved June 15, 2016, from https://www.youtube.com/watch?v=y3eHHGpwtQo

Thuwayni, M. al-. (2005). *al-Shaykh Salih bin Ibrahim al-Bilayhi wa Juhuduhu al-'Ilmiyya wa al-Da'awiyya*. Riyadh, Saudi Arabia: Dar al-Muslim.

Tibi, B. (2002). *The Challenge of Fundamentalism: Political Islam and the New World Disorder*. Berkeley: University of California Press.

Tibi, B. (2009). *Islam's Predicament with Modernity: Religious Reform and Cultural Change* London, UK: Routledge.

Toumi, H. (2012, February 8). Saudi King Orders Controversial Columnist's Arrest. *Gulf News*. Retrieved June 15, 2016, from http://gulfnews.com/news/gulf/saudi-arabia/saudi-king-orders-controversial-columnist-s-arrest-1.977785

Trofimov, Y. (2007). *The Siege of Mecca*. New York, NY: First Anchor Books.

Tschannen, O. (1991). The Secularization Paradigm: A Systematization. *Journal for the Scientific Study of Religion, 30*(4), 395–415. http://www.jstor.org/stable/1387276

Turner, B. S. (1991). *Religion and Social Theory* (2nd ed.). London, UK: Sage Publications.

Twasul. (2011, February 20). Wafd min Mashayikh al-Qasim Yaltaqi Nai'b Wazir al-Ta'lim al-'Ali. Retrieved November 6, 2015, from http://twasul.info/1757/

Um al-Qura University. (2005). Bayan al-'Ulama wa Talabat al-'Ilm Hawl Qiyadat al-Mar'a Li-l-sayyara. Retrieved November 2, 2015, from https://uqu.edu.sa/lib/ar/35462

'Umar, N. al-. (2013, April 14). D. al-Umar: Ma Hadath fi "al-Janadiriyya" Ab'aduhu Khatira wa Nantaziru Mawqafan Haziman min al-mas'ulin (video). Retrieved September 29, 2013, from http://www.almoslim.net/node/181936

Umaym, A. al-. (2012, February 4). Ibrahim al-Bilayhi - Muthaqaf la Yas'am min al-Tikrar. *al-Sharq al-Awsat*. Retrieved June 15, 2016, from http://www.aawsat.com/leader.asp?section=3&issueno=12121&article=661965;

'Uqaylan. (2011). al-Mafhum al-Madani Li-l-'Uluhiyyah. Retrieved November 2, 2015, from http://www.falsafh.com/vb/t8203.html

US Department of State. (2015). 2014 Human Rights Reports: Saudi Arabia. Retrieved November 6, 2015, from http://www.state.gov/j/drl/rls/hrrpt/2014/nea/236620.htm

Useem, J. (2002). Banking on Allah Devout Muslims Don't Pay or Receive Interest. So How Can Their Financial System Work? Retrieved September 29, 2013, from http://archive.fortune.com/magazines/fortune/fortune_archive/2002/06/10/324525/index.htm

Usmani, M. T. (2013). Slavery in Islam. Retrieved November 6, 2015, from http://www.deoband.org/2013/01/hadith/hadith-commentary/slavery-in-islam/

Usul al-Fiqh. (2015). In J. Esposito (Ed.), *The Oxford Dictionary of Islam*. Oxford, UK: Oxford University Press.

ʿUtaybi, A. al-. (2008, January 7). Islam al-Nas wa Islam al-Siraʿ. *al-Riyadh*. Retrieved June 15, 2016, from http://www.alriyadh.com/306977

ʿUwayjan, K. al-. (2010). ʿudu Hayʾat Kibar al-ʿUlama: man Yutalib Bi-ʾIqaf al-ʾIbtiʿath Afkaruhu "Khayaliyya." *al-Sharq al-Awsat*. Retrieved June 15, 2016, from http://www.aawsat.com/details.asp?issueno=11700&article=562405#.UlAg-yRkOFU

van Dun, T., Versteeg, P., & Roeland, J. (2015). Virtualization of Ritual: Consequences and Meaning. *Annual Review of the Sociology of Religion*, 6, 34–47. doi:10.1163/9789004302549_004

van Harskamp, A. (2008). Existential Insecurity and New Religiosity: An Essay on Some Religion-Making Characteristics of Modernity. *Social Compass*, 55(1), 9–19. doi: 10.1177/0037768607086494

van Oort, J. (2015). "Manichaeism." In *Religion Past and Present*. Brill Online. Retrieved June 15, 2016, from http://referenceworks.brillonline.com/entries/religion-past-and-present/manichaeism-COM_13501.

Vogel, F. E. (2003). The Public and Private in Saudi Arabia: Restrictions on the Powers of Committees for Ordering the Good and Forbidding the Evil. *Social Research: An International Quarterly*, 70(3), 749–768. http://www.jstor.org/stable/40971639

Voll, J. (1991). The Revivalist Heritage. In Y. Y. Haddad, J. O. Voll, & J. L. Esposito (Eds.), *The Contemporary Islamic Revival: A Critical Survey and Bibliography* (pp. 23–31). Westport, CT: Greenwood.

wa7eed6. (Producer). (2012). Rad al-Shaykh Muhammad al-ʿUrayfi ʿala al-Maʿfuna Hessah Al al-Shaykh. Retrieved June 15, 2016, from https://www.youtube.com/watch?v=H1A7klxdToA

Wakalat. (2011). al-Bayan al-Khitami li-l-Muʾtamar al-ʿAalami "Thahirat al-Takfir" bi al-Madina al-Munawwara. Retrieved October 6, 2015, from http://fiqh.islammessage.com/NewsDetails.aspx?id=3644

Walsh, R. (2009). *Education and Islamic Radicalization in the Arabian Peninsula*. The College of William and Mary VA. Retrieved June 15, 2016, from https://digitalarchive.wm.edu/bitstream/handle/10288/1203/WalshRachel2009.pdf?sequence=1

Wardi, A. al-. (1995). *Wuᶜᶜath al-Salatin*. London, UK: Dar Kufan.

WAS. (2010, April 29). Al- Lajnah al-Daʾima Li-l-Buhuth al-ʾIlmiyyah wa al-ʾIfta Tuʾakkid ʾala Wujub Salat al-Jamaʾah fi al-Masjid. *al-Riyadh*. Retrieved October 25, 2014, from, http://www.alriyadh.com/520981

WAS. (2014, March 8). Idraj Tanthimat al-Qaᶜidah wa Daᶜish. *al-Riyadh*. Retrieved October 25, 2014 from, http://www.alriyadh.com/916236

Wasatiyyah al-. (2002). Hiwar Maftuh ʾajrahu Muntada al-Wasatiyya maᶜ Mansour al-Nogaidan. Retrieved June 1, 2013, from http://alnogaidan.com/28-12-2002/

Wasella, J. (2011). *al-Tamarrod ᶜala al-Salafyia: Abdullah al-Qasimi* (M. Kabibo, Trans.). Beirut, Lebanon: Jadawil.

Watt, W. M. (1988). *Islamic Fundamentalism and Modernity* London, UK: Routledge.

Weber, M. (1919/2004). Politics as a Vocation (R. Livingstone, Trans.). In D. Owen & T. B. Strong (Eds.), *The Vocation Lectures*. Indianapolis, IN: Hackett.

Weber, M. (1919/2009). Science as a Vocation. In H. H. Gerth & C. W. Mills (Eds.), *From Max Weber: Essays in Sociology* (pp. 129–156). London, UK: Routledge.

Weeam al-. (2012). Muhibbu "Turki al-Hamad" Yuwaqiᶜun Khitaban Li-Hurriyyatihi wa Takrimihi. Retrieved November 2, 2015, from http://www.alweeam.com.sa/176614/

Weeam al-. (2014, October 16). "Kibar al-ᶜUlama Tusdir Bayanan Nassa ᶜAla 'Hurmat" al-ʾIktitab Bi "al-Bank al-ʾAhli." Retrieved November 6, 2015, from www.alweeam.com.sa/297013/هيئة-كبار-العلماء-تصدر-بياناً-نص-فيه-عل/

Weigert, A. J. (1974). Whose Invisible Religion? Luckmann Revisited. *Sociology of Religion, 35*(3), 181–188. doi: 10.2307/3710648

Wensinck, A. J. (2015). K̲h̲aṭīʾa. In M. T. Houtsma, T. W. Arnold, R. Basset, & R. Hartmann (Eds.), *Encyclopaedia of Islam, First Edition (1913–1936)*. Brill Online. Retrieved June 15, 2016, from http://referenceworks.brillonline.com/entries/encyclopaedia-of-islam-1/khatia-SIM_4141.

Wensinck, A. J., & Gardet, L. (2015). Iblīs. In P. Bearman, Th. Bianquis, C. E. Bosworth, E. van Donzel, & W. P. Heinrichs (Eds.), *Encyclopaedia of Islam Second Edition*. Brill Online. Retrieved June 15, 2016, from http://referenceworks.brillonline.com/entries/encyclopaedia-of-islam-2/iblis-SIM_3021.

Whitaker, B. (2006, September 14). A Bad Joke. *Guardian*. Retrieved June 15, 2016, from http://www.theguardian.com/commentisfree/2006/sep/14/abadjoke

Whitaker, B. (2014). *Arabs Without God*. CreateSpace Independent Publishing Platform.

Wilcke, C. (2008). The Ismailis of Najran: Second-Class Saudi Citizens. Retrieved June 15, 2016, from http://www.hrw.org/sites/default/files/reports/saudiarabia0908web.pdf

Wilson, B. (2014). The Failure of Nomenclature: The Concept of "Orthodoxy" in the Study of Islam. In M. Fierro (Ed.), *Orthodoxy and Heresy in Islam* (Vol. 1, pp. 153–176). Oxon, UK: Routledge.

Withnall, A. (2014, April 1). Saudi Arabia Declares All Atheists Are Terrorists in New Law to Crack Down on Political Dissidents. *The Independent*. Retrieved June

15, 2016, from http://www.independent.co.uk/news/world/middle-east/saudi-arabia-declares-all-atheists-are-terrorists-in-new-law-to-crack-down-on-political-dissidents-9228389.html

Yahia, E. (Producer). (2010). Abaleeso wa ʿAhdadh Asalib al-Muʾakasah. Retrieved March 20, 2019, from https://www.youtube.com/watch?v=LdW_ddwTVIw

Zahrani, A. al-. (Producer). (2012). Tawbat Hamza Kashgari La Tusqit al-ʿUquba. Retrieved June 15, 2016, from https://www.youtube.com/watch?v=boqOxsEnd1E

Zahrani, S. al-. (2010). Ush-hidu Allah ʿala Bughdhi li "Turki al-Hamad." *al-Madinah*. Retrieved June 15, 2016, from http://www.al-madina.com/node/213540

Zaman, M. Q. (2015). Sin, Major and Minor. In J. D. McAuliffe (Ed.), *Encyclopaedia of the Qurʾān*. Brill Online. Retrieved June 15, 2016, from http://referenceworks.brillonline.com/entries/encyclopaedia-of-the-quran/sin-major-and-minor-EQCOM_00184?s.num=14&s.q=f%C4%81siq+.

Zaman, M. R. (2008). Usury (Riba) and the Place of Bank Interest in Islamic Banking and Finance. *International Journal of Banking and Finance, 6*(1).

Zaydan, K. al-. (2007, June 21). Al-Shakyk al-Fawzan Li "al-Riyadh": La ʾArdha Bi-Tawthif al-Fatwa fi Ghayr Mahalliha wa ʾIstighlaliha fi Takfir al-ʾAshkhas Dun Dhawabitiha al-Sharʿiyyah. *al-Riyadh*. Retrieved June 15, 2016, from http://www.alriyadh.com/258720

Zekri, M. al-. (2004). *The Religious Encounter Between Sufis and Salafis: Issue of Identity* (PhD dissertation). University of Exeter. Retrieved June 15, 2016, from http://ethos.bl.uk/OrderDetails.do?uin=uk.bl.ethos.410772

Zirikly, K. al-. (1988). *al-Wajiz fi Sirat a-Malik Abdulaziz* (5th ed.). Beirut, Lebanon: Dar Alʾilm Liʾlmalayin.

Zito, G. V. (1983). Toward a Sociology of Heresy. *Sociology of Religion, 44*(2), 123–130. http://socrel.oxfordjournals.org/content/44/2/123.abstract doi:10.2307/3711397

Zubaida, S. (2000). Trajectories of Political Islam: Egypt, Iran and Turkey. *Political Quarterly, 71*, 60–78. doi: 10.1111/1467-923X.71.s1.7

Zubaida, S. (2011). *Beyond Islam: A New Understanding of the Middle East*. London, UK: I.B. Tauris.

Zuckerman, P. (2007). Atheism: Contemporary Numbers and Patterns. In M. Martin (Ed.), *The Cambridge Companion to Atheism* (pp. 47–66). New York, NY: University of Cambridge Press.

Index